Impeachment – A Political Sword

How the Johnson, Nixon and Clinton Battles with Congress Shaped Impeachment

Scott S.Barker

Published in the United States of America by

History Publishing Company LLC PO Box 700
Palisades, NY 10964 www.historypublishingco.com

ISBN 9781940773704

SAN:850-5942

Printed in the United States on acid print paper 9 8 7 6 5 4 3 2

PRESIDENTIAL IMPEACHMENT – FROM CHECK AND BALANCE TO PARTISAN POLITICAL WEAPON

DEDICATION

To my father, Paul Winston ("Bill") Barker, a departed career Air Force pilot who flew into harm's way in two wars and who taught me by example what it means to protect and defend the Constitution of the United States of America.

ACKNOWLEDGEMENTS

My deepest appreciation to my beloved wife, Joan, who has been a marvelous companion and astute adviser as I have traveled the road from trial lawyer to author. Many thanks to my friends, Bob Bearman, Fred Ritsema and John Vaught, who have reviewed my drafts, discussed them with me and provided valuable feedback that I know has improved both my analysis and my prose. Finally, my gratitude to my editor, Mary Gottschalk, whose careful and insight- ful review and suggested revisions made my story about presidential impeachment so much better.

CONTENTS

PREFACE

"WE THE PEOPLE of the United States, in Order to form a more perfect Union, establish Justice, insure domestic Tranquility, promote the general Welfare, and secure the Blessings of Liberty to ourselves and our Posterity, do ordain and establish this Constitution for the United States of America."

1

This book tells the story of presidential impeachment. I wrote it for the everyday citizen, the "PEOPLE" for whom the Constitution was created. Together we will explore how and why impeachment was added to the United States Constitution, how the framers and their contemporaries viewed it and what has happened to the presiden- tial impeachment power as a result of the two times that it has been invoked, as well as the "near impeachment" of Richard Nixon.[2] We will learn that, while the framers saw presidential impeachment as a kind of "check and balance of last resort," the politicians have rarely used it that way, but instead have wielded it as a blunt edged political sword.

---

1 *Preamble to the U.S. Constitution*

2 *Andrew Johnson and Bill Clinton were the only two Presidents who were impeached, but they were not convicted. Impeachment resolutions were introduced in the House of Representatives against Presidents John Tyler, Grover Cleveland, Herbert Hoover, Harry S. Truman, Richard M. Nixon, Ronald Reagan and George H.W. Bush. Of these, articles of impeachment were voted by the House Judiciary Committee only against President Nixon, but he resigned before the House voted on them. No serious action was taken by the House of Representatives against the remainder of the Presidents.*

Now seems an opportune time to undertake this comprehensive examination of the presidential impeachment power. Even before Don- ald J. Trump took the presidential oath of office on January 20, 2017, rumblings of impeachment began reverberating across the American

political landscape. Politicians, media commentators and private cit- izens have been speculating on the air waves, on the cable networks, in print, on social media, around the water cooler and the kitchen table about President Trump's chances of being impeached, and whether, if impeached, he would be convicted. Each new indictment or guilty plea generated by the independent counsel investigation – or sometimes an ill-considered presidential tweet -- sparks another round of impeach- ment thunder.

I have found the public discussion about impeachment unhelpful. There seems to be pervasive ignorance about what the Constitution requires to impeach and to convict a president. There is also virtually no discussion of the history of presidential impeachment and what that history tells us about this important, even if little-used, constitution- al power. Perhaps it's because we live in a world of sound bites that doesn't allow for a meaty discussion about anything, let alone "other high crimes and misdemeanors." Or perhaps the politicians and the media haven't done their homework.

What stands out most distinctly about this public discussion is its fixation on whether Donald Trump has committed a crime. Did he "collude" or "conspire" with the Russians during the Presidential cam- paign of 2016? Did he "obstruct justice" by firing FBI Director James Comey, who was investigating the connection between the Russians and the Trump campaign? The unstated assumption seems to be that, if no crime had been committed, there would be no grounds for im- peachment.

Alexander Hamilton's Federalist 65 says something quite different.[3] Here is what he said about presidential impeachment in March 1788:

3 *The Federalist Papers are a collection of newspaper articles, what we would call today "op-eds," written under the pseudonym of "Publius" to support ratification of the Constitution in New York, although they also had broader impact. Hamilton, who took the lead, wrote fifty-one of the eighty-five essays and Madison penned twenty-nine. Hamilton and Madison were delegates to the*

> "The subjects of [Presidential impeachment] are those offenses which proceed from the misconduct of public men, or, in other words, from the abuse or violation of some public trust. They are of a nature which may with peculiar propriety be denominated POLITICAL, as they relate chiefly to injuries done immediately to society itself."[4]

Prompted by Hamilton, I decided to seek my own answers to the questions about impeachment. I am a civil trial lawyer by education and profession. Over the fifty years or so of my adult life I have been an avid student of American history, with a particular interest in the founding generation of our remarkable country and its presidents. I have also long revered the Constitution. My father was a career Air Force pilot, whose job it was to protect and defend the Constitution and who did so in two wars. I took the same oath he did when I was sworn in as a second lieutenant in the Air Force, and I like to think I lived up to that oath in the eight years I served my country at home and abroad. I have kept a copy of the Constitution close to my desk for almost forty years and quite often refer to it, not just for work, but as a fundamental reference point to current political events.

A lot of words have been written about presidential impeachment, almost all of which have been directed at professional historians and law professors. The existing literature also tends to compartmentalize the subject. For example, much has been written about the history of impeachment under English law and its impact on the version of im- peachment that was adopted by the framers at the 1787 Constitutional Convention. There are also books and law review articles that delve deeply into either the

Constitutional Convention and had also signed the founding document. John Jay, like Hamilton and Madison, supported a strong national government based on his unhappy attempts to provide leader-ship to the United States under the Articles of Confederation. He was boxed out of participation in the Convention by the political leaders in New York, who wanted to preserve the state's sovereignty. Due to an illness, Jay wrote only five of the papers. Written in 1787-1788, these articles are viewed by students of constitutional history as valuable tools in helping to determine what the framers and ratifiers meant at the time.

4 *The Federalist Papers, (Odins Library Classics, 2018) (hereafter The Federalist Papers), 165. The all capitals in "POLITICAL" are in the original.*

Andrew Johnson or the Bill Clinton impeach- ments and trials. And, o course, there is a mountain of material written about Watergate and wha I call Richard Nixon's "near impeachment." What I found to be missing is a comprehensive, single-volume treatment of the history of presidentia impeachment for non-academ- ics. This is my effort to plug that gap. I have endeavored to trace pres- idential impeachment to its origins in English law and to discern what the founders meant by including impeachment in the Constitution as revealed by the debates at the Convention and other 18thcentury sources. Then, I have looked at the impeachments and trials of Presidents Johnson and Clinton, as well as the circumstances that led to President Nixon's resignation in the face of what otherwise would have been his certain impeachment and likely conviction.

The story of presidential impeachment is rich with irony and the surprises that fortune dishes out unexpectedly. What would have hap- pened if Abraham Lincoln had not gone to Ford's Theater on April 14, 1865, only to unexpectedly meet his death by an assassin's bullet? What if Bill Clinton had never encountered Monica Lewinsky? What if that Watergate security guard had not noticed the masking tape that the Watergate burglars had placed on the lock to keep the door into the building open?

The story also proves the validity of Ralph Waldo Emerson's aph- orism: "there is properly no history; only biography." What if Andrew Johnson had not been a stubborn Southern outsider who clung to views about blacks that, so far as the Radical Republicans were concerned, had been vanquished by the Union's victory in the Civil War? What if Bill Clinton had not been an unrepentant womanizer who was willing to demean his presidency by bringing his affairs into the White House? What if Richard Nixon had not been so paranoid that he countenanced illegal "dirty tricks" to ensure the defeat of an opponent that he was going to trounce anyway, and then orchestrated a cover-up to prevent the public from knowing what had happened? Indeed, the history of presidential impeachment is, in a very real sense, the story of these three presidents and the circumstances in which the efforts to remove them from office unfolded.

All of this was in the unknown and unknowable future when the framers met in Philadelphia in the summer of 1787 to create a nation. What I have learned – and what I want to share – is the creative maj- esty of our fundamental law, what can justifiably be described as an historical miracle worked by a unique group of American aristocrats, who were both "doers" and "thinkers." At the same time, what these miracle workers gave to the PEOPLE was not a guarantee for all time, but rather a challenge to each succeeding generation of Americans to remain faithful to the principles embodied in the Constitution and, in so doing, to "... secure the Blessings of Liberty to ourselves and our Posterity."

As I contemplate how our generation can remain faithful to these principles, my mind travels back to the four years of my young adult- hood that I spent as a cadet at the United States Air Force Academy, located in the shadow of the Rampart Range of the Rocky Mountains. Those were hard, exhilarating and deeply formative years for me and my classmates. Although we didn't have much time to enjoy it, our campus (the "cadet area" in military speak) was beautiful. Like all

college campuses, it was, and still is, dotted with statues and other memorabilia designed to connect the collective heritage of past gen- erations to the present. One of the most poignant statues is the "Eagle and Fledglings," a carved black stone image of a mother eagle stand- ing above her two fledglings and protecting them with her outstretched wings. Etched below the eagles are these words: "Man's flight through life is sustained by the power of his knowledge."

Those words have stuck with me for 52 years. They can be para- phrased as follows for all Americans: "The power of a democracy is fueled by the knowledge of its citizens." I hope that this book will contribute to your knowledge of our founding document, including the proper use of the impeachment power, enabling you better to fuel the power of our democracy.

PART 1

THE CONSTITUTION

CHAPTER 1
THE BIG PICTURE

"The President . . . shall be removed from Office on Impeach- ment for, and Conviction of, Treason, Bribery, or other high Crimes and Misdemeanors."[5]

The words chosen by the framers to define an impeachable offense do not necessarily make sense to a 21st century American. We know that treason is bad. In fact, the Constitution itself defines it: "Treason against the United States shall consist only in Levying War against them, or in adhering to their Enemies, giving them Aid and Comfort."6[6] We would all certainly vote to remove a president from office who had engaged in war against his country or gave aid and comfort to an enemy of the United States. Although "bribery" is not defined in the Constitution we know instinctively that it would be a bad thing for a President to take a bribe. So far, so good.

Then we get to "other high Crimes and Misdemeanors." What in the world does that mean? If you take that phrase along with "trea- son" and "bribery," you might very easily conclude that impeachment requires a crime of some sort. But what kind of crime are we talking about? To us, a misdemeanor is a "small crime," like a traffic ticket. Did they really mean to allow a president to be removed for such mi- nor offenses? That doesn't

5 *U.S. CONST., art. II, § 4.*
6 *U.S. CONST., art. III, § 3.*

make sense. So, what if "high" also modi- fies "misdemeanor"? What is a "high misdemeanor"? Is it like a felo-

ny? In order to understand what this all means, are we left to parse the definition of an impeachable offense like a grammarian? The answer is no. As it turns out, there is a wealth of information bearing on the meaning of this key term.

As a result of battles for power between Parliament and the Crown over a long period of time, the law in England developed a process, called impeachment, to remove ministers of the king, who himself could not be removed. Over time, what constituted an impeachable offense came to be embodied in the phrase "high crimes and misde- meanors." The framers of our Constitution were well aware of that law and the meaning of that term. They drew upon it when they wrote the constitutional definition of impeachment, adapting it to their particu- lar circumstances, replacing an unimpeachable king with an impeach- able president.[7] For present purposes, it is worth taking another look at what Alexander Hamilton, who was at the Convention and signed the Constitution, had to say about it:

> "The subjects of [presidential impeachment] are those offenses which proceed from the misconduct of public men, or, in other words, from the abuse or violation of some public trust. They are of a nature which may with peculiar propriety be denominated POLITICAL, as they relate chiefly to injuries done immediately to society itself."

Thus, drawing on English law, and adapting it to their particular needs, the framers included presidential impeachment as a check and balance of last

7 *Berger, Raoul, Impeachment, the Constitutional Problems, Enlarged Edition, (Harvard University Press, 1974), (hereafter Berger, Impeach- ment, the Constitutional Problems), 58; see also Constitutional Grounds for Presidential Impeachment, Report by the Staff of Impeachment Inquiry, Committee on the Judiciary, House of Representatives, Ninety-Third Congress, Second Session, February 1974, (U.S. Government Printing Office, 1974) (hereafter 1974 House Judiciary Committee Staff Report), 4-8.*

resort to protect against abuse of the awesome powers they we in the executive under Article II of the Constitu- tion.[8] A preside removed from office for a major breach of the public trust that rel conduct of his official duties as president. It certainly could be a crime, but it need not be. It was a last resort, in part, because of the political passions its invocation was likely to excite. Once again, Alexander Hamilton's words in Federalist No. 65 are worth quoting:

> "The prosecution of them [impeachments] . . . will sel- dom fail to agitate the passions of the whole communi- ty, and to divide it into parties, more or less friendly or inimical, to the accused. In many cases, it will connect itself with the pre-existing factions, and will inlist [sic] all their animosities, partialities, influence and interest on one side, or on the other; and in such cases there will always be the greatest danger, that the decision will be regulated more by the comparative strength of the parties than by the real demonstrations of innocence or guilt." [9]

Certainly, Hamilton and all political leaders in late 18th century America themselves participated in "factions." Indeed, the ratifica- tion debates were conducted by two rough factions, the "Federalists," who favored ratification of the new governing document, and the "An- ti-Federalists," who opposed it. However, the concept of a political party, in the sense of a group of people with a shared set of valuesand goals, that is in continual existence and

8 *Those powers included serving as the commander-in-chief of the armed forces, his responsibility to conduct the foreign policy of the United States, and the power to pardon. Those powers are far more awesome today than the founding fathers could have fathomed. As just one example, today the president's constitutional role as the commander-in-chief includes a war making power and consequent risk to the country that would have been unimaginable to an 18th century American.*

9 *The Federalist Papers, 165. At least one scholar has cited this quote from Hamilton as proof that the Framers knew that impeachment would be the subject of partisan politics. See, e.g., Turley, Johnathan, "Senate Trials and Factional Disputes: Impeachment as a Madisonian Device," 49 Duke L.J. 1 (Oct. 1999) (hereafter Turley, "Senate Trials and Factional Disputes"). However, on its face, Hamilton is not saying that existing political parties would invoke impeachment to advance their political agendas. Rather, he is saying that the impeachment itself would generate divisions.*

coordinates efforts to achieve political power through the electoral process was still in its infancy. It wasn't until Martin Van Buren's time in the 1830s[10] that political parties as we know them today began developing. By the time of the Civil War, political parties were well-established and constituted the primary mechanism for articulating political positions in electionsand implementing policies when political leaders were elected to govern.

As we shall see, partisan passion was the motivating force behind the impeachments and trials of both Andrew Johnson and Bill Clin- ton, thereby perverting the safety-valve check and balance view ofthe founders.

10 Van Buren, a New Yorker, was a founder of the Democratic Party and served as president from 1837-1841.

CHAPTER 2
IMPEACHMENT UNDER ENGLISH LAW

". . . the [English] common law was [for the Framers] a 'brood- ing omnipresence.'"[11]

We start with English law because the framers borrowed from it in crafting the American version of impeachment embodiedin the Constitution. The record of the Constitutional Convention reveals sub- stantial knowledge of impeachment as it had developed in England.[12] No less an authority than Alexander Hamilton acknowledged that the institution of impeachment in the Constitution was "borrowed" from Great Britain.[13] The terms "treason, bribery or other high crimes and misdemeanors" were "lifted bodily from English law."[14]

Over the course of hundreds of years, the English version of im- peachment developed as a mechanism for Parliament to remove min- isters of the Crown, or others, whom it found were pursuing policies or engaging

11 Berger, Impeachment, the Constitutional Problems, 58. Professor Berger's book is an excel- lent source for those who want to delve deeply into the history of English impeachment.
12 See, e.g., Turley, "Senate Trials and Factional Disputes," 9, 34-35. Professor Turley in- cludes a succinct history of English impeachment at pages 9-21.
13 Federalist No. 65, The Federalist Papers, 165.
14 Berger, Impeachment, the Constitutional Problems, 58; see also 1974 Judiciary Committee Staff Report, 4-12.

in acts offensive to the interests of the state. Since the king himself could not be removed, the attacks were made against the agents of the Crown.

Impeachment first appeared in England during the so-called Good Parliament of 1376, when it was initially used as a means of initiating criminal proceedings.[15] By 1399, during the reign of Henry IV, a set of procedures and precedent had been developed.[16] Impeachment fell out of use after the mid-15th century, but was revived in the 17th century when it was used repeatedly by Parliament to rein in Crown officials during the clash between Parliament and the Stuarts, who sought ab- solute power for the Crown.[17] From 1621 to 1679, Parliament wielded impeachment against numerous high level ministers to the Crown, in- cluding the 1st Duke of Buckingham, the Earl of Stafford, Archbishop William Laud, the Earl of Clarendon and Thomas Osborne, Earl of Danby, in whose case it was decided that the king's pardon could not stop the process.[18] Use of impeachment gradually waned again in the 18th century and, once it was established in the early 19th century that the government was beholden to Parliament, not the Crown, impeach- ment was no longer deemed necessary.[19]

Under English procedure, the House of Commons conducted a truncated trial (the defense was not allowed to present testimony) to determine if an impeachable offense had occurred. If the answer was yes in the judgment of the House of Commons, it would issue articles of impeachment and the matter was transferred to the House of Lords. There, another trial was held, at which the defense presented its case. The Lords had the power to convict and also to assess punishment, which was not limited to removal from office, but could also include fines, forfeiture, imprisonment and, rarely, death. All citizens, except members of the royal family, were subject to impeachment.

---

15 "Impeachment Law," https://www.britannica.com/topic/impeachment.

16 1974 House Judiciary Committee Staff Report, 11.

17 Ibid., 12 -14.

18 Ibid, 11.

19 Ibid. In addition, government officials were subject to removal pursuant to a Bill of Attain- der, a legislative act that inflicted capital punish- ment on persons supposedly guilty of high offenses, but without trial or other judicial proceeding.

This in- cluded members of Parliament.[20] By 1769, it was proclaimed in the House of Commons that impeachment was the "chief institution for the preservation of government."[21]

Although the primary use of impeachment was to charge and prosecute crimes against Crown ministers who were otherwise beyond the reach of the law, the grounds for impeachment in England were broad and varied, going beyond criminal behavior. The term "high crimes and misdemeanors" was first clearly applied in the 1386 trial of Michael de la Pole, Earl of Suffolk, who was accused of a "host of impeachable offenses, including the 'appointment of incompetent of- ficers and advising the King to grant liberties and privileges to certain persons to the hindrance of the due execution of laws.'"[22]

Thus, under English practice, impeachment was for "political crimes" that injured the state. It was injury to the state that distin- guished "high crimes and misdemeanors" from an ordinary misde- meanor.[23] Professor Raoul Berger has compiled the following list of impeachable offenses, constituting a potpourri of malfeasance, butnot necessarily criminal conduct: applying appropriated funds for purpos- es other than specified; procuring offices for people who were unfit and unworthy of them; commencing but not prosecuting suits; allow- ing contracts for greatly needed powder to lapse for want of payment; thwarting Parliament's order to store arms and ammunition in arsenals; preventing a political enemy from standing for election and causing his illegal arrest and detention; losing a ship through neglect to bring it to mooring; assisting the Attorney General in drafting a proclamation to suppress petitions to the King to call a parliament; and accepting 5,500 guineas from the East India Company to procure a charter for confirmation."[24]

20 *Ibid., 9-10.*

21 *Sunstein, Cass, Impeachment, A Citizen's Guide, Harvard University Press (2017) (hereafter Sunstein, Impeachment, A Citizen's Guide), 35.*

22 *1974 House Judiciary Committee Staff Report, 11-12.*

23 *Gerhardt, Michael J. The Federal Impeachment Process, A Constitutional and Historical Analysis, Princeton University Press (1996) (hereafter, Gerhardt, The Federal Impeachment Process), 103-104; see also 1974 House Judiciary Committee Staff Report, 7.*

24 *Sunstein, Impeachment, A Citizen's Guide, 37, quoting from Berger, Impeachment, the Con-*

Three things stand out from the English practice to assist us in interpreting our Constitution. First, impeachment was deployed as a check on the power of the Crown when it was perceived to be under- mining the interests of the king's subjects, often as expressed in acts of Parliament.[25] Second, England had developed a bicameral procedure under which the House of Commons would consider evidence to de- termine if there were sufficient grounds for issuing articles of impeach- ment, after which the House of Lords would try the accused, determine guilt or innocence and assess punishment if there were a conviction. Third, and perhaps most informative, under the rubric of "high crimes and misdemeanors," impeachable offenses included non-criminal con- duct in the discharge of official duties.

Following America's independence, several of the states included an impeachment mechanism in their constitutions, including Delaware, Massachusetts, New York, North Carolina and Pennsylvania.[26] During the 1780s, the list expanded to include Georgia, New Hampshire and South Carolina. The standards for impeachment varied among the states. For instance, in Delaware, impeachable offenses were defined as "offending against the state by maladministration, corruption, or other means, by which the safety of the commonwealth might be en- dangered."[27] In New Hampshire and Massachusetts, officers could be impeached for misconduct or maladministration, and in New York impeachment was available against all officers for "mal and corrupt" conduct. Thus, even before the Constitutional Convention in 1787, the practice had been imported into the republican forms of various state governments, with impeachment available for non-criminal conduct.[28]

---

stitutional Problems, 71-72.

25 *1974 House Judiciary Committee Staff Report, 7.*

26 *Sunstein, Impeachment, A Citizen's Guide, 39.*

27 *Ibid., 39-40.*

28 *Ibid.; see also 1974 House Judiciary Committee Staff Report, 7.*

CHAPTER 3
THE ROAD TOTHE CONSTITUTIONAL CONVENTION

"... the Confederation appears to me to be little more than an empty sound and Congress a nugatory body."[29]

As all of us learned in school, the Constitution was drafted at a Convention of delegates from the states/former colonies that was held in Philadelphia in the summer of 1787. Ratification followed two years later. The Constitutional Convention of 1787 was a seminal event in American history, constituting what many scholars believe to have been the second American revolution.

Articles of Confederation .

The Constitutional Convention grew out of the failure of the Articles of Confederation that were drafted in 1777 and ratified in 1781. The Confederation had been formed by the states/former colonies, which remained sovereign.[30] There was a "Congress," made up of delegates

---

29 *George Washington quoted in Ellis, Joseph J., The Quartet, (Vintage Books, 2015) (hereafter Ellis, The Quartet), 108-109.*

30 *Articles of Confederation, art. II.*

appointed by the legislatures of the states.[31] Because this Confedera- tion Congress did not derive its authority from the people, it had no power to tax or regulate commerce. Therefore, the Confederation Con- gress could request money from the states, but had no way to compel compliance with the requests. All decisions relating to war-making, including raising an army and raising the money to pay for combat, required a vote of at least nine of the thirteen member States.[32] Absen- teeism was a problem. For example, the Confederation Congress was initially unable to assemble a quorum to ratify the Treaty of Paris end- ing the Revolutionary War or to accept General George Washington's highly symbolic resignation.[33]

As a vehicle for managing the war, the Confederation Congress was sorely lacking. George Washington and his Continental Army bore the brunt of its inadequacies. Troop quotas sent to the state legislatures were regarded as requests and none of the states complied.[34] The mon- ey to support the troops that did show up was never sufficient. As a result, Washington's troops were plagued by the lack of food, clothing and ammunition. Washington summed it up by saying, "[c]ertain Iam that unless Congress speaks in a more decisive tone; unless they are vested with powers by the several states competent to the great pur- pose of War . . ., that our Cause is lost . . . I see one head gradually changing into thirteen."[35]

The Confederation "Executive" was actually a cumbersome "Committee of the States" (with a rotating "president") that only sat when Congress was in recess.[36] The delegates to the Constitutional Convention viewed the absence of an "energetic" executive as one of the most glaring short-comings of Confederation "governance."[37]

31 *Ibid., art. IX.*
32 *Ibid.*
33 *Ellis, The Quartet, 74.*
34 *Ibid., 17-18.*
35 *Ibid., 18.*
36 *Articles of Confederation, art. IX.*
37 *Sunstein, Impeachment, A Citizen's Guide, 28.*

By 1787, the Confederation was on the verge of dissolution.[38] Washington's assessment quoted at the head of this chapter was correct and widely accepted. Something had to be done. Although the Confed- eration was nominally the official sponsor of the Convention, its orga- nizing energy came from the efforts of James Madison and Alexander Hamilton, efforts that ultimately won the imprimatur of Washington. All three had become convinced that the amending the Articles of Confederation was not a practical alternative because to do so required the unanimous approval of all the states.[39] That requirement had torpedoed efforts in 1781, 1783 and 1784 to amend the Articles to allow the Confederation Congress to collect duties on imports as an independent source of revenue (1781 and 1783) and to regulate foreign commerce (1784).[40]

In yet another attempt to amend theArticles to allow for congres- sional authority over foreign trade, at Virginia's invitation, a group of twelve "commissioners" from five states (Virginia, New York, Penn- sylvania, Delaware and New Jersey) gathered in Annapolis in Sep- tember 1786.[41] Madison and Hamilton were both there, but not Wash- ington. Those in attendance did not believe that they had sufficient representation to act. Not willing to abandon the project, Hamilton claimed there was unanimous support at the Annapolis convention for another convention in Philadelphia in May 1787, with a broad man- date to address "all salient issues" under the Articles of Confederation. There was, of course, no guarantee that the states would respond to such a clarion call for change.

Two things happened to develop the momentum necessary to at- tract delegates to the Philadelphia Convention. First, Shays Rebellion, which unfolded in Massachusetts from the summer of 1786 to the win-

38 *Ibid., xvii.*

39 *Articles of Confederation, art. XIII.*

40 *Rakove, Jack N., editor, The Annotated U.S. Constitution and Declaration of Independence, (Harvard University Press, Cambridge, 2009) (hereafter Rakove, The Annotated Constitution), 26; see also Ellis, The Quartet, 99-100; Stewart, David O., The Summer of 1787,(Simon & Schuster Paperbacks, 2007) (hereafter Stewart, The Summer of 1787), 9-10.*

41 *Stewart, The Summer of 1787, 9-11.*

ter of 1787, dramatically underscored the failure of government un- der the Confederation.[42] Motivated by crushing debt and burdensome taxes, the rebels sought to avoid being hauled into a court that always seemed to favor the creditors threatening to repossess mortgaged farm- land. The first skirmish in the rebellion occurred in the summer of 1786 when crowds of Massachusetts farmers prevented the court from con- vening in Northampton.[43] In October, the Confederation Congress met in New York City to authorize troops to restore order in Massachusetts. However, the states refused to pay for the troops, a stinging reminder of the impotence of the Confederation Congress.[44] Massachusetts was left to its own devices to blunt the rebellion, raising a force of 4,000.

By the winter, the rebellion had a name and a leader, Daniel Shays, who was thrust into leadership by virtue of his military experience. On a snowy day in late January 1787, Shays was in command of one of three columns that advanced on an arsenal in Springfield defended by the state troops. The attack failed and the state troops pursued the rebel force for another week and surprised the rebels who were holed up in Petersham. The leaders fled to Vermont and most of the rebels simply went home.[45] With that, the rebellion sputtered to its end.

Shays and his ragtag rebels were, in truth, not much more than an annoyance. But these events sent shock waves through the political leadership of the Confederation. Within a decade of the Declaration of Independence, Americans were fighting each other over some of the very issues that motivated their war against the British Empire. The Confederation seemed incapable of dealing with the underlying issues and the minor threat posed by Shays rebels. As Henry Knox, Washington's Revolutionary War artillery commander, put it in a letter to the General, the rebellion ". . . wrought prodigious changes in the minds of men . . . respecting the

42 *Ibid.,11-16.*
43 *Ibid., 12.*
44 *Ibid., 12-13.*
45 *Ibid., 14-15.*

powers of government –everybody says they must be strengthened."[46]

The second big attraction to the Convention was Washington, if he agreed to attend. While he believed that the Articles of Confedera- tion were a governmental disaster, he nonetheless needed to be coaxed out of retirement to get him to the Convention, and thereby require Washington to renege on his pledge that, once retired, he would re- main a private citizen. Washington's most prized possession was his integrity and he was reluctant to go back on his word, unless there was a good chance that the states would show up. Madison, Hamilton, Washington's wartime aide de camp, and John Jay joined with Knox, eventually persuading Washington to enter the fray. But it wasn't easy. As late as March of 1787, Washington indicated privately that he would not attend the Convention.[47] That same month, Knox advised Washington to attend. Washington trusted Knox, who had been with him from the very beginning when the General took command over the Continental Army outside of Boston in 1776. Equally persuasive was Madison's state-by-state poll that showed there would be a quo- rum this time. That put the issue over the top for Washington and he agreed to attend, thereby assuring that a Convention would be held.[48] Republicanism in America before the Constitutional Convention.

While the Confederation was unraveling, the states had become hot houses of republicanism.[49] By 1787, every state had drafted at least one constitution, each of which experimented with one form or an- other of

46 *Ibid., 15.*

47 *Ellis, The Quartet, 110.*

48 *For a detailed description of the campaign to recruit Washington from retirement to preside at the Convention see Stewart, The Summer of 1787, 97-120.*

49 *"Republican" government was one of three forms of government that late 18th century lead- ers recognized as deriving legitimacy from the consent of the governed. A "republic" was a form of representative government without a hereditary executive, what we think about today as "representative democracy." In contrast was a constitutional monarchy, which featured a hereditary executive. The third form, "democracy," was thought of as the direct voice of the people in government, invariably occurring in small homogenous populations. See Ketcham, Ralph (ed.), The Anti-Federalist Papers and the Constitutional Convention Debates (Signet Classics, New York, 2003) (hereafter Ketcham, The Anti-Federalist Papers), xiv-xv. This book contains a helpful compendium of the key documents and debates at the Convention, with explanatory notes, as well as Ketcham's excellent introductory survey of the political and governmental landscape leading to the Convention.*

separation of powers, but almost all of which featured strong legislatures with relatively weak governors. According to Thomas Jefferson's rough arithmetic, the thirteen new states each had eleven years — collectively a total of nearly 150 years — of experience with republican government.[50] By the time of the 1787 Convention, Amer- icans had experimented with a variety of forms of representative gov- ernment. They had a strong sense of the good and the bad and brought those opinions to Philadelphia. Among other things, the shortcomings of a weak executive had become apparent. As Madison said about the weak executive under the Virginia constitution, it was "the worst part of a bad constitution."[51]

50 *Ibid., xi.*
51 *Ibid., xii.*

CHAPER 4 THECONSTITUTIONAL CONVENTION AND AMERICAN EXCEPTIONALISM

"Thus I consent, Sir, to this Constitution because I expect no better, and I am not sure that it is not the best."[52]

The Background .

The Constitutional Convention began its work on May 25, 1787, in the East Room of the Pennsylvania Statehouse in Philadelphia, the very same room in which The Declaration of Independence had been debated and signed.[53] The 55 delegates from 12 states[54] were relatively young, well-educated, tested by war and steeped in politics, including, most significantly, the politics of failure under the Articles of Confederation. The average age was 44. Twenty-nine had college degrees. Twenty-nine had also studied law. Thirty-five had served in the Continental Army. Forty-two had served in the Confederation Congress.[55] If you're looking for American exceptionalism, here it was. As Thomas Jefferson, who was serving as the Confederation Minister to France at the time, said in a letter to John Adams,

52 *Benjamin Franklin, as read on his behalf by James Wilson, on the last day of the Constitutional Convention, September 17, 1787, as quoted in The Quartet, 153.*

53 *This was the date at which a quorum was assembled, eleven days after the proposed start on May 14th. See Rakove, The Annotated Constitution, 31-33.*

54 *Rhode Island did not send a delegation.*

55 *Stewart, The Summer of 1787, 140.*

who was serving the Confederation in England, "it is really an assembly of demigods."[56]

It might be worth highlighting some of the luminaries in attendance. George Washington, among those representing Virginia, was the central figure at the Convention and the first to sign the Constitution. He had been the embodiment of the Revolution even before the Declaration of Independence had been signed, and had led a bedraggled and ignored Continental Army to outlast the British expeditionary forces sent byKing George III to bring the colonies to heel. He was revered even more during his lifetime than he is today. Indeed, it is hard for us completely to fath- om the magnitude of his dominance at the time. He contributed virtually nothing to the substance of the Constitution, his remarks consuming only five lines of Madison's notes of the Convention. But his presence in the presiding chair was the essential ingredient that gave hope for success. As the "father of his country,"[57] Washington's absence would have doomed the effort before it started.[58]

Benjamin Franklin, one of eight delegates representing the host state of Pennsylvania, was by far the senior statesman. At 81, he was old enough to be Washington's father, and grandfather to many of the delegates. He added revolutionary "street cred," tempered by worldly wisdom and political experience. As the quote at the head of this chap- ter indicates, he also had an uncanny instinct for weighing in when restoring balance was necessary. He was the one who left us the most memorable quip coming out of the Convention. When asked "what have you given us, a monarchy or a republic?" he replied, "a republic if you can keep it."

---

56 Ibid., 25.

57 The "father of his country" honorific was apparently first bestowed on the General by Knox in a letter to Washington in March 1787, urging him to participate in the Constitutional Convention. See Ellis, The Quartet, 111-112.

58 As a fitting postscript to George Washington's legacy, it would be well to note that, in his will written in the summer of 1799, he directed that his slaves be given their freedom and directed his estate to support freed slaves who were too old to work and to pay to educate others. See Stewart, The Summer of 1787, 257. At least one of the founders paid penance for the sin of slavery embedded in the country's governing charter.

James Madison was there too as what might be called the "Pre- parer in Chief." He was the architect of the Virginia Plan that con- tained the constitutional structure that set the agenda for the debates at the Convention. At five foot four and 120 pounds, Madison was a well-educated, gnomish figure and a practical politician who was able to bring his intellect and prodigious preparation to bear on the thorny and contentious issues that were debated. In advance of the Conven- tion, Madison had borrowed from Thomas Jefferson, and then studied, the contents of several crates of books that represented the latest Euro- pean wisdom on political philosophy, adding to his already substantial knowledge on the topic, as well as his practical experience.[59]

Alexander Hamilton, who had served as one of General Wash- ington's aides-de-camp during the Revolutionary War, had long been a strong and vocal advocate for scrapping the Articles of Confedera- tion in favor of a new national government that was not beholden to the states, nor hamstrung by the absence of effective and energetic leadership. Hamilton was instrumental in pushing the states toward the Convention. He vigorously supported a national government and a strong executive within that scheme. Hamilton's role in writing many of the Federalist Papers was instrumental in winning ratification and his service as Washington's first Secretary of the Treasury is credited with building the foundation of America's national economy.

Gouverneur Morris, from Pennsylvania, was the most vocal spokesman for a strong national government and a strong executive at the Convention and was the only delegate who spoke more than Madi- son. While many delegates contributed to the creation of the Constitu- tion, it was Morris who actually wrote it in its final form.[60] He was the author of the majestic words of the Preamble, which he changed from the pedestrian "We the people of the States of New Hampshire, Massa- chusetts, etc.," to the more poetic, "WE THE PEOPLE." This deft edit also placed the source of the

59 *Stewart, The Summer of 1787, 126.*

60 *Ibid., 150-151.*

new nation's legitimacy on "the People," as opposed to the existing states.[61] He later served as Washington's ambassador to England and France, and also represented Pennsylvania in the U.S. Senate.

George Mason, a Virginia delegate, was Washington's long-time friend and political compatriot. He wrote Virginia's Declaration of Rights in early June 1776, from which Jefferson borrowed heavily in drafting the Declaration of Independence later that month.[62] Mason also played an important cameo role in the final debate on the defi- nition of an impeachable offense on September 8, 1787. However, he eventually parted company with his fellow Virginians, including Washington and Madison, refusing to sign the Constitution and oppos- ing it during the ratification debates because he thought it violated the sovereignty of the states.

While Washington, Madison, Hamilton, Morris and a few others came to the Convention bent on creating a national government that was not dependent on the states for its sovereignty, there were oth- ers at the Convention who believed that such a government would be unworkable and an abandonment of the very principles on which the American Revolution had been founded. These "moderates" preferred amendments to the Articles of Confederation, rather than a wholesale change, and they did not want to sacrifice the sovereignty of the states provided by the Confederation. Moreover, with the exception of two members of the New York delegation,[63] all those opposed to a nation- al republic boycotted the Convention. Although the absence of these Anti-Federalists facilitated the creation of the Constitution, their views remained to be reckoned with in the ratification phase of the endeavor. Alexander Hamilton, speaking at the very beginning of the in- augural Federalist Paper, expressed the historical importance of this self- conscious creative act and the special role that history had assigned to the framers:

---

61 *Stewart, The Summer of 1787, 234.*

62 *Ibid., 36-37.*

63 *The only New York delegate to sign the Constitution was Alexander Hamilton.*

> "It has frequently been remarked that it seems to have been reserved to the people of this country, by their conduct and example, to decide the importantquestion, whether societies of men are really capable or not of es- tablishing good government from reflection and choice, or whether they are forever destined to depend for their political constitutions on accident and force."[64]

History has shown that the answer to Hamilton's question is a re- sounding "yes!" When they were finished, the founders had created a new form of government by choice of the people. Whereas the kings and queens of Europe ruled as of divine right from God, the Constitution took its authority from the consent of the people who were to be governed.[65] This document has been the central rallying flag for Americans throughout the history of the Republic, which we have kept for 239 years.

The Constitutional Convention and the Executive .

Article II of the Constitution begins with a simple declaration: "The executive Power shall be vested in a President of the United States of America."[66] That executive power included taking care that the laws enacted by Congress are "faithfully executed;"[67] serving as the Com- mander in Chief of the armed forces;[68] sharing treaty making and ap- pointment power with the Senate;[69] the power of "reprieves and par- dons," except in cases

---

64 *Federalist No. 1, The Federalist Papers, 1.*

65 *The people themselves were not consulted in some massive continent-wide referendum. But the existing state legislatures were bypassed in favor of independently selected "ratification con- ventions" of the states. Many scholars believe that this was not a philosophical statement, but rather a political gambit by Madison and the other promoters of the document to avoid the existing state legislatures that would not have ratified the Constitution in the form it emerged from Philadelphia in September 1787. And, of course, the people decidedly did not include the millions of African American slaves who were relegated to the status of 3/5 personage with no rights until the 13th and 14th amend- ments that were extracted from the body politic as a result of the Civil War.*

66 *U.S. CONST., art. II, § 1.*

67 *Ibid., art. II, § 3.*

68 *Ibid., art. II, § 2.*

69 *Ibid.*

of impeachment;[70] and wielding a limited veto power over bills passed by Congress.[71] This final formulation was by no means predictable at the outset of the Constitutional Convention.

The framers were well-steeped in and committed to the "separa- tion of powers" doctrine that found its first developed statement in the writings of a French philosopher, Montesquieu, who posited a triad of power: "that of enacting laws, that of executing the public resolu- tions, and of trying the causes of individuals."[72] This tripartite form of republican government had already been widely adopted by the states following independence. It was generally accepted that the national government would be built upon that same tripartite foundation, with checks and balances among the three departments to preclude domi- nance of any one over the other two.

With that three-branch structure, it must also be remembered that the presidency harbored within itself the ghost of despotism that was at the very heart of the American Revolution. In Jefferson's soaring prose in the Declaration of Independence:

> ". . . But when a long train of abuses and usurpations, pursuing invariably the same object evinces a design to reduce them under absolute Despotism, it is their right, it is their duty, to throw off such a Government, and to provide new Guards for their future security – Such has been the patient suffering of these Colonies; and such is now the necessity which constrains them to alter their former Systems of Government. The history of the present King of Great Britain is a history of repeated injuries and usur- pations, all having in their direct object the establishment of an absolute tyranny over these States. . . ."[73]

---

70 *Ibid.*

71 *Ibid., art. I, § 7.*

72 *Quoted in Rakove, Jack N., Original Meanings – Politics and Ideas in the Making of the Constitution, (Alfred A. Knopf, New York, 1996) (hereafter Rakove, Original Meanings), 248.*

73 *Preamble to Declaration of Independence of 1776.*

Having won their independence from what they believed to have been a despotic king, Americans, with the possible exception of Alexan- der Hamilton, were not about to turn around and install a new king.[74] Yet, by 1787, those actively involved in government had concluded that the absence of an executive was one of the greatest defects of the Articles of Confederation.[75] Alexander Hamilton, Gouverneur Morris and James Wilson of Pennsylvania were the most out-spoken advocates for an "energetic executive."[76] Madison was ambivalent, but he was certain of one thing: it was imperative to create an independent executive capable of withstanding manipulation by the legislature.[77] Washington, who said nothing on this or virtually any of the subjects that came up, was the most reliable living example of what the executive could and should be.

There was no question that an executive was going to be one of the three "departments" of the government. Beyond that, it was mushy. The delegates faced a "Goldilocks dilemma." As expressed by Gou- verneur Morris:

> "It is most difficult rightly to balance the executive. Make him too weak, the legislature will usurp his powers. Make him too strong and hewill usurp the legislature."[78]

So, the balance between the legislature and the executive had to be "just right." As a result, the debates on the executive took up more time and energy than any other issue.[79] The issues were interdependent.

---

74 *Hamilton was an advocate for a strong "Magistrate," arguing in a speech at the Convention that the English model was a good one and that President should be elected for life and should have the power of an absolute veto over laws passed by the legislature, a view that gathered virtually no support. See The Summer of 1787, 95.*

75 *Sunstein, Impeachment, A Citizen's Guide, 28.*

76 *Rakove, Original Meanings, 255-256.*

77 *Ibid.*

78 *Stewart, The Summer of 1787, 157*

79 *Ellis, The Quartet, 142-143. In addition to The Quartet, the description of the debates on the executive and impeachment is drawn from the following: Berger, Impeachment, the Constitutional Problems; Rakove, Original Meanings; Sunstein, Impeachment, A Citizen's Guide; Stewart, The Summer of 1787; Gerhardt, The Federal Impeachment Process; and Turley, "Senate Trials and Factional Disputes."*

For instance, the longer the term of the executive, the more concerns there were about the powers given to him and the more pressure there was for an impeachment mechanism to remove him from office if he abused his authority. As another example, the mode of election raised questions about his independence vis a vis the legislature, as well as the difficult issues regarding the relative power allocated to the states versus the "people" in electing the legislature (the "big state" versus "small state" issue). The more the delegates debated the executive, the more puzzled they became. Their consideration of this department was "frustratingly episodic and even circular."[80]

In this picture, impeachment was the tail on the dog and the tail was definitely not wagging the dog. Since impeachment was included as a check on the executive, its final form was intertwined with the conception of the presidency as finally enshrined in the Constitution. Closure on impeachment could not be achieved until the form of the executive had taken definite shape, and that did not occur until almost the very end of the Convention.

The delegates' first decision was that the executive would be "uni- tary," a buzz word for one person.[81] At the same time, they soundly rejected Hamilton's motion to give the executive an absolute veto, but did agree to a limited veto power. That happened on June 4th, about two weeks after a quorum had been achieved on May 25th.

Then, during late July, the framers turned their attention to the interlocking issues of how the executive would be elected, length of term, "re-eligibility" for office, impeachment and the so-called "coun- cil of

---

80 Original Meanings, 256.

81 The proposal for a single executive was made on June 1, 1787, by James Wilson of Penn- sylvania and passed by a seven to three vote on June 4th. See Farrand. Max (ed.), The Records of the Federal Convention of 1787, Vol. I, 97. This decision was an easy one, given the bad experience with the "executive by committee" under the Articles of Confederation and problems that had surfaced under the state constitutions. Alexander Hamilton devoted Federalist 71 to a discussion of the benefits of a single executive as compared to a committee, or to a single executive obligated to consult with a "council," as was the case in some of the states. See The Federalist Papers, 176-180.

revision."[82] On July 26th, the Convention designated a"Commit- tee c Detail" to compile a document that contained what had been agreed upon to that date and to make proposals on issues that were still undecided. On August 6th, the Committee produced the first draft of the Constitution.[83] The executive was addressed in Article X. It called for the executive power to be "vested in a single person," to be elected by the legislature. His powers included: "duly and faithfully executing the laws of the United States;" commissioning of officers of the United Sates; serving as commander and chief of the armed forces; and acer- emonial role in foreign affairs, but not treaty making, which was left to the Senate. It provided that the President could be removed from office when impeached by the House and convicted by the Senate for "treason, bribery or corruption."

The draft prepared by the Committee on Detail was a major step forward, but much remained to be done. The mode of election and issues relating to the allocation of responsibilities, especially between the executive and the Senate, continued to be debated in August, but without resolution. On August 31st, a committee (the "Committee of Eleven") was appointed to propose solutions to "such parts of the Con- stitution as have been postponed."[84]

The Committee of Eleven reported back to the assembly on Sep- tember 4th, with a proposal that was close to a final resolution. It in- cluded an executive elected by an electoral college for a four-year term, with eligibility for reelection, shared responsibility by the President and the Senate for treaty making and administrative appointments, and a removal procedure under which the House would impeach the Pres- ident and the Senate would conduct the trial, as had previously been contemplated under the August 6thdraft.

82 Rakove, Original Meanings, 258 -262. The text of the debate can be found in The Records of the Federal Convention of 1787, Vol. II., 64- 70. . The "council of revision" was a proposal to create a body made up of the executive and the judiciary to wield veto power over legislation. Among other considerations, the framers were concerned that either of the other two branches acting alone would not have sufficient "gravitas" to keep the legislature in check. The proposal was defeated by a narrow margin, four states to three, with two divided. At the same time, a limited executive veto was unanimously affirmed.

83 The text of this document is in The Anti-Federalist Papers, 122-134.

84 Rakove, Original Meanings, 264.

chment Debates .

ed to presidential impeachment there were essentially four ; that unfolded at the Convention: whether the President should be subject to impeachment in the first place; the proper forum for impeachment trials; the grounds for impeachment; and thenumber of votes necessary for conviction/removal.[85]

The most extensive debate on the propriety of presidential im- peachment occurred on July 20th, while the delegates were still wran- gling over a number of other issues about the shape of the executive. Three positions were advanced during the debate. The day before, Gouverneur Morris, who, like Hamilton, favored an "energetic executive," had spoken against including a power to impeach the President in the Constitution, warning that impeachment would "render the president dependent on those who are to impeach him."[86] At the other extreme was Roger Sherman's view, which received little support, that the leg- islature should have the unfettered power to remove the President.[87]

As the debate unfolded, it gravitated toward a middle view advocated by a number of delegates, including James Madison, who argued that it was "indispensable" to provide for presidential impeachment. Otherwise, the president might "pervert his administration into a scheme of peculation and oppression. He might betray his trust to foreign powers."[88] Franklin noted in a morbid comment that, without impeachment, "recourse was had to assassination in which he [the "Magistrate"] was not only deprived of his life but of the opportunity of vindicating his character."89[89] George Mason, who played a major role in the final debate that was yet to come,

85 *Gerhardt, The Federal Impeachment Process, 5-10.*

86 *Ibid., 7.*

87 *Sunstein, Cass, "Impeaching the President, An Essay," 147 Univ. Penn. L. Rev. 279 (December 1998) (hereafter Sunstein, "Impeaching the President"), 286.*

88 *Ibid., 287.*

89 *The Records of the Federal Convention of 1787, Vol. II, 65.* *89 The Records of the Federal Convention of 1787, Vol. II, 65.*

stated that "[n]o point is of more importance than that the right of impeachment could be continued. Shall any man be above justice? Above all shall that man be above it, who can commit the most extensive injus- tice."[90] Edmund Randolph favored impeachment because the Executive "will have great opportunit[ie]s of abusing his power; particularly in time of war when the military force and in some respects the public money will be in his hands."[91]

Having heard these comments, Gouverneur Morris agreed that impeachment was necessary, but urged that the "cases ought to be enumerated & defined."[92] Accordingly, on July 26th, the Convention reaffirmed what had been the tentatively decided on July 20th, that the President shall be "removed for impeachment and conviction of malpractice or neglect of duty."[93] From this point forward, impeachment was included as a mechanism for removing the President, but significant issues remained over the impeachment process and what the grounds for impeachment would be. However, the "trend of the discussion was toward allowing a narrow impeachment power by which the President could be removed only for gross abuses of public authority."[94]

Madison, Hamilton and others preferred to have the nationaljudicia- ry try impeachments. The other leading candidate to determine convic- tion was the Senate. At the time of the appointment of the Committee of Eleven on August 31st, no choice between the two had been made. In its report of September 4, the Committee provided for impeachment in the House and a trial in the Senate, essentially adopting the well-established bicameral procedure under English law, under which the House of Com- mons had the impeachment power, with the House of Lords determining conviction and punishment. It also proposed that conviction would require atwo-thirds

90 *Ibid.*
91 *Ibid., 67.*
92 *Ibid., 65.*
93 *Ibid., 121.*
94 *Sunstein, "Impeaching the President," 287.*

super-majority.[95] All of these were agreed to by the assembly and they became part of theConstitution.

The remaining question became the most significant in the im- peachments and trials of Presidents Johnson and Clinton: on what ba- sis can the President be impeached and, if convicted, removed from office? There was a circuitous route to the final standard of "treason, bribery, or other high crimes and misdemeanors" that was incorporat- ed into the Constitution. Various standards were suggested throughout the course of the Convention, including "mal-" and "corrupt admin- istration," "misconduct in office" and "neglect of duty, malversation, or corruption." As already noted, the August 6th draft used the term "treason, bribery or corruption."

On September 4th , the Committee of Eleven proposed that re- moval of the President should be limited to "treason or bribery." Re- membering the various far more expansive formulas suggested by the delegates over the course of the three months they had been together in Philadelphia, the following brief but important exchange occurred on Saturday, September 8th, as recorded in Madison's notes:

> Col. Mason. Why is the provision [as contained in the Committee's report] restrained to Treason & bribery only? Treason as defined in the Constitution will not reach many great and dangerous offenses. Hastings is not guilty of Treason. Attempts to subvert the Constitution may not be Treason as above defined – as bills of attainder which have saved the British Constitution are forbidden, it is more necessary to extend the power ofimpeachments.
>
> He moved to add after "bribery" "or maladministra- tion." Mr. Gerry seconded him–
>
> Mr. Madison: So vague a term will be equivalent to a tenure during pleasure of the Senate.

95 Ibid., 8-9.

Mr. Govr. Morris, it will not be put in force & can do no harm – An election every four years will prevent maladministration.

Co. Mason withdrew "maladministration" & substitutes "other high crimes & misdemeanors agst. the State."[96]

Mason's reference to "Hastings" was to a celebrated English impeachment case ongoing at the time of the Convention and well- known to the delegates. Hastings, the Governor-General of India, was charged with "high crimes and misdemeanors" in the form of mal- administration, corruption in office and cruelty toward the people of India.[97] Mason's point was that, under English law, treason was not the only grounds on which impeachment could be based. His substitute language of "high crimes or misdemeanors" was also known to the delegates as a term of art under English law that included a range of se- rious criminal and non-criminal conduct for which impeachment was available.[98] Mason had said earlier in the Convention that the President should be punished "when great crimes were committed."[99] The fact that he included the words "against the state" indicated that he under- stood that the impeachable conduct had to be directed at the state.

With one exception, the language that resulted from the exchange made it into the final version of the Constitution. When the Committee on Style produced the final document the words "against the state" were removed.[100] This odd bit of drafting history has provided a hook for those who argue that the removal of the qualifying language re- flected a decision by the Convention to open up impeachment for conduct by the President that does not relate to his official duties. This became a significant interpretation issue during the impeachment of President Bill Clinton.

96 *The Records of the Federal Convention of 1787, Vol. II., 550. A Bill of Attainder was a special legislative act that inflicted capital pun- ishment upon persons supposed to be guilty of high offenses, such as treason and felony, without conviction in the ordinary course of judicial proceedings. As Mason said, Bills of Attainder were excluded under the Constitution in what became art. I, § 9.*

97 *1974 House Judiciary Committee Staff Report, 7.*

98 *Berger, Impeachment, the Constitutional Problems, 66.*

99 *Ibid., 91, f.n. 158.*

100 *The Records of the Federal Convention of 1787, Vol II, 600.*

That argument ignores the fact that the Committee on Style did not have the authority to change the meaning of the language of the document as it was submitted to them for "polishing up."[101] It also fails to account for the impeachment debates during the Convention that the framers and ratifiers were concerned about significant breaches of trust by the President and their adverse effect on the body politic.

101 *Sunstein, "Impeaching the President," 288.*

CHAPTER 5
WHAT IS AN IMPEACHABLE OFFENSE?

Like so much else in the Constitution, there is a lot packed into the eight words defining an impeachable offense: "treason, bribery, or other high crimes and misdemeanors." The last four words seem espe- cially wide open on their face. As you might expect, there are different views about what they mean. But, before we get to those, let's remind ourselves of what the people who drafted and ratified the Constitution had to say.

We start with the fact that, under English law, impeachment was available to remove ministers who had engaged in non-criminal con- duct. As we have already seen, the framers were aware of and drew upon this English law when they adopted the English term of art, "high crimes and misdemeanors." Second, the debates on impeachment at the Constitutional Convention referred to such non-criminal conduct as "neglect," "maladministration," and the like when they spoke of the grounds for removing the President. The key exchange among Mason, Madison and Governeur Morris on September 8th quoted above at pag- es 28 and 29 underscores the point.

The political tracts issued and statements made at some of the ratification conventions further support the conclusion that the Consti- tution authorizes impeachment for non-criminal conduct. Hamilton's definition of impeachment in Federalist 65 is telling. Impeachment, according to Hamilton, one of the signers of the Constitution and an active participate in promoting its ratification, "proceeds from the mis- conduct of public men . . . from the abuse or violation of a public trust." The offenses that support impeachment . . . may with peculiar propriety be denominated POLITICAL, as they relate chiefly to inju- ries done immediately to society itself."

The historical record also includes statements made at both the Virginia and North Carolina ratifying conventions that reveal an un- derstanding that impeachment was not limited to criminal conduct. In Virginia, James Madison, George Nicholas, John Randolph and Ed- mund Randolph all stated that impeachable offenses were not limited to indictable crimes.[102] John Randolph elaborated that "[in] England, those subjects which produce impeachments are not opinions . . . It would be impossible to discover whether the error in opinion result- ed from a willful mistake of the heart, or an involuntary fault of the head," stressing that only willful conduct, not errors of opinion would be impeachable.[103]

At the North Carolina convention, the most significant remarks on the scope of impeachable conduct were made by James Iredell, who was later appointed as an associate justice of the Supreme Court. He noted the complexity, if not impossibility, of describing the bounds of impeachable conduct other than to acknowledge that it involves serious injuries to the federal government. He understood impeachment to be "calculated to bring [great offenders] to punishment for crime which it is not easy to describe," although he gave the following examples: giv- ing false information to the Senate; bribery, or, more broadly, "acting from some corrupt motive or other."[104] He also distinguished between "want of judgment" (not impeachable) and "willfully abusing[ing] his trust" (impeachable).[105] As

102 *Gerhardt, The Federal Impeachment Process, 9.*

103 *Ibid; see also 1974 House Judiciary Committee Staff Report, 14.*

104 *Ibid., 18-19.*

105 *Ibid.*

an example of impeachable conduct Iredell cited a situation President had received a bribe . . . from a foreign power, a influence of that bribe, had address enough with the Senate, by misrepresentations, to seduce their consent to a pernicious trea

One scholar has looked for but been unable to find "a single ex- ample of an impeachable offense advanced on the record that did not involve [the abuse of public power]."[107] Echoing Hamilton's Federalist 65, Justice Joseph Story wrote in his Commentaries on the Constitution in 1833 that impeachment applies to offenses of a "political char- acter" that are so varied as to be impossible of exact definition:

> "Not but that crimes of a strictly legal character fall within the scope of the power . . .; but that it has a more enlarged operation, and reaches, and reaches, what are a termed political offenses, growing out of personal misconduct or gross neglect, or usurpation, or habitual disregard of the public interests, in the discharge of the duties of political office. These are so various in char- acter, and so indefinable in their actual involutions, that is almost impossible to provide systematically for them by positive law. They must be examined upon very broad and comprehensive principles of public policy and duty."[108]

In summary, it is clear from the framers' understanding of En- glish common law, as well as the Convention and ratification de- bates that those who drafted and ratified the Constitution meant to make a president removable from office for certain non-criminal conduct. It is also clear that the non-criminal conduct was not to be unlimited. The debates at the Convention, and especially Madison's concerns expressed in the debate on September 8th, show that the framers wanted there to be limits on "high crimes and

---

106 *Sunstein, "Impeaching the President," 289 107 Ibid., 290.*

107 *Ibid., 290.*

108 *Quoted in 1974 House Judiciary Committee Staff Report, 16-17.*

isdemean- ors." Otherwise, in Madison's words, the President would end up with a "tenure during the pleasure of the Senate." This theme was carried forward into the ratification debates, which reveal that, in Hamilton's words, impeachable conduct had to relate to the vio- lation of some public trust, with ". . . injuries done immediately to society itself." Others were keen to assert that the conduct had to constitute some "great offense." The words that were chosen to describe impeachable conduct underscore that point: "a scheme of peculation [i.e. embezzlement] and oppression," "corrupt," or "willful breach of trust," as opposed to "want of judgment."

Based on this record, there are two mainstream arguments that together are widely accepted. Under both these views, a president may be impeached for conduct that is not indictable as a crime, but there are limits on Congress's power to do so.

The "Originalist" View .

One of the mainstream views is that the meaning of the impeachment phrase must be determined by looking at what the term "high crimes and misdemeanors" meant under English common law as understood by the framers at the time the Constitution was drafted and ratified, as reflected in the text of the Constitution and contemporaneous state- ments made by the framers and ratifiers, as well as the historical con- text surrounding its drafting and ratification.

The most prominent modern proponent of this view is Professor Raoul Berger. He contends that, while Parliament claimed an unlimited to right to define impeachable conduct, the framers had amore limited view with respect to the American adaptation. They included a tight definition of treason in the Constitution and listed bribery along with it. To broaden the ambit of impeachable offenses, they adopted the English phrase "high crimes and misdemeanors" because they thought the words had a limited technical meaning.[109] They further conceived that the President would be impeachable not just for indictable crimes, but for other "great offenses" such as "corruption or perfidy." The conduct needs to be limited to a cause that would win the assent of "all right thinking men."[110]

A "Living Meaning" of Impeachable Offense.

The other, which begins with the same material relied upon by the "originalists," also asserts that, given the difficulties in imagining all of the complex, unpredictable situations that might justify removal, the framers meant for the scope of impeachment to be worked out in the future on a case-by-case basis, but constrained by the principles derived from the "original materials." Professor Michael Gerhardt is a well-regarded advocate of this view. He concludes that the framers made a decision loosely to define "other high crimes and misdemean- ors" with the content to be developed later as the cases arose.[111] Profes- sor Sunstein has pointed out that the fact that the impeachment power has been so little used is itself an indication that it has been reserved by the Congress for truly exceptional cases.[112]

Perhaps the most eloquent statement of this view was authored by Senator William P. Fessenden in his written opinion in support of his votes to acquit Andrew Johnson of the impeachment charges brought against Johnson in 1868:

> ". . .It is evident, then, as it seems to me, that the offence [sic] for which the Chief Magistrate is removed from of- fice, and the power intrusted [sic] to him by the people transferred to

---

109 Berger, Impeachment, the Constitutional Problems, 310-311.

110 Ibid.

111 Gerhardt, Michael J., "The Presidency: Twenty-Five Years After Watergate, Putting the Law of Impeachment in Perspective," 43 St Louis U. L. J. 905 (1999). See also Weeden, Darnell, "The Clinton Impeachment Indicates a Presidential Impeachable Offense is Only Limited by Constitutional Process and Congress' Political Compass Directive," 27 Williams Mitchell Law Review, Vol. 27: Iss. 4, Article 7 (2001) (hereafter Weeden, "The Clinton Impeachment"); Gerhardt. The Federal Impeachment Process, 103-111; Sunstein, Impeachment, A Citizen's Guide , 64- 79; 1974 House Judiciary Committee Staff Report, 25.

112 Sunstein, "Impeaching the President," 293-298.

> other hands . . . should be of such a charac- ter as to commend itself at once to the minds of all right thinking men as, beyond all question, an adequate cause. It should be free from taint of party; leave no reasonable ground for suspicion upon the motives of those who inflict the penalty; and address itself to the country and the civ- ilized world as a measure justly called for by the gravity of the crime, and the necessity for its punishment. . . ."[113]

Given the fact that the historical record contains only two presi- dential impeachments, the differences in outcome between these two schools of thought is, at least so far, without any real distinction. To- gether they stand for the proposition that a president may be removed for non-criminal conduct that amounts to a serious breach of trust causing injury to the political "community," and that the Congress's ability to do so is not unlimited.

Impeachable Conduct Is What The Congress Says It Is .

The mainstream positions are book-ended by two extreme views. First, there is the open-ended view that an impeachable offense is whatever the House and the Senate together agree is impeachable as they ex- ercise their respective constitutional roles in the process. This view was most famously espoused by then-Congressman Gerald Ford when he proposed the impeachment of Supreme Court Justice William O. Douglas in 1970. He asserted that an impeachable offense is whatever the House of Representatives, with the requisite concurrence of the

Senate, considers it to be.[114] It also receives at least some support from academia. For example, Professor L. Darnell Weeden has opined that "I believe the words 'high crimes and misdemeanors,' for purposes of presidential impeachment, mean whatever the requisite majority in Congress want them to mean."[115]

113 Trial of Andrew Johnson, President of the United States, before the Senate of the United States, Impeachment by the House of Representa- tives for High Crimes and Misdemeanors, Vol. III, Government Printing Office (1868), 30.

114 Berger, Impeachment, the Constitutional Problems, 56 and f.n. 1.

115 Weeden, "The Clinton Impeachment," 2516.

There is some superficial appeal to this unfettered view of "high crimes and misdemeanors," since it is clear from the text of the Consti- tution and the contemporaneous materials that the Constitution assigns no substantive role to the judiciary in the impeachment process. This was made clear in a Supreme Court case decided 23 years after Con- gressman Ford made his claim on behalf of Congress to the power to define the grounds for impeachment as they please. In Nixon v. United States,[116] the petitioner was Walter L. Nixon, a former Chief Judge of the United States District Court for the Southern District of Mississip- pi. He was convicted by a jury of two counts of making false statements before a grand jury impaneled as part of an investigation into reports that Nixon had accepted a gratuity from a Mississippi businessman in exchange for asking a local district attorney to halt the prosecution of the businessman's son. He was sentenced to prison.

However, Judge Nixon refused to resign his position as a federal judge and continued to collect his federal paycheck during his incar- ceration. Impeachment was necessary to terminate this unseemly use of taxpayers' money. The House sent three articles of impeachment to the Senate, which invoked a Senate rule under which a committee of Senators was appointed to receive evidence and take testimony. The Senate committee held four days of testimony from ten witnesses, in- cluding Nixon himself. The committee presented to the full Senate a transcript of the proceedings before the committee and a report stating the uncontested facts and summarizing the evidence on the contested facts. Nixon and the House impeachment managers submitted briefs to the full Senate and delivered arguments from the Senate floor during the three hours set aside for oral argument in front of that body. The full Senate voted to convict Nixon.

Nixon argued that, under the Constitution, the trial must be con- ducted in its entirety before all the Senators. Since that had not hap- pened, he asked the trial court to rule his impeachment conviction in-

116 506 U.S. 224 (1993).

valid and to restore his salary and other privileges. Both lower courts rejected this argument, as did the Supreme Court. In a deferential opin- ion for the court, Chief Justice Rehnquist concluded that there was no textual basis for limiting the Senate's discretion in deciding what pro- cedure it would use to fulfill its obligation to "try" the official, in this case a judge, on the articles of impeachment delivered to the Senate by the House.

The Chief Justice pointed out that the framers had considered sce- narios in which the power to try impeachments was placed in the fed- eral judiciary, including a proposal by Madison that the Supreme Court should have that power. The ultimate version gave the sole power to the Senate for reasons explained by Hamilton in Federalist 65. First, according to Hamilton, the Senate was the "fit depositary for this im- portant trust because its members are representatives ofthe people."[117] Second, the Supreme Court was not the proper body because the framers "doubted whether the members of that tribunal would, at all times, be endowed with so eminent a portion of fortitude as would be called for in the execution of so difficult a task" or whether the Court "would possess the degree of credit and authority" to carry out its judgment if it conflicted with the accusation brought by the legislature, the people's representative.[118] The Constitution assigns no role in the process to the judiciary and it seems evident that the Senate has broad discretion to conduct the trial in any manner it chooses as a body.[119] In addition, the framers believed that the Court was too small. Hamil- ton says, "The awful discretion, which a court of impeachments must necessarily have, to doom to honor or to infamy the most confidential and the most distinguished characters of the community, forbids the commitment of the trust to a small number of persons."[120]

---

117 The Federalist Papers, 165.

118 Ibid.

119 Both the House and the Senate have the Constitutional authority to ". . . determine the Rules of its Proceedings. . ." U.S. CONST., art. I, § 5, cl. 2.

120 The Federalist Papers, 165.

Although the only issue before the Court was a procedural one related to the Senate's unilateral ability to define the makeup of the "trial" called for by the Constitution, the decision is widely read as standing for the proposition that questions relating to impeachment are not "justiciable," meaning that the courts do not have jurisdiction to decide the dispute, in this case because the Constitution is clear that

the judiciary does not have any role in the impeachment process.[121] This, however, does not give the Congress unfettered discretion to de- cide what grounds will justify removing a President from office. That issue was not before the Court and it is unlikely that it ever will be.

The assumption of unfettered discretion ignores the clear record from the Constitutional Convention and the ratifying debates, as well as commentary from others writing in the early 19th century familiar with the founding generation, that there are limits to the scope of conduct that will support removal of a president. It is well to remember that there was substantial concern expressed during the Convention debates that the formula could not be such as to invite the legislature to impeach a president based solely on their disagreement with his actions. In Madison's words, such a vague term as "maladministration" would be "equivalent to a tenure during the pleasure of the Senate." The Ford position of unfettered discre- tion, if adopted, would subject the President to "votes of no confidence" as in the British system. This would make the President completely beholden to Congress, a practice that is at odds with the separation of powers at the heart of the Constitution.

121 See, e.g., Gerhardt, The Federal Impeachment Process, 118-124.

Presidents May Be Removed Only for Indictable Crimes .

This argument was first advanced in 1867 amidst the debates in Congress over the impeachment of Andrew Johnson. Professor Theodore W. Dwight wrote an article in March 1867 that elaborated the view, based on his reading of English common law, that impeachment must be based on an indictable crime under federal law.[122] Those who op- posed impeachment and were looking for a way to reduce Johnson's exposure seized on Professor Dwight's analysis, which found its way into a Judiciary Committee Minority Report on Impeachment issued in December 1867.[123] It was also seized upon by Senators who voted to acquit President Johnson in his impeachment trial in 1868. Finally, it was picked up by James St. Clair in a February 1974 memorandum when he was chief defense counsel for Richard Nixon, "fighting like

hell" to keep the impending threat of Nixon's impeachment at bay.[124]Just this year, this argument has been resurrected by Professor Alan Dershowitz.[125]

This position was rejected by the staff of the House Judiciary Committee in the Nixon case[126] and receives virtually no support from constitutional scholars.[127] It ignores the English cases, well-known to the framers, where

122 Dwight, Theodore, "Trial by Impeachment," The American Law Register (1852-1891), Vol. 15, No. 5, New Series Volume 6 (Mar. 1867) (hereafter Dwight, "Trial by Impeachment"), 257-283. Dwight's analysis was effectively refuted in an article by former Judge and Congressman William Lawrence of Ohio, published in The American Register in September 1867. See "The Law of Impeachment," The American Register, (1852-1891), Vol. 15, No. 11, New Series Volume 6 (Sep. 1867) (hereafter Lawrence, "The Law of Impeachment"), 641-680.

123 House Report No. 7, 40th Congress, 1st Session (Republican Minority Report), 59-105.

124 Berger, Impeachment, the Constitutional Problems, 331.

125 Dershowitz, Alan, The Case Against Impeaching Trump (Hot Books, New York, 2018). However, he acknowledges that the overwhelming weight of opinion is against him. Ibid., 143, f.n. 37.

126 1974 House Judiciary Committee Staff Report, 14-15.

127 On November 9, 1998, as part of the Clinton impeachment proceedings, nineteen law professors, political scientists and historians tes- tified before the House Subcommittee on the Constitution regarding the grounds for presidential impeachment. While there was disagreement about what those grounds are, they all unanimously agreed that the President can be removed for conduct other than indictable crimes. See Impeachment of President William Jefferson Clinton, The Evidentiary Record Pursuant to S. Res. 16, Vol. XX, Hearing of the Subcommittee on the Constitution, "Background and History of Impeachment" (November 9, 1998) Ser. No. 63, U.S. Government Printing Office (1999); see also 1974 House Judiciary Committee Staff Report, 22-25.

impeachment was based on non-criminal conduct. More importantly, it brushes aside the debates at the Constitutional Convention and during the ratification process that the phrase "high crimes and misdemeanors" was meant to embrace "political crimes" amounting to great breaches of trust. Confining it to indictable crimes would be incompatible with the intent of the framers to provide a mechanism broad enough to maintain the integrity of constitutional government. Impeachment is a constitutional safety valve that must be sufficiently flexible to deal with circumstances that are not foresee- able.[128]

128 1974 Judiciary Committee Staff Report, 25.

CHAPTER 6
IMPEACHMENT AND TRIAL UNDER THE CONSTITUTION

The Bifurcated Procedure .

The impeachment procedure established by the Constitution roughly mimics the respective roles of the lower and upper legislative chambers in the British process. Like the House of Commons, impeachment is committed to the assembly that is more directly tied to the people, the House of Representatives,[129] which ". . . shall have the sole Power of Impeachment."[130] This is an official charge against the person being impeached, taking the form of "articles of impeachment," approved by a majority of the House. The Senate, like the House of Lords, then conducts the trial, with the Senators under oath.[131] When the President is being tried, the Chief Justice of the United States presides.[132] Conviction requires a "super majority" of two thirds of the members present.[133]

---

129 Before the 17th Amendment was ratified in 1913, Senators were elected by the state legislatures, not by popular vote.

130 U.S. CONST., art. I, § 2, cl. 5. For a description of the impeachment process and the trial conducted before the Senate, see Weeden, "The Clinton Impeachment."

131 U.S. CONST., art. I, § 3, cl. 6.

132 Ibid. This is the only role assigned to the judiciary in the impeachment/trial process. It is largely ceremonial. As the impeachment trials of Presidents Johnson and Clinton have demonstrated, the rulings made by the Chief Justice can be overruled by vote of the Senators.

133 Ibid.

As described in Walter Nixon v. United States, there was some support during the Convention debates for a judicial role in the im- peachment process, which was rejected by the Convention. As a prac-

tical matter, this has meant that Congress is in a position to take action that cannot be checked by the other branches of the government. Thus, the House and Senate are left to exercise constitutional restraint on their own conduct. Against the risk that Congress will not rise above partisan pressures to encroach on the powers of the executive are the bifurcation of the process between the House and the Senate and the "super majority" requirement for conviction in the Senate, which saved both Andrew Johnson and Bill Clinton from being convicted.

Other Procedural Provisions .

The Constitution dispenses with a number of other procedural is- sues in terse language. Significantly, the only remedy upon conviction for impeachment is removal from office: "Judgment in cases of Im- peachment shall not extend further than to removal from Office, and disqualification to hold and enjoy any Office of honor, Trust, orProfit under the United States."[134] However, ". . . the Party convicted shall nevertheless be liable and subject to Indictment, Trial, Judgment and Punishment, according to Law."[135]

The Constitution expressly exempts trial by jury for impeach- ment.[136]Other than that, the House and Senate are free to adopt what- ever rules they deem appropriate to manage the impeachment process in the House and to conduct the trial in the Senate.[137] The President's pardon power does not extend to persons convicted on impeachment: "he shall have Power to grant Reprieves and Pardons for Offenses against the United State, except in Cases of Impeachment."[138]

134 U.S. CONST., art. I, § 3, cl. 7
135 Ibid.
136 U.S. CONST., art. III, § 2.
137 Both the House and the Senate have the constitutional authority to ". . . determine the Rules of its Proceedings. . ." U.S. CONST., art. I, § 5, cl. 2.
138 U.S. CONST., art. III, § 2.

The Constitutionasratified in 1789 contained both a standard forremoval of a president and a procedure to accomplish it. The first time the mechanism was activated against a president was 79 years later as the Civil War wound down and the national political leadership struggled with its consequences.

PART 2

PRESIDENT ANDREW JOHNSON

CHAPTER 7
THE WRONG MAN FOR TROUBLED TIMES

"Andrew Johnson was the queerest character that ever occupied the White House."[139]

When John Wilkes Booth's bullet placed the mantle of the Presidency on Andrew Johnson in April 1865, fortune played a transformative trick on America. The assassinated President had not only steered the Union through the travails of the most devastating event in the history of the Republic, but his views about slavery and the place of blacks in American society had also been transformed. He captured his vision for a reimagined and healed America in the soaring words of his Second Inaugural Address delivered in his high pitched voice from the steps of the Capitol to a mud-soaked crowd on March 4, 1865, just 41 days before his assassination.

As the election season opened in 1864, it was by no means certain that Abraham Lincoln would see a second term. It wasn't until the Union battlefield victories in the late summer of 1864 that his re-elec- tion was secured. On Inauguration Day, the war was not over, but it seemed to

139 Assessment of Johnson by a contemporary, as quoted in Berger, Impeachment, the Constitutional Problems, 269.

have been won, and the President directed his eloquence to the future. For whatever reason the war may have started, Mr.Lincoln made it clear that it would end only with the demise of slavery:

> "... Fondly do we hope, fervently we do pray, that this mighty scourge of war may speedily pass away. Yet, if God wills that it continue until all the wealth piled by the bondsman's two hundred and fifty years of unre- quited toil shall be sunk, and until every drop of blood drawn with the lash shall be paid by another drawn with the sword, as was said three thousand years ago, so still it must be said 'the judgments of the Lord are true and righteous altogether.'"

The slaves were to be freed.[140] But what of those who had en- slaved them and sought to rip the Union asunder? To them, heextend- ed this olive branch:

> "With malice toward none, with charity for all, with firmness in the right as God gives us to see the right, let us strive on to finish the work we are in, to bind up the nation's wounds, to care for him who shall have borne the battle and for his widow and his orphan, to do all which may achieve and cherish a just and lastingpeace among ourselves and with all other nations."

In March 1865, as Lincoln saw it, the nation was already on its way to "reconstructing" itself. On December 8, 1863, Lincoln had is- sued his Proclamation of Amnesty and Reconstruction, a template for restoring the full stature of the seceded states. It provided for pardons to individual Confederates who took a loyalty oath and agreed to ac- cept that slavery had been abolished. An ex-Confederate state could form a new government

140 They had already been freed in the South by Lincoln's Emancipation Proclamation on January 1, 1863, which declared "all persons held as slaves within any State or designated part of a State, the people whereof shall then be in rebellion against the United States, shall be then, thencefor- ward, and forever free." In addition, as noted in the text, at the time of the Lincoln's Second Inaugural Address, the 13th Amendment had been passed by Congress, but not yet ratified by the states.

when the number of Southerners who took the oath amounted to ten percent of the votes cast in the 1860 election. The new state constitutions would have to abolish slavery, but unspec- ified "temporary measures" could be employed to transition the freed people into their new status. Property, except as to slaves and where the "rights of third parties shall have intervened," was restored to those who took the oath. There was no mention of black suffrage.[141] Howev- er, Lincoln left room for modifications of the structure created in his Proclamation: ". . . while the mode presented is the best the Executive can suggest, with his present impressions, it must not be understood that no other possible mode would be acceptable."

Congress also spoke on emancipation. On January 13, 1865, the 13th Amendment abolishing slavery passed Congress and was ratified by the states on December 6, 1865, eight months after Lincoln's death. Thus, the country was irretrievably committed to the emancipation of the slaves as a bedrock for rebuilding the South.

As important as these measure were, they were just the begin- ning of the process of "binding up the nation's wounds." There was much work to be done and, even within Lincoln's party, there was not a consensus about what would be undertaken in the future to redeem the former slaves and reintegrate the ex-Confederate states back into the Union. We will never know what would have happened if Lincoln had not been shot. What we do know is that his replacement, Andrew Johnson, was the wrong man for these troubled times. His approach to Reconstruction and hidebound personality led to a pitched battle with his own party in Congress and ultimately to his impeachment.[142]

141 The Proclamation of Amnesty and Reconstruction by the President of the United States, December 8, 1863, http://www.freedmen.umd. edu/procamn.htm; see also Gordon-Reed, Annette, Andrew Johnson, (Times Books, Henry Holt and Company, New York, 2011) (hereafter, Gordon-Reed, Andrew Johnson), 108-109. There were exemptions from the amnesty, including Confederate military officers above a certain rank and members of Congress who had withdrawn from their positions to "aid the rebellion."

142 Johnson was never really a Republican. He always saw himself as a "Jacksonian Democrat." His nomination for the Vice Presidency on the "Republican Unity Party" ticket was designed to garner broader support in the 1864 Presidential Campaign. While President, Johnson unsuccessfully

Abraham Lincoln and Andrew Johnson shared much incommon. They were the same age, they both grew up in poverty, Lincoln had lit- tle formal schooling, Johnson had none, they were ambitious, and they had both achieved material comfort before the Civil War.[143] But their personalities and political skills were strikingly different. Lincolnwas a gifted leader. He was the master of nuance and compromise amidst complex issues, with an uncanny ability to gauge the political winds and tack to them, while keeping his ultimate destination in mind. In contrast, Johnson lacked Lincoln's political antennae and his genius for compromise and leadership.[144] Complex problems frustrated him and he sought refuge from them in general rules to govern all situa- tions. Once he made up his mind he would not yield his point, but in- stead would fight to sustain his position with every weapon at hand.[145]

Andrew Johnson was born to Jacob and Mary ("Polly") Johnson in 1808 in a log cabin in Raleigh, North Carolina. Jacob and Mary were average uneducated working people. They were both illiterate.[146] Jacob was known to have occupied a "humble but useful station," having served as the "city constable, sexton and porter to the State Bank."[147] At the age of three, Johnson's father died, leaving his mother to raise her two surviving children, both boys, although she soon remarried.

---

sought the Democratic nomination for the Presidency in the 1868 election.

143 Foner, Eric, Reconstruction, America's Unfinished Revolution, 1863-1877 (Updated Edition) (Harper Perennial Modern Classics, New York, 2002) (hereafter Foner, Reconstruction); 176; see also Hearn, Chester G., The Impeachment of Andrew Johnson, (McFarland & Company, Inc., New York, 2000) (hereafter Hearn, Impeachment of Andrew Johnson), 3.

144 Berger, Impeachment, the Constitutional Problems, 265.

145 Benedict, Michael Les, The Impeachment and Trial of Andrew Johnson (W.W. Norton & Company, New York, 1999) (hereafter Benedict, The Impeachment and Trial of Andrew Johnson), 3.

146 Gordon-Reed, Andrew Johnson, 18.

147 Quoted from a newspaper article that appeared after his death in the Raleigh Star in Trefousse, Hans L., Andrew Johnson, A Biography (W.W. Norton & Company, New York, 1991) (hereafter, Trefousse, Andrew Johnson), 20.

When Johnson was ten, he was apprenticed to a tailor, like his older brother before him. This apprenticeship supplied him with a trade and a means to support himself and ultimately his family.[148] His ap- prenticeship also provided the fortuitous circumstance by which he learned to read. Among his master's customers was an eccentric gen- tleman who regularly visited the shop and read aloud from books and newspapers to young Andrew. He soon learned to read and, once he did, Johnson regularly devoted two or three hours to study at the end of the working day. After he was married in 1827, his wife taught him how to write and do arithmetic.[149]

After bouncing around in North and South Carolina, Johnson landed in the eastern Tennessee village of Greenville, the county seat of Green County in 1826.[150] He was able to establish a successful tailor shop and generate enough revenue to begin buying real estate. These two ventures allowed Johnson to prosper. Greenville was also where he got his start in politics, being elected as an alderman in 1829, at the age of 21. In 1834, he was selected by the other aldermen as Greenville's mayor. Thereafter, in rapid fashion, he was elected to the Tennessee state legislature (1840) and the state Senate (1841). Beginning in 1845, he served three terms as a U.S. Representative. In 1853 he was elected Governor of Tennessee and was re-elected in 1855. In 1857, he was elected by the state legislature as a U.S. Senator.[151]

Although slavery existed in Johnson's home base of eastern Tennes- see and Johnson himself owned a number of house slaves,[152] the economy and culture in that part of the state were dominated by small subsistence farmers

148 *Ibid.*

149 *Harper's Weekly Article, May 13, 1865, http://www.impeach-andrewjohnson.com/03BackgroundOf AJ/i-7.htm. Harper's Weekly was the most important national periodical in the Reconstruction period. It had a circulation exceeding 100,000 and its estimated readership was over half a million. Its news and editorial columns were comparable to today's Time Magazine and CNN News. http://www.andrewjohnson. com/01Introduction/Introduction.htm.*

150 *Trefousse, Andrew Johnson, 26.*

151 *Foner, Reconstruction, 176; see also Harper's Weekly Article, September 15, 1866, http://impeach-andrewjohnson.com/03Background- OfAJ/i-10.htm.*

152 *In 1860, he owned one adult couple and three children. See Trefousse, Andrew Johnson, 45.*

who remained loyal to the Union during the Civil War. Through- out his political career, Johnson identified himself as a populist who sup- ported the white "yeomanry" against the "slaveocracy" of the large plan- tations that dominated the politics of Tennessee and the rest of the South. True to the Unionists of this political base, Johnson was the only U.S. Senator from a seceding state that remained in the Senate. This earned him the trust and gratitude of Abraham Lincoln, who appointed Johnson as the military governor of Tennessee in 1862. While still serving as military governor, Johnson was nominated on the Republican Union Party ticket as Vice President.[153] In March 1865, he resigned as military governor in order to assume his duties as Lincoln's Vice President.

Without a doubt, Johnson was an accomplished and successful politician. Indeed, he was one of the most experienced politicians ever to become the President of the United States. He was upright and hon- est, and his doggedness and courage had served him well.[154] He was an accomplished stump orator who spoke from the gut and could whip an audience into a frenzy.[155] Although not a successful legislator, he had been an effective military governor, serving during trying times that, along with his loyalty to the Union, had earned him the Vice Presidency. At the same time, Johnson came to the presidency with signifi- cant shortcomings. While successful, his life had been "one intense, unceasing desperate upward struggle."[156] This desperate struggle had taken a toll on his psyche. According to Jefferson Davis, Johnson had ". . . an intense, almost morbidly sensitive pride."[157] His fellow Ten- nessean and former President, James K. Polk, said that Johnson was ".. . very vindictive and perverse in his character."[158] Privately,

153 Lincoln pushed for adding "Union" to the name of the Republican Party as an emblem of the unification of the country that would occur once the war had ended.

154 Berger, Impeachment, the Constitutional Problems, 269.

155 Gordon-Reed, Andrew Johnson, 4-5.

156 Benedict, The Impeachment and Trial of Andrew Johnson, 3.

157 Rehnquist, William H., Grand Inquests, The Historic Impeachments of Justice Samuel Chase and President Andrew Johnson (William Morrow and Company, Inc., New York, 1992), (hereafter Rehnquist, Grand Inquests), 200.

158 Ibid.

he was self-absorbed and lonely, with few friends. His Secretary of the Navy and ally, Gideon Welles, remarked that "he has no confidants and seeks none."[159] He lacked flexibility and sensitivity to public opinion. He was unable to give any credit to his opponents' views and he never understood that he was expected to bargain with Congressional lead- ers.[160] To sum it up, one of his of his contemporaries described Johnson as ". . . the queerest character that ever occupied the White House."[161] Perhaps even more troubling in retrospect was that the man whom fortune had put in Lincoln's chair was an unwavering white suprem- acist. The message he delivered to Congress on December 3, 1867 contains proof enough. In remarking on the 1867 Reconstruction Act passed by Congress over his veto, which he had previously said was designed to "protect niggers,"[162] the President had this to say:

> "It is not proposed merely that they [the "Negroes"] shall govern themselves, but that they shall rule the white race, make and administer State laws, elect Pres- idents and members of Congress, and shape to a greater or less extent the future destiny of the whole country. Would such a trust and power be safe in such hands? . . . It is the glory of white men to know that they have had the qualities in sufficient measure to build upon this continent a great political fabric and to preserve its sta- bility for more than ninety years . . . But if anything can be proved by known facts, if all reasoning upon evi- dence is not abandoned, it must be acknowledged that in the progress of nations Negroes have shown less ca- pacity for government than any other race of people."[163]

159 Foner, Reconstruction, 177.

160 Berger, Impeachment, the Constitutional Problems, 269.

161 Ibid.

162 Trefousse, Hans L., Impeachment of a President – Andrew Johnson, the Blacks and Reconstruction (Fordham University Press, New York, 1999) (hereafter, Trefousse, Impeachment of a President), 5.

163 President Andrew Johnson's Third Annual Message to Congress, December 3, 1867. https://millercenter.org/the-presidency/presiden- tial-speeches/december-3-1867.

Andrew Johnson's stubborn commitment to rebuilding the South by placing the political power in the hands of the white race would run head long into an equally stubborn group of so-called Radical Republicans who based their plan for the South on the bedrock of black suffrage. This was the grist of the impeachment mill that ground over the next three years, culminating in Johnson's impeachment in February 1868, just shy of three years after the presidential mantle was placed on his shoulders.

CHAPTER 8
ROUND ONE OF THE RECONSTRUCTION BATTLE

"Sir, I am right. I know I am right and I am damned if I don't adhere to it."[164]

"Reconstruction" is one of those fuzzy events that lurk in the recesses of our minds. It is something that we packed into our brains in simplified form for a test in American history class in high school and then promptly forgot about. The word itself is an unintended pun, with two different but interdependent meanings. The South was both physically decimated and deprived of function- ing governments by the Civil War. The economy had to be rebuilt ("reconstructed"). Before that could really happen, it was necessary to rebuild ("reconstruct") the governments that had collapsed in such a way that recognized the Union victory and the huge new reality of the American economy and body politic: 4,000,000 souls who had been enslaved were now free. This was a two-pronged problem ofphenom- enal complexity and difficulty.

Andrew Johnson's vision of Reconstruction was based on two things: a strict reading of the Constitution and white supremacy. John- son had an "extreme reverence for the Constitution," with an "almost hypnotic

164 *President Andrew Johnson to his private secretary on January 2, 1866.*

determination to follow what he conceived its spirit and let- ter."[165] In his mind, the Union and the Constitution were inseparable.[166]

He believed that the states that had purportedly seceded from the Union never really left it, because the Constitution provided no mechanism for that to happen. Therefore, the ordinances of secession" were "mere nullities."[167] The rebelling states were entitled to a republican form of government under Article IV, Section 4 of the Constitution. As part of that guarantee, Johnson believed that all states, including those that had attempted to secede, had an unfettered right to determine which of its citizens had the right to vote.

Since Johnson also believed that the freed slaves should not be enfranchised, the work of Reconstruction would be left in the hands of "loyal" whites.[168] Except as to slavery, " the states are to retain the character which belonged to them before the war."[169] In this regime, there was no commitment to civil equality or a political role for blacks. Johnson did not think that the status of blacks should be an obstacle to Reconstruction.[170] In his own words, "[w]hite men alone mustmanage the South."[171] Johnson would dedicate the resources of his Presidency to making that happen.[172]

As you would expect, when Andrew Johnson was inaugurated on April 15, 1865, the day after Lincoln's assassination and six days after Lee surrendered to Grant at the Appomattox Courthouse, there was no unanimity on what needed to be done. To understand the reasons for Johnson's impeachment, it is necessary to look at the battle over Reconstruction between Johnson and the Republican Party, which en- joyed a two-thirds majority in both Houses

---

165 Berger, Impeachment, the Constitutional Problems, 269.

166 President Andrew Johnson's Third Annual Message to Congress, December 3, 1867. https://millercenter.org/the-presidency/presiden- tial-speeches/december-3-1867.

167 Ibid., 3.

168 Ibid., 6-7; see also Harper's Weekly Article, May 13, 1865. http://www.impeach-andrew-johnson.com/03BackgroundOf AJ/i-7.htm.

169 Harper's Weekly Article, May 13, 1865. http://www.impeach-andrewjohnson.com/03Back-groundOf AJ/i-7.htm

170 Foner, Reconstruction, 178-180.

171 Ibid., 180.

172 Trefousse, Impeachment of a President, 29.

of Congress throughout Johnson's Presidency, a key fact in the political struggles to come.[173]

The Republican Party itself was by no means a monolith. To the contrary, it was a big tent with much conflict among the three rough groups that populated it. The Radical Republicans were the most doc- trinaire on the issues of black suffrage and the need to vanquish the Confederate leadership just as the Union Army had defeated the rebels on the battlefield. They became wedded to removal of President Johnson as early as 1866 and pushed hard and repeatedly for his impeach- ment from that time.Their leader in the House of Representatives was Thaddeus Stevens of Pennsylvania, a long-time abolitionist and fire breathing hater of the South. In the Senate, Benjamin Wade of Ohio was their leader. As the President pro tempore of the Senate, he stood next in line after Johnson for the Presidency.

The Moderate Republicans occupied the middle of the political landscape. At least initially, they agreed with Johnson about black suf- frage, but parted ways with him on a number of other issues related to Reconstruction. Prominent among the Moderates were Senators Wil- liam P. Fessenden of Maine, who served briefly as Lincoln's Secretary of the Treasury, James W. Grimes of Iowa, and Lyman Trumbull of Illinois, co-author of the 13th Amendment. Both Fessenden and Grimes detested the Radical leadership.[174] Representative James Wilson of Iowa was a prominent Moderate in the House. As Chair of the House Judiciary Committee, he played a leading role in the House impeach- ment proceedings.

The Conservative Republicans were at the opposite end of the po- litical spectrum from the Radicals. They did not endorse the Radicals' Reconstruction policy and generally supported Johnson's Reconstruc- tion

173 The discussion of Reconstruction is not intended to be exhaustive or definitive. The purpose is to provide enough information for the reader to understand the issues and the vehement disputes over those issues sufficient to place Johnson's impeachment in its historical context. A detailed treatment of Reconstruction can be found in Eric Foner's Reconstruction, widely recognized as the definitive modern textbook on the subject.

174 Trefousse, Impeachment of a President, 22.

measures. The Conservatives also frequently found themselves agreeing with northern Democrats on a number of economic and polit- ical issues unrelated to Reconstruction.

While Johnson's white supremacy and racism cries out as offen- sive to the modern reader, his approach wasn't that much different from the structure Lincoln created in his December 8, 1863 Proclamation of Amnesty and Pardon. Both approaches committed to republican forms of government for the rebelling states, leaving the issue of black suf- frage up to them, Lincoln by implication, Johnson by assertion. Im- portantly, as usual, Lincoln, who had indicated before his death a will- ingness to grant at least limited black suffrage, had left himself wiggle room. Johnson never did.

Johnson's views on black suffrage and the lot of the freed slaves were actually in the mainstream at the time, as a majority of Johnson's countrymen shared his racial prejudices.[175] Only five states, all in New England, allowed blacks to vote on the same terms as whites.[176] At the close of the Civil War, for most Americans, Reconstruction meant the proscription of "rebels," not the recognition of the rights of blacks.[177] Few Republicans, apart from the Radicals, seemed anxious to make black suffrage a reason to repudiate the President. Northern Democrats supported Johnson.[178] Moreover, powerful Northern economic inter- ests supported revival of the cotton trade, which favored stabilityover reform, especially radical reform.[179] Most Northerners would proba- bly have been satisfied with two requirements for Reconstruction: that the 13th Amendment would be ratified by the rebelling states and that high-ranking Confederates would be banned from office.[180]

The Radical Republicans were further to the left than the main- stream of America. With the exception of Thaddeus Stevens, who was from

175 *Trefousse, Impeachment of a President, 17.*
176 *Foner, Reconstruction, 222.*
177 *Ibid., 186.*
178 *Ibid., 217.*
179 *Ibid., 220.*
180 *Rehnquist, Grand Inquests, 204.*

Pennsylvania, their constituencies were centered in New England and the band of states to the west along the Great Lakes. In these states, the superiority of the free labor system appeared evident, pre-war re- form had flourished and the Republican Party enjoyed overwhelming majorities.[181] The Radicals adamantly believed that the Republican North had not fought and won the Civil War merely to surrender that victory to unrepentant rebels.[182] In 1865, they were the only political group that supported black suffrage, which was the centerpiece of their Reconstruction program.[183]

In their view, without the black vote, the old Southern ruling classes – the great planters and their allies – would be back in con- trol. If allowed, these former rebels would align with the Northern Democrats and, with the nullification of the 3/5 compromise, after 1870 the South would have greater strength in Congress than ever before.[184] Added to this political motivation was the Radicals' be- lief that allowing blacks to vote was the only way to secure their civil rights. The Radicals based their program on a vision of free enterprise grounded on private property and small land holdings, which included the eventual integration of blacks into the Ameri- can economy and political community.[185]

Despite the rabid confrontations to come, President Johnson en- joyed the proverbial, but very brief, honeymoon at the beginning of his unexpected Presidency. At first, the Radicals, who had a rocky relation- ship with Lincoln, viewed Johnson as a godsend. A group of Radical lawmakers, including Benjamin Wade, met with Johnson right away to sound him out. They went away heartened by Johnson's exclamation that "I hold this: . . . treason is a

181 Foner, Reconstruction, 228.

182 Berger, Impeachment, the Constitutional Problems, 267.

183 Rehnquist, Grand Inquests, 221.

184 Under Article I, §, cl. 2 of the Constitution, slaves were counted as 3/5 of a person for determining representation in the House. Once the slaves were freed under the 13th Amendment, they presumably could be counted as "whole persons," a presumption that was confirmed by Section 2 of the 14th Amendment, which was ratified on July 9, 1868.

185 Trefousse, Impeachment of a President, 17.

crime and crime must be punished."[186] Congress went home in May and, by the end of the month, the honeymoon was over. On May 8th, Johnson, whose Cabinet was even- ly divided on black suffrage, recognized the Southern governments in Arkansas, Louisiana, Texas and Virginia that had been created under Lincoln's December 1863 Proclamation, none of which had extended the vote to blacks. This was a slap in face of the Radicals.[187] Then, on May 29th, Johnson publicly announced his Reconstruction program, with his own Proclamation of Amnesty and Reconstruction.[188] John- son left in place Lincoln's program for reconstructing the Southern governments, which did not provide for black suffrage. This allowed Johnson to claim fidelity to Lincoln's vision of Reconstruction while supporting the white Southerners who, like Johnson, were adamant- ly opposed to black suffrage. This meant that, under Johnson's plan, Southern politics would be limited to the white population, leaving the freed slaves at the mercy of their former masters.

Like Lincoln, Johnson included an amnesty oath in his Procla- mation, with certain exclusions similar to Lincoln's, but adding a pro- vision that excluded ex-Confederates who owned property valued at more than $20,000. This seemed to be aimed at the "slaveocracy" that Johnson had vilified for years. Significantly, Johnson also allowed for individual pardons for those who were otherwise exempted, "and such clemency will be liberally extended as may be consistent with the facts of the case and the peace and dignity of the United States." This turned out to be the path by which the pre-war Southern political class found its way back into power. As the months unfolded, Johnson liberally granted clemency. Although he wanted to hold off on clemency to the main Confederate leaders, he was ready to begin a broad policy of forgiveness. Generals, cabinet members and diplomats asked for and were given either pardons or parole.[189]

---

186 Foner, Reconstruction, 177; see also Harper's Weekly Article, May 13, 1865, http://www.impeach-andrewjohnson.com/03BackgroundO- fAJ/i-7.htm (attributing this statement to Johnson: "[traitors] must not only be punished, but impoverished.")

187 Foner, Reconstruction, 182; see also Rehnquist, Grand Inquests, 202.

188 The Proclamation can be found at https://cwnc.omeka.chass.ncsu.edu/items/show/13.

189 Trefousse, Andrew Johnson, 227.

On May 29th, President Johnson issued another Proclamation, this one "Reorganizing a Constitutional Government in North Carolina," a state that had not been addressed in Lincoln's December 1863 Procla- mation.[190] The Proclamation appointed William W. Holden provisional Governor of North Carolina. Noting that the Constitution guaranteed the states the right to a republican form of government, Johnson direct- ed Governor Holden, "at the earliest practicable period," to convene a convention to draft a new constitution. Delegates to the convention were to be "loyal people," that is, those who took the oath called for in his May 29th Proclamation for Amnesty and Reconstruction.

Blacks were effectively foreclosed from this process because the people who chose the delegates and those who were eligible to serve as such were limited to people who had been eligible to vote under the state constitution in effect at the time of North Carolina's secession from the Union. These people did not include the former slaves. The military commander responsible for North Carolina and all other mil- itary personnel were ". . . enjoined to abstain from in any way hinder- ing, impeding, or discouraging the loyal people from the organization .

. ." of the North Carolina government as called for in the Proclamation. This Proclamation was consistent with Johnson's view that the white man should govern the South, which directly opposed the Radicals' views.

In July 1865, Johnson's Attorney General, James Speed, began to restrict enforcement of the Confiscation Act of July 17, 1862. That Act called for the seizure of real and personal property in the South owned by major Confederate officeholders and all Confed- erates who did not return an oath of allegiance within sixty days of a presidential warning proclamation. However, title to the proper- ty had to be secured by court action and the forfeiture was limit- ed to the life of the Confederate whose

190 The Proclamation can be found at http://www.presidency.ucsb.edu/ws/index.php?pid=72403.

property was confiscated, which minimized the utility of the statute.[191] The confiscated land was to be used to aid black people in the transition from slavery to freedom.[192] At first, Speed limited the restriction to Florida, but in September he ordered the cessation of confiscation in Virginia and ruled that the law could not be invoked against corporate property. From September 1865 to December 1867, the confiscation program was at a virtual standstill.[193]

The Southern legislatures elected pursuant to Johnson's policies tended to be dominated by arch-conservatives and secessionists. Em- boldened by Johnson's support, they enacted what came to be known as black codes that imposed a regime that, while not slavery in name, amounted to slavery in fact. For example, freedmen quitting work in violation of their contracts could be forcibly returned to their employ- ers. They could also be auctioned off for "vagrancy," and their chil- dren, if not properly provided for, could be apprenticed against their will. The President refused to intervene.[194]

As a result of Johnson's program, by the time Congress returned to Washington in December 1865, all of the Southern states except Texas had returned to Confederate leadership.[195] The President be- lieved that Reconstruction was just about over. With no sympathy for the desires of northern Republicans to protect blacks and their liberty, he felt no need for further interference in the politics and economy in the South.[196] Southern politicians had been given the opportunity to form republican governments and they had done it.

On the other hand, reports from the South convinced many North- erners that Presidential Reconstruction was no Reconstruction at all. These

191 Benedict, Impeachment and Trial of Andrew Johnson, 36.

192 Ibid.

193 Ibid., 41.

194 The description of the black codes in the text is taken from Trefousse, Andrew Johnson, 230; see also Foner, Reconstruction, 199-209.

195 Benedict, The Impeachment and Trial of Andrew Johnson, 40; see also Berger, Impeachment, the Constitutional Problems, 265.

196 Benedict, The Impeachment and Trial of Andrew Johnson, 7.

reports spoke of the white Southerners' refusal to accept the consequences of their defeat, to adjust to the end of slavery and to cease the widespread mistreatment of blacks, Unionists and Northern- ers living in the South and attempting to participate in Reconstruc- tion.[197] The Radicals were outraged that Johnson had encouraged white Southerners in their adamant refusal to grant blacks any voting rights at all, or any semblance of equality. For them, the most difficult prob- lem was the persistent prejudice against blacks in both the North and the South.[198] While the majority of Republicans agreed that it was politically impossible to force a realignment of power in the South by giving blacks the right to vote, they were not ready to accept what Johnson had helped to create.

Thus, as Congress convened, the door stood open for the Presi- dent to embrace the emerging Republican consensus that the former slaves were entitled to civil equality short of suffrage and that wartime Unionists must play a prominent role in Southern politics. But John- son slammed the door shut. On January 2, 1866, he told his private secretary, "Sir, I am right. I know I am right and I am damned if I don't adhere to it."[199]

197 *Foner, Reconstruction, 224-225.*
198 *Trefousse, Impeachment of a President, 23.*
199 *Ibid., 16*

CHAPTER 9
CONGRESS FIGHTSBACK

The President was itching for a fight and he was about to get it. The first thing that the Congressional Republicans did on their return to business was to exercise their constitutional power to determine the qualifications of their own members by refusing seats to Senators and Representatives from any of the Southern states.[200] Signaling their intent to legislate their own Reconstruction program, they also voted to establish a Joint Committee on Reconstruction. These measures drew broad support among Congressional Republicans, including Senators William Fessenden of Maine and James Grimes of Iowa, both Moderate Republicans who detested the Radical leadership.[201]

At least initially, the Congressional leadership was hoping that the President would cooperate with them, a hope that was fed by a meeting a delegation from the Joint Reconstruction Committee had with the President in early January. Among others, Senator Lyman Trumbull had understood Johnson to be supportive of the committee's agenda. However those hopes were soon dashed.

The first sign of the battles ahead came in Johnson's February 19th veto of a bill sponsored by Moderate Republican Senator Lyman Trumbull to extend the Freedmen's Bureau Act of 1865, which was designed to assist

200 Rehnquist, Grand Inquests, 204; see also Trefousse, Impeachment of a President, 22.
201 Ibid.

the transition of the former slaves to freedom.[202] Trumbull thought he had secured Johnson's approval for the measure.

He and the great majority of the members of Congress were outraged by the veto.[203]

In his veto message, the President drew a sharp line between him- self and Congressional Republicans.[204] He declared that the Bill was not needed because ". . . most of the States . . . have been fully re- stored," and objected to enacting legislation affecting Southern states while they remained unrepresented in Congress. He also attacked the notion of helping freedmen when ". . . the Government . . . has never felt itself authorized to expend the public money for the thousands, not to say, millions, of the white race who are honestly toiling from dayto day for their subsistence."

Johnson next rubbed salt in Congress's wounded expectations during an impromptu speech that he delivered from the steps of the White House to a crowd of well-wishers on Washington's Birthday, February 22nd. Warned in advance not to make a speech, he got carried away by the energy of the crowd and ended up giving a strident and offensive stump speech that was widely reported in the press.[205] The speech began innocently enough, with Johnson thanking the crowd for their support and eulogizing George Washington as "first in peace, first in war, first in the hearts of his countrymen."[206] It went

202 *The existing Act was due to expire one year after the conclusion of the war, or sometime in the spring of 1866. In general, it established a "Bureau for the Relief of Freedmen and Refugees" to provide food, shelter, clothing, medical services, and land to displaced Southerners, including former slaves. It also established schools, supervised contracts between freedmen and employers, and managed confiscated or aban- doned lands. Following Johnson's veto, a more moderate Bill was proposed in May and passed by the House and Senate on July 3rd. Congress overrode Johnson's veto of this Bill and it became law on July 16th, extending the work of the Bureau for two more years. See United States Senate, Freedmen's Bureau Acts of 1865 and 1866, https://www.cop.senate.gov/artand history/history/common/generic/FreedmensBureau.htm.*

203 *Trefousse, Impeachment of a President, 27; see also Trefousse, Andrew Johnson, 243; Benedict, The Impeachment and Trial of Andrew Johnson, 11-12.*

204 *The February 19, 1866 veto message can be found at http://teachingamericanhistory.org/library/document/veto-of-the-freedmens-bureau- bill/*

205 *Trefousse, Andrew Johnson, 243-244.*

206 *The text of the speech can be found at http://teachingamericanhistory.org/library/document/speech-to-the-citizens-of-washington/. This would not be the last time that Johnson would lash*

downhill from there. In a clear reference to the Radicals, Johnson railed against "the two parties," one in the South, the other in the North that were engaged as "traitors" in an effort to disrupt the government: ". . . [t]hey agreed in the destruction of the Government, the precise thing which I have stood up to oppose. Whether the disunionists come from South Caro- lina or the North I stand now where I did then, to vindicate the Union of these States and the Constitution of the country." Goaded repeatedly by voices from the crowd to provide names, Johnson finally gave in:

"A gentleman calls for names. Well, suppose I should give them. I say [Representative] Thaddeus Stevens of Pennsylvania (tremendous applause). I say Charles Sumner [Senator from Massachusetts] (great applause). I say Wendell Phillips [a well- known abolitionist]."

Showing how carried away he was, Johnson likened himself to Christ as the savior of the Union: "If my blood is to be shed because I vindicate the Union and the preservation of this Government in its original purity and character, let it be shed; let an altar to the Union be erected, and then, if necessary, take me and lay me upon it, and the blood that now warms and animates my existence shall be poured out as a fit libation to the Union of these States (Great applause)."

Johnson's speech ended up being a low-brow verbal assault that horrified not only the Radicals, but even the most moderate Republi- cans.[207] Moreover, the speech was broadly reported and widely con- demned. For example, Harper's Weekly had this to say about it:

> "That the President of the United States should have been incited by a shouting crowd of his fellow-citizens to denounce

out at his enemies. Later in the year, during a campaign speech in support of Ohio Democrats in Cleveland, Johnson excoriated his opponents in the language of the stump: "While this gang – this common gang [Congress] of cormorants [greedy and rapacious people] and bloodsuckers have been fattening themselves for the past four or five years – men never going into the field, who growl at being removed from their fat offices, they are the patriots!" See Cleveland Speech, September 3, 1866, http:www.let.rug.nl/usa/ presidents/Andrew-johnson/cleveland-speech-september-3-1866

207 *Trefousse, Andrew Johnson, 244.*

> by name a Senator, a Representative and a private citizen, and to speak of another citizen in the slang of the stump, is something unprecedented and astounding that, while every generous man will allow for the excitement of passion, there is no self-respect- ing American citizen who will feel humiliated that the chief citizen of the Republic, in such a place, on such a day, should have been utterly mastered by it."[208]

In March, Congress passed the Civil Rights Act of 1866.[209] The Act officially conferred citizenship on the former slaves: ". . . all per- sons born in the United States and not subject to any foreign power, excluding Indians not taxed, are hereby declared to be citizens of the United States." It then guaranteed the freed slaves ". . . the same right .

. . to make and enforce contracts, to sue, be parties, and give evidence, to inherit, purchase, lease, sell, hold, and convey real and personal property, and to full and equal benefit of all laws and proceedings for the security of person and property, as enjoyed by white citizens . . ." Any person convicted of depriving a citizen of his/her rights covered by the Act was deemed guilty of a misdemeanor, punishable by a fine not exceeding one thousand dollars, or imprisonment not exceeding one year, or both. Seeking to avoid local bias, exclusive jurisdiction over enforcement of the Act was granted to the federal courts.

This was not a radical measure and drew strong support in Con- gress. It was expected that the President would sign the Bill, but instead he vetoed it.[210] Congress promptly overrode the veto and the Bill be- came law on April 9th. In his veto message, Johnson repeated his states' rights refrain by noting that the bill legislated in areas that, in his view, were the province of the individual states. He also complained about the purportedly discriminatory

208 *Harper's Weekly Article, March 10, 1866, http://www.impeach-andrewjohnson.com/05AJ-FirstVetoes/iia-7.htm.*

209 *The Civil Rights Act can be found at http://teachingamericanhistory.org/library/document/the-civil-rights-act-of-1866.*

210 *The veto message can be found at Richardson, ed., Messages and Papers, Vol. VI., 405 ff.*

impact of the bill on whites, which he claimed ". . . establish[es] for the colored race safeguards which go infinitely beyond any that the General Government has ever provided for the white race. In fact, the distinction of race and color is by the Bill made to operate in favor of the colored against the white race."

Despite all these controversial moves by the President, in 1866 most Republicans remained wedded to their moderate legislative pro- gram.[211] Forsaking black suffrage for measures to promote the equality and advancement of the former slaves, the Republican Congress asked two things of the Southern governments built under Johnson's Recon- struction plan: that they ratify the 14th amendment and that theyrepeal the laws that discriminated against blacks.[212] This moderate approach was politically attractive and it brought the Republicans major victo- ries in the 1866 mid-term elections.[213] The drubbing of the Democrats also put the issue of black suffrage on the political table.[214]

When the second session of the 39th Congress convened on De- cember 3, 1866, the Republicans were confident. They knew that their legislative program would be essentially veto-proof, as had been demonstrated by the events of 1866. Senator James Grimes of Iowa expressed the prevailing mood: "The President has no power to con- trol or influence anybody and legislation will be carried on entirely regardless of his opinions or wishes."[215] In other words, the Republi- cans thought they had the President in a legislative hammer lock. They under-estimated the wily and determined opposition from the Chief Executive they would encounter as 1867 unfolded.

Congress quickly went on the offensive, enacting the Reconstruc- tion Act of 1867 that was passed over Johnson's March 2nd veto by the 40th Congress that convened on March 4th, immediately following the

211 *Benedict, Impeachment and Trial of Andrew Johnson, 14-15.*

212 *Ibid.*

213 *Ibid., 15-16; see also Trefousse, Impeachment of a President, 40.*

214 *Foner, Reconstruction, 271-280.*

215 *Ibid., 271.*

dissolution of the 39th Congress, once again without Southern representation.[216] The Reconstruction Act refused to recognize the govern- ments that had been formed under the Lincoln and Johnson Proclama- tions of December 1863 and May 1865, except for Tennessee, which had ratified the 14th Amendment. It essentially placed Reconstruction in the hands of the military by dividing the remaining ten Southern states into five military districts with a federal general responsible for the implementation of the program within his district.[217] The district commanders were given broad civil administrative and judicial pow- ers. Voters in the districts would include black males and these voters would elect delegates to conventions that would draft new state consti- tutions. To re-enter the Union, a state had to ratify the 14th Amendment. The Reconstruction Act essentially nullified the regime imple- mented by Johnson in the South in 1865 and 1866. It included black suffrage and, through the requirement that the states ratify the 14th Amendment, it established a legal structure designed to protect the rights of blacks and give them "equal protection under thelaw." However, Congress had not eliminated the President's role in Reconstruc- tion. Section 2 of the Act directed the President to ". . . assign to the command of each of the said districts an officer of the army, not below the rank of brigadier general." Moreover, as Commander-in-Chief, Johnson wielded authority over the military officers apart from the Act. Congress did, however, attempt to side-line Johnson by adding a provision to the 1867-68 Army Appropriations Act that required the President to issue all military orders through the General of the Army stationed in Washington, D.C., who could not be removed without Senate consent.[218] Not accidentally, that person happened to be Ulyss- es Grant, the most popular general, if not the most popular person, in the country. The General was viewed

216 Two "Supplementary Acts" were passed on March 23, 1867 and July 19, 1867, both over Johnson's vetoes. The text of all three Acts can be found at https://www.tsl.texas.gov/ref/abouttx/secession/reconstruction.html; see also Impeachment and Trial of Andrew Johnson, 16-21.

217 The First District was Virginia; the Second District included North and South Carolina; the Third District included Florida, Alabama and Georgia; the Fourth District included Arkansas and Mississippi; and the Fifth District included Texas and Louisiana.

218 Trefousse, Impeachment of a President, 45; see also Berger, Impeachment, the Constitution-

as independent of the President and likely to side with the Congressional Republicans on issues relat- ed to Reconstruction. Accordingly, they saw Grant as a check on any attempt by Johnson to obstruct their plans. Johnson concluded that this legislation was an unconstitutional attempt to interfere with his powers as Commander-in-Chief and he ignored it, placing what he viewed as conservative generals in command in the South.[219]

Johnson returned to the offensive in August 1867. Using his pow- ers as Commander-in-Chief and those given to him by the Recon- struction Act, Johnson reshuffled the military commanders who were in charge of Reconstruction, creating a more conservative administra- tion to his liking. This included the recall of General Sheridan, who was exercising his powers under the Reconstruction Act in Texas and Louisiana to actively assist Unionists and the Republican party and to remove officeholders who refused to cooperate in implementing the Act.[220] Sheridan's removal was opposed by all members of his Cabinet except Welles.[221] Johnson also issued an amnesty Proclamation that pardoned all but a handful of Confederates. These moves greatly agi- tated the country, including both Radicals and Moderate Republicans in Congress. However, the President had been careful not to violate any of the statutes he had vetoed.

---

al Problems, 271.

219 *Ibid.*

220 *Foner, Reconstruction, 307.*

221 *Ibid., 82.*

CHAPTER 10 THE TENURE OF OFFICEACT

Now we come to what turned out to be the linchpin to Andrew Johnson's impeachment, the Tenure of Office Act, enacted by Congress over the President's veto on March 2, 1867.[222] Eight of the eleven articles of impeachment were based on Johnson's alleged violation of this Act. It is, therefore, worth spending some time on it.

The main provision in the Act was designed to constrain Presi- dent Johnson's power of patronage, that is, the power to appoint thou- sands of federal officials throughout the country. In the 19th century, in the days before the civil service system was created, this patronage brought tremendous political power to the President and his party be- cause the appointees were obliged to and did contribute their time and money to support their "patron" and his political party in election cam- paigns. In addition to this general concern, Congressional Republicans wanted to limit Johnson's ability to staff federal positions in the South with people sympathetic to his view of Reconstruction.[223]

The key provision was in Section 1:

---

222 *The text of the Tenure of Office Act can be found at http://teachingamericanhistory.org/library/document/tenure-of-office-act/*

223 *Trefousse, Impeachment of a President, 43-44.*

> "Be it enacted that every person holding any civil office to which he has been appointed by and with the advice and consent of the Senate, and every person who shall hereafter be appointed to any such office, shall hereaf- ter be appointed to any such office, and shall become duly qualified to act therein, is, and shall be entitled to hold such office until a successor shall have been in a like manner appointed and duly qualified, except as herein otherwise provided: Provided, That the Sec- retaries of State, of the Treasury, of War, of the Navy, and of the Interior, the Postmaster-General and the At- torney general, shall hold their offices respectively for and during the term of the President by whom they may have been appointed and for one month thereafter, sub- ject to removal by and with the advice of the Senate." (emphasis added)

The Act also allowed for "suspension" of civil officeholders subject to Senate confirmation during a Senate recess and designation of a tempo- rary replacement who could serve in the absence of the Senate's approval. If the President suspended an official, he had to give his reasons for the suspension within twenty days of the Senate's reconvening. If the Senate disagreed, the suspended official would be returned to office.

In what was clearly an impeachment set up, the final Section of the Act declared that any violation of the Act, including a prohibited removal by the President, would be a "high misdemeanor," punishable by a fine not exceeding ten thousand dollars, or imprisonment not ex- ceeding five years, or both.[224]

As Chief Justice William Rehnquist has said, this Act was an "ex- traordinary exercise of Congressional authority."[225] Although the lan- guage is dense, the thrust of this provision was to require the President to get

224 *Turley, "Senate Trials and Factional Disputes," 86-87.*

225 *Rehnquist, Grand Inquests, 252.*

Senate approval for the removal by him of an official whose ap- pointment had required the advice and consent of the Senate. This was a serious obstacle to the ability of the executive effectively to manage the departments of government. Not surprisingly, serious questions were raised about its constitutionality when it was passed. Johnson's cabinet, including Secretary of War Edwin Stanton, advised the Presi- dent that they thought the Act was "likely unconstitutional" and Stan- ton saw it as a "flagrant abuse."[226] President Johnson was not the only Chief Executive to object to the Act. Presidents Grant and Cleveland after him urged that it be repealed, and it was in 1887.[227]

It wasn't until 1926 that the Supreme Court had the opportunity to address the constitutionality of Congressional attempts to limit the removal power of the President. That year, in Myers v. United States,[228] the Supreme Court considered the constitutional validity of an 1876 law that required the Senate's consent to remove postmasters. With Chief Justice William Howard Taft, himself a former President, writ- ing the opinion, the Supreme Court held the statute to be unconstitu- tional because it attempted to make the President's power of removal dependent on the Senate's consent. In explaining the decision, Chief Justice Taft had this to say about the Tenure of Office Act: ". . . the Act . . ., insofar as it attempted to prevent the President from removing [an] executive officer who had been appointed by him with the advice and consent of the Senate, was invalid."[229]

However, in March 1867, it was Congress's judgment that the Act was constitutional and it expected the President to abide by it. By this time it was known that Secretary of War Edwin Stanton, a Lincoln holdover, and the President were at odds with one another. Stanton was Lincoln's right hand man in the prosecution of the Civil War. However, his sharp intellect and prodigious work ethic were compromised by his negatives. His anger was

226 *Hearn, The Impeachment of Andrew Johnson, 118.*
227 *Rehnquist, Grand Inquests, 259-261.*
228 *272 U.S. 52 (1926)*
229 *Ibid.; see also Impeachment, the Constitutional Problems, 292-298.*

legendary and he was prone to make hasty and sometimes rash decisions.[230] A contemporary who worked with Stanton described him as ". . . arbitrary, capricious, tyrannical, vindic- tive, hateful, and cruel."[231]

Stanton's politics, not to mention his personality, were bound to put him at odds with President Johnson sooner or later. As early as the summer of 1866, one of Stanton's friends remarked that he was staying in Johnson's cabinet as a watchdog for the Radicals.[232] The Radicals themselves conceded that Stanton had close ties to them and that he "sneaked out Cabinet secrets to the Radicals." By August 1867, John- son had decided that Stanton would have to go, although he was not yet ready directly to confront Congress over the Tenure of Office Act. On August 5th, with the Senate in recess, the President asked for Stanton's resignation. Had Stanton resigned, the Tenure of Office Act would not have been triggered. Recognizing that fact and wishing to support his Radical allies in Congress, Stanton refused to resign, John- son then "suspended" him and appointed General Grant as the inter- im Secretary of War.[233] Significantly, although Johnson used the word "suspend" from the Tenure of Office Act, his written order claimed the right to suspend "[b]y virtue of the power and authority vested in me as President by the Constitution and laws of the United States."[234] The President was apparently trying to avoid provoking Congress while reserving the argument that the Tenure of Office Act was unconstitu- tional.

Because of the public perception that Grant opposed the Presi- dent's Reconstruction policy, his agreement to accept the interim ap- pointment shocked Republicans.[235] Johnson wanted Grant as his Sec- retary of War

---

230 Stahr, Walter, Stanton, Lincoln's Secretary of War (Simon & Schuster, New York, 2017), 539.

231 Ibid.

232 Trefousse, Impeachment of a President, 36, 78.

233 Benedict, Impeachment and Trial of Andrew Johnson, 58; see also Trefousse, Impeachment of a President, 79-81.

234 The text of the order is contained within Johnson's December 12, 1867: Message Regarding the Suspension of Secretary Stanton, https:// millercenter.org/the-presidency/presidential-speeches/de- cember-12-1867-message.

235 Trefousse, Impeachment of a President, 68. Grant, who was popular with conservative Re-

for the opposite reason: it gave him the appearance of Grant's support. In any event, Grant's acceptance ensuredthat Stanton would be removed from Johnson's Cabinet at least until Congress re- convened in December. The suspension of Stanton, who was widely identified as a supporter of Congress's Reconstruction policy, coupled with the reshuffling of the military commanders and Johnson's broad amnesty Proclamation, spread support for impeachment beyond the Radicals. Moderate Republicans began to speak of impeachment and even conservatives, who tended to favor the President, were uneasy.[236] Public sentiment in the fall of 1867 was reflected in an editorial that appeared in the October 5th edition of Harper's Weekly:[237] "The subject of impeachment has received fresh impulse from recent events." The removal of General Sheridan was "popularly accepted" as proof that Johnson was bent on thwarting Congress's Reconstruc- tion program.[238] The editorial proclaimed that ". . . while Andrew John- son is President it is impossible that the great work of reconstruction can properly proceed." Prominent opponents of impeachment, including Representative James Wilson, the Chairman of the House Judi- ciary Committee were ". . . converted to the belief of its necessity." Yet, ". . . up the present moment the President has not violated the law," either in removing General Sheridan or in "suspending" Sec- retary Stanton. While noting that ". . . public sentiment would justify impeachment . . .," the editorial concluded by asserting that ". . . [a]cts must be fully proved which are a violation of law, or which imply an unmistakable intention to thwart the honest execution of laws and to endanger the safety of the country."

---

publicans who generally supported Johnson, was beginning to position himself for a run at the Republican nomination for President in 1868.

236 Ibid., 82-83

237 Harper's Weekly Editorial, "Impeachment," October 5, 1867. http://www.andrewjohnson.com/09)vertObstructionOfCongress/v-23.htm.

238 General Phillip Sheridan had served under Grant during the Civil War and the two had a close professional and personal bond. In 1867, Sheridan was serving as the commander of one of the military districts established by the Reconstruction Act. He was widely viewed as effec- tively implementing the Act in his district and clashed with Johnson as a result. Johnson removed Sheridan over Grant's objection. See Trefousse, Andrew Johnson, 292.

Within eighteen months of taking the oath of office, the President had managed to squander the support of the Moderate Republicans, who were now joining the Radicals in calling for his impeachment. As a matter of political necessity, President Johnson needed to be re- moved. However, as the Harper's Weekly editorialist pointed out, there did not appear to be constitutional grounds for his impeachment.

CHAPTER 11
JOHNSON'S IMPEACHMENT BY THEHOUSE

The process that led to Andrew Johnson's impeachment had begun in the summer of 1866, when the Radicals became convinced that the President was and always would be determined to block any program designed to give the blacks a vote, or to provide them with any chance of achieving equality and economic well-being in the South. There is no question that the Radicals wanted Johnson removed as a matter of partisan politics, nothing more, nothing less. To them, with Johnson as President, there was no hope whatsoever of vindicating the hard-won victory in the Civil War. Emboldened by the results of the 1866 Congressional elections, when the 39th Congress reconvened in December 1866, they were determined to take action, even though they were way out ahead of their Moderate and Conservative Republi- can colleagues, as well as public opinion.

There were three attempts by the Radicals to convince the House to impeach the President. The first attempt died in the Judiciary Com- mittee just before the 39th Congress dissolved in March 1867. The sec- ond attempt, in November and December 1867, when the 40th Con- gress convened, made it out of the Judiciary Committee, but was voted down by the House. The third attempt, in February 1868, immediately following Johnson's removal of Secretary Stanton, worked.

The First Impeachment Attempt, January 1867.

While his conduct was aggravating in the extreme, at the time of the first impeachment attempt in January 1867, the President hadviolated no laws. As expressed in December 15, 1866 Harper's Weekly editori- al: "There have been many rumors of an intention of impeachment at the present session. But nothing is clearer than that the country does not demand that the President shall be impeached for any thing [sic] which he is known to have done."[239]

Ignoring the obvious lack of public support, on January 7, 1867, Radical Republican John Ashley of Ohio introduced an impeachment resolution before the House. Ashley had vowed that he would ". . . give neither sleep to his eyes nor slumber to his eyelids" until he had brought articles of impeachment against the President.[240] His resolu- tion asserted that President Johnson had committed "high crimes and misdemeanors" by "usurping power" and "violating the law." The charges were vague. Ashley accused the President of having"corrupt- ly used" his appointment, pardoning and veto powers; corruptly dis- posed of public property of the United States; and corruptly interfered in elections. The resolution asked that the Judiciary Committee be ". . . authorized to inquire into the official conduct of Andrew Johnson . . . and to report whether, in their opinion" the President ". . . has been guilty of acts which are . . . high crimes and misdemeanors."[241]

On the same day, the House voted in favor of Ashley's resolutionby a vote of 105 to 39, with 27 members not voting,[242] and the matter was referred to the Judiciary Committee. Apparently recognizing the absence of any evidence upon which to impeach the President, on March 2nd, two days

239 *Harper's Weekly Editorial, "Impeachment and General Butler," December 15, 1866, http://www.andrewjohnson.com/06FirstImpeacment- Discussions/iiib-16.htm.*

240 *Ibid.*

241 *Quoted in Congressional Resolutions on Presidential Impeachment: A Historical Overview, Updated September 16, 1998, Congressional Research Service, The Library of Congress, p. CRS-4 (hereafter 1998 CRS Report).*

242 *Ibid.*

before the end of the 39th Congress, the Committee recommended that the matter be given further study by the next Congress.[243]

During the eight months between the 39th and 40th Congresses, two competing views of what constituted an impeachable offense were debated. Democrats and Republicans who opposed impeachment ar- gued for a narrow definition, i.e., that it must be based on an indictable crime, as set out by Professor Theodore Dwight in a scholarly article published in March, 1867.[244] In September, Judge William Lawrence

published a rebuttal to Professor Dwight's article, contending that an indictable crime was not necessary to impeach, remarking, somewhat tartly, that the assertion that impeachment could only be based on crimes ". . . is a view not yet a year old, which has not been held at any prior time in England or America."[245] Not surprisingly, those who supported impeachment argued for this broader view.

As always, "ultra" Radicals like Thaddeus Stevens and Benjamin Butler, both of whom participated on behalf of the House in Johnson's Senate trial, took the extreme (and unconstitutional) view that, when it came to impeachment, Congress was a "law unto itself" because it was the sole sovereign power. They wanted to impeach and convict Johnson because he wouldn't obey Congress.[246]

Also, as we have already seen, between March and November of 1867, the President had continued his determined effort to block Con- gress's

---

243 *Ibid.*

244 *Dwight, "Trial by Impeachment," 257-283. Professor Dwight's contention that the impeachable conduct must be indictable as a crime is now widely rejected. See the discussion in the text above at 40-41. In any event, Congress covered that base in the Tenure of Office Act by making its violation a "high misdemeanor."*

245 *Lawrence, "The Law of Impeachment," 658.*

246 *Berger, Impeachment, the Constitutional Problems, 274-275. With regard to Stevens, Professor Berger quotes Fawn Brodie, a Stevens biographer, as saying, "[Stevens] would redefine the power relationship in the government in his own terms; and those terms were: first, that Con- gress was to be the sole sovereign power, and second, that none of this power was to be shared with the President or the Court." Ibid., 275, f.n. 81*

Reconstruction policy by vetoing the Reconstruction Acts, "sus- pending" Secretary of War Stanton and shuffling the roster of district commanders whose jobs it were to implement the Reconstruction Act. As a result, when the 40th Congress convened on the second Tuesday in No- vember, the support for impeachment had broadened beyond the Radicals. However, impeachment was still not popular with large seg- ments of the Republican Party.[247] Moreover, the President had still remained careful not to overstep the law. He had "suspended" Stan- ton, a move that was authorized by the Tenure of Office Act and installed the popular Grant as the interim Secretary of War. The personnel changes he made in the military districts were within his authority under the Reconstruction Act. He had properly exercised his constitutional pardon power in issuing his latest amnesty proclamation.

The Second Impeachment Attempt, November-December 1867 .

Nonetheless, after holding a series of inconsequential hearings, on November 25th, the House Judiciary Committee voted 5-4 for impeachment.[248] The majority report, recommending impeachment, was written by Representative Thomas Williams of Pennsylvania and joined by George Boutwell, Francis Thomas, William Law- rence and John C. Churchill. It contained 17 charges based almost entirely on Johnson's efforts to foil Congress's Reconstruction policy.[249] It has been described as "an inflammatory indictment of the President, injudicious in language, even violent in spirit."[250] It was characterized by broad, hyperbolic denunciations of the President, supported by disorganized factual allegations.[251] It was not persua- sive.

---

247 Trefousse, Impeachment of a President, 109-113.

248 Ibid., 105-107; see also Benedict, Impeachment and Trial of Andrew Johnson, 73-74; House Report No. 7, 40th Congress, 1st Session; November 25, 1867, Majority Report, pp. 1-59.

249 Trefousse, Impeachment of a President, 107.

250 Trial and Impeachment of Andrew Johnson, 74.

251 Stewart, David O., Impeached, the Trial of President Andrew Johnson and the Fight for Lincoln's Legacy (Simon & Schuster Paperbacks, New York, 2010) (hereafter Stewart, Impeached), 102-103. Here is a sampling of the venomous tone of the majority report: Johnson had issued "imperial proclamations;" Johnson exhibited "a boldness unequalled even by Charles I, when, he too, undertook to reign without Parliament;" Johnson "exercised . . . powers as absolute as those of any monarch in Christendom." See House Report No. 7, 40th Congress, 1st Session, November 25, 1867 (Majority Report), 3,4,47.

James Wilson, the Committee Chair, refused to join the ma- jority and was joined in dissent by his Republican colleague, Fred- erick Woodbridge.[252] Wilson was a lawyer and one of the founding fathers of Iowa Republicanism. His minority report argued that im- peachment required proof of an indictable crime and, since there were no allegations of such crimes in the majority report, there should be no impeachment.[253] Summarizing the minority's argu- ment, and presaging history's judgment about Johnson's impeach- ment, Wilson wrote:

"The report of the majority resolves all presumptions against the President, closes the door against all doubts, affirms facts as established by the testimony in support of which there is not a particle of evidence before us which would be received by any court in the land. We dissent from all this, and from the temper and spirit of the report. The cool and unbiased judgment of the fu- ture, when the excitement in the midst of which we live shall have passed away, will not fail to discover that the political bitterness of the present times has, in no inconsiderable degree, given the tone to the document which we decline to approve."[254]

On December 3rd, the President used his Third Annual Message to Congress as an opportunity to poke yet another stick in Congress's eye.[255] He repeated his oft-stated canons of Reconstruction. The Con- federate states never left the Union, because they could not do so under the Constitution. The work to restore them to the Union under repub- lican governments was completed. He called for repeal of the Recon- struction Acts which placed ". . . ten of the Southern states under the domination of military masters." He lashed out again at black suffrage. Giving blacks the vote, he wrote, would result in a "subjugation of the States to Negro domination . . ." that ". . . would be worse than the military despotism under which they are now suffering."

---

252 House Report No. 7, 40th Congress, 1st Session, November 25, 1867, Minority Report, pp. 59-105. The two Democrats on the Committee, S.S. Marshall and Charles A. Eldridge, also submitted a separate report refusing to join the majority. Ibid., 106-115.

253 Benedict, Trial and Impeachment of Andrew Johnson, 74.

254 House Report No. 7, 40th Congress, 1st Session, November 25, 1867, 59.

255 The text of the Message can be found at https://millercenter.org/the-presidency/presiden-tial-speches/december-3-1867-third-annual.

Two days after the President delivered his inflammatory Message to Congress debate began on the Judiciary Committee reports. Repre- sentative George Boutwell of Massachusetts, senior signer of the ma- jority report, argued in favor of impeachment.[256] Boutwell was a former Democratic governor of Massachusetts who made his start in politics in the temperance movement and ended up as a Radical Republican with a violent passion to remove Johnson.[257] In urging the adoption of what most agreed was a poor majority report, Boutwell had a difficult task. He spoke for a total of about two hours, spread over two days. He first delivered an extensive and eloquent argument in favor of the view that impeachment did not require that the President be charged with an indictable crime.[258] He reminded his colleagues that the purpose of impeachment was to remove, not punish, citing, among others author- ities, Alexander Hamilton's words from Federalist 65 that the subject of impeachment was ". . . the misconduct of public men, or, in other words, the violation of some public trust."[259]

Using this standard, Boutwell admitted that the Judiciary Com- mittee had not charged the President with "a specific, heinous, novel offense. . . ." Instead, it had charged him with "political crimes," offering this summary of the majority's case for impeachment: the President had ". . . misused as necessity and circumstances dictated, the great powers of the nation with which he was intrusted [sic], for the purpose of reconstructing this Government in the interest of the rebellion, . . ."[260] This was the Radicals' view in a nutshell. The President should be removed because he opposed Congress's policy of Reconstruction. James Wilson followed Boutwell. Sensing that he had the high ground, Wilson spoke for only about an hour.[261] He finessed the "indictable crime" argument, concentrating instead on the

256 *Impeachment, Speech of Hon. George S. Boutwell, of Massachusetts in the House of Representatives, December 5 and 6, 1867.*
257 *Stewart, Impeached, 108-109.*
258 *Ibid., 2-12.*
259 *Ibid., 8.*
260 *Ibid.,12.*
261 *Ibid., 110.*

difficulty of defining a "political crime" for purposes of impeachment. He asked rhetorically if impeachment could be based simply on "the doing of something that the dominant party in the country does not like?" He al- lowed that Johnson was "the worst of Presidents," but that the remedy should be found through the "suffrages of the people."

The House was not yet willing to vote for a purely political im- peachment. On December 7th, 57 Representatives (all Republicans) voted in favor of impeachment, with 106 (including sixty-eight Re- publicans) voting against. Twenty-two Congressmen did not vote. Johnson may have been unfit for the presidency, but, in the absence of any hard evidence that the President had violated any law or the Con- stitution, the votes for impeachment weren't there. Ironically, most of those voting against impeachment relied on Wilson's minority report that claimed impeachment had to be based on an indictable crime, de- spite the fact that the weight of authority held the other way.[262]

In late 1867 there were also broader political factors that worked against impeachment. The Republicans had lost ground in the 1867 local elections, which were a disaster for the Radicals. This made Moderate Republicans leery about impeachment.[263] The principal ad- vocates of impeachment, Butler, Stevens and Wade had problems of their own. They had become identified with a plan to pay off part of the national bonds that helped to finance the war with "greenbacks," as op- posed to hard currency backed by gold. The result would be inflation that was of great concern to the financial community.[264] The impactof impeachment on the 1868 presidential race also came into play. Sena- tor Ben Wade, who was President, pro tempore, of the Senate , would become president if Johnson were removed. This would be an obstacle to the nomination of Grant, who was viewed as a better candidate than Wade.[265]

262 *Benedict, Impeachment and Trial of Andrew Johnson, 85.*

263 *Ibid., 69-70; see also Trefousse, Impeachment of a President, 85-97.*

264 *Trefousse, Andrew Johnson, 302-303.*

265 *Ibid.*

Moreover, despite his aggressive rhetoric in his December 3rd Message to Congress, the President had eased off on his provocative moves. For example, after August 1867, he removed no more military commanders in the South and he did not replace his Republican Cabi- net with Democrats, despite strong pressure to do so.[266]

The Third and Successful Impeachment Attempt, February 1868 .

The Radicals had been foiled once again. Unless the President did something more egregious to provoke Congress, it looked as if impeachment was off the table. That something turned out to be lurking in the sleeping dog controversy over the status of Secretary Stanton, who, it will be recalled, had been "suspended" since August 12th,, with General Grant serving temporarily in his Cabinet spot pending the re- convening of Congress. Now that Congress was back in session, under the Tenure of Office Act, the President was obliged to inform the Sen- ate of the reasons for Stanton's suspension, which he did on December 12th, about a week after impeachment was voted down in the House.[267] The President's suspension message to the Senate skewered Stanton and exposed him for what he was – the instrument of Senators who were opposed to the President's Reconstruction policy, a circumstance that was abhorrent to the constitutional separation of powers between the executive and legislative branches of government.[268] Johnson point- ed out that, when the Tenure of Office Act was sent to the President, all members of his Cabinet, including Stanton, had agreed that it was unconstitutional. The President avowed that ". . . Stanton's condemna- tion of the law was the most elaborate and emphatic . . ." and that ". . . he advised me that it was my duty to defend the power of the President from usurpation and to veto the law." That was March of 1867. By Au- gust of that year, Stanton had reversed field and invoked the Tenure of Office Act to argue that he could not be suspended

266 *Benedict, Impeachment and Trial of Andrew Johnson, 71.*

267 *Ibid., 95; Trefousse, Impeachment of a President, 117.*

268 *December 12, 1867: Message Regarding the Suspension of Secretary Stanton, https://millercenter.org/the-presidency/presidential-speech- es/december-12-1867-message.*

without the consent of the Senate. The President then made the practical point that, under such circumstances, it made no sense for Stanton to have continued in Johnson's cabinet.

Turning to Reconstruction policy, Johnson reminded Congress that, at the beginning of his Presidency, his Cabinet, all holdovers from the Lincoln administration, agreed that the executive had the power to implement a Reconstruction program and that Stanton himself had prepared one for Lincoln. Stanton and the rest of Johnson's Cabinet agreed on the program announced in the May 29, 1865 Proclamations. Johnson acknowledged that, over time, significant differences arose between Stanton and himself over Reconstruction. He pointed outthat three other Cabinet members who also had such disagreements had resigned and argued that Stanton should have followed their lead. All in all, the message was a stout justification for removing Stanton. The Senate was due to respond by January 1868.

In the meantime, rather than continuing to lay low, Johnson de- cided to go back on the offensive once again by reshuffling the military commanders in an effort to inhibit Congress's Reconstruction policy.[269] These moves were opposed by Johnson's Cabinet and drew condem- nation from the public.[270] At the same time, progress in implementing the Reconstruction Act energized many Congressional Republicans. Southerners were registering to vote again, but this time with freed- men participating. For instance, in Virginia, 105,000 blacks registered to vote for delegates to a new constitutional convention, along with 120,000 whites. Of the 102 delegates elected to Virginia's constitu- tional convention, 24 were blacks and a majority were Republicans.[271] Against this backdrop, Congress continued its campaign against the President. On January 13, 1868, the Senate voted not to concur in Stanton's suspension.[272] This meant that Johnson could rid

269 *Benedict, Impeachment and Trial of Andrew Johnson, pp. 89-91; Trefousse, Andrew Johnson, 303; Trefousse, Impeachment of a President, 115-130.*

270 *Ibid.., 116-117.*

271 *Stewart, Impeached, 115-116.*

272 *Trefousse, Andrew Johnson, 306.*

himself of Stanton only if the Senate agreed to his replacement. The ball was back in his court. It did not seem that, at this point, Johnson was willing to remove Stanton over the Senate's objection, as evidenced by his attempts to find other alternatives. First, prior to January 13th, Johnson had sounded out Grant on whether he would agree not to physically relinquish the War Department office if the Senate did not uphold Stan- ton's dismissal. Based on a private conversation with the General, the President thought that Grant had agreed to do that. Grant vehemently denied that he made such a commitment.[273] Precisely what Johnson had in mind is unclear, but he apparently saw some advantage to keep- ing Stanton off the physical premises.[274]

On January 11th, Grant informed Johnson that, if the Senate re- fused to support Stanton's removal, he would have no choice but to relinquish the position to Stanton. Believing that he had been duped, Johnson was furious.[275] Nonetheless, on January 14th, Grant resigned his temporary position as Secretary of War and turned the keys to the War Office over to Stanton, who now held a title with an office.[276] But he did not participate in the operation of Johnson's government.

Johnson next sought out a candidate to replace Stanton whom he thought would be acceptable to the Senate. He quickly settled on General William Tecumseh Sherman, second only to Grant in the pantheon of Union generals. He was best known for capturing Atlanta and thereafter conducting the scorched earth "march to the sea." Sherman was also politically well-connected, with a brother who was a Senator from Ohio. Senate confirmation of a Sherman appointment as Secretary of War

273 *This disagreement, which became public, was a major rupture in their relationship that was never repaired. See Stewart, Impeached, 118- 120.*

274 *Ibid., 118-119. Stewart suggests, as do others, that perhaps Johnson was contemplating a court challenge to the constitutionality of the Tenure of Office Act and that having physical control over the War office premises would facilitate that. Ibid.*

275 *Trefousse, Impeachment of a President, 126.*

276 *Benedict, Impeachment and Trial of Andrew Johnson, 99.*

seemed likely.[277] In short, Sherman's star power was attractive. Johnson also liked the fact that, before the war, Sherman had lived in Louisiana and was familiar with and accepting of Southern culture and sympathetic to Southern whites.[278]

Wanting Sherman was one thing. Recruiting him to the task was another. Sherman and Grant had gone through the crucible of a brutal war together and had forged a bond that neither would break. Sherman had always been subordinate to Grant, so there were both profession- al and personal reasons for him to avoid offending Grant. Moreover, Sherman was, by his own assessment, unsuited to the political tempest integral to service at the highest levels of government. Despite John- son's determined campaign to land Sherman, the General resolutely refused the Cabinet appointment.[279] Angry, frustrated and feeling be- trayed, sometime in the middle of February, the President decided that he would remove Stanton over the Senate's objection, even if it meant his impeachment.[280] As Johnson put it, his self-respect demanded it.[281] At the other end of Pennsylvania Avenue, Thaddeus Stevens, the aged and ill, but not yet exhausted, fire breathing Radical had his own problems to deal with. His determined campaign to impeach the Pres- ident whom he hated had been twice rejected by his Congressional colleagues. However, by February he had returned to the impeachment battlefield. Sorely disappointed in the Judiciary Committee's inability to get the job done and seeking to avoid its impeachment detractor Chairman, James Wilson, on February 10th, Stevens induced the House to transfer the impeachment issue to the Reconstruction Committee that he chaired.[282] Three days later, Stevens submitted a resolution to his committee to commence impeachment proceedings based on the argument that Johnson

---

277 *Stewart, Impeached, 127-130.*
278 *Ibid.*
279 *Ibid.*
280 *Trefousse, Andrew Johnson, 311.*
281 *Ibid., 312.*
282 *Trefousse, Impeachment of a President, p. 129.*

had attempted to induce Grant to violate the Tenure of Office Act.[283] Like all the impeachment measures before it, this one failed too.

Stevens did not have to long lament this latest loss. The immov- able object, Andrew Johnson, was about to meet the irresistible force, Thaddeus Stevens. Eight days later, on Friday, February 21st, Johnson removed Stanton and appointed Adjutant General Lorenzo Thomas as Secretary of War "ad interim" in a move that many felt was a clear violation of the Tenure of Office Act and an insult to the Senate. The removal united the Republicans against the President.284[284] The impeach- ment dam burst.

When Stanton received the removal order, he said he wanted time for reflection, but was actually determined to resist it. He conferred with Grant who supported him in that decision.[285] Meanwhile, the news of Stanton's removal struck Capitol Hill like a thunderbolt. In the Senate, Lyman Trumbull was delivering a speech when the news ar- rived. The Senators rushed to surround Benjamin Wade's desk to read Johnson's order.[286] A group of four Republican Senators immediately went to the War Department to urge Stanton to resist the President's order, and then walked across the street to let Grant know of their sup- port for Stanton.[287] Messages from other Senators poured in to Stanton, including Sumner's one word telegram, "Stick."[288] The Senate went into executive session to consider what to do. Believing that the House needed some bolstering, the Senators passed a resolution that the Pres- ident had no right to suspend Stanton.[289]

283 *Ibid.*

284 *Benedict, Impeachment and Trial of Andrew Johnson, 101-103. Benedict quotes this critique of Johnson's action from his Secretary of the Navy and ally: "A little skillful management would have made a permanent break in that party [Republican], . . . [b]ut the President had no tact himself to affect it, he consulted with no others, the opportunity passed away, and by a final hasty move, without preparation, without advising with anybody, he took a step which consolidated the Radicals of every stripe." Ibid., 103-104*

285 *Trefousse, Andrew Johnson, 313.*

286 *Stewart, Impeached, 135.*

287 *Ibid.*

288 *And "stick" he did. A kind of keystone cops scenario unfolded with Stanton hunkered down in the War Department office, arresting and then releasing Johnson's appointee, yet performing no official duties. See Stewart, Impeached, 139-142, for a description of the chaos having two competing Cabinet secretaries set off in the capital city. This proud and arrogant man had become just a pawn in the chess game being played by the Congress and the President.*

289 *Ibid. The operative portion of the resolution read as follows: "That we do not concur in the action*

The reaction in the House was even more heated. When the Speaker announced the Stanton firing, small groups of Representatives gathered to commiserate on the floor of the House. Thaddeus Stevens went from group to group repeating, "Didn't I tell you so? What good did it do you? If you don't kill the beast, it will kill you."[290] John Bing- ham, a Moderate, exclaimed that the President had revived "a contest which can exert no other than evil influence upon the welfare of the country."[291] Working quickly, Stevens's Reconstruction Committee re- ported an impeachment resolution to the House the next day, Saturday, February 22nd, which was passed on Monday, February 24th, by a party line vote of 128 to 47, with fifteen not voting. A committee was ap- pointed to draw up specific charges.[292]

On February 29th, the House committee reported ten articles of impeachment. After debate, the number was reduced to nine, all but two of which were based on Johnson's alleged violation of the Tenure of Office Act. On March 2nd, the House adopted these nine and added two more, for a total of eleven.[293]

The Articles of Impeachment .

In considering the eleven articles of impeachment it is important to remember that the only new element in the equation was Johnson's suspension/removal of Stanton. As a result, that became the focus of the charges against the President.

> Article I accused Johnson of intentionally violating the Tenure of Office Act when he issued the order to re- move Stanton.

---

of the President . . .; that we deny the right of the President to act, under the existing law, without the consent of the Senate." See Benedict, Impeachment and Trial of Andrew Johnson, 102.

290 *Trefousse, Andrew Johnson, 313; Benedict, Impeachment and Trial of Andrew Johnson, 101.*

291 *Ibid., 101.*

292 *Trefousse, Andrew Johnson, 314-315; Trefousse, Impeachment of a President, 137.*

293 *Ibid., 138-139. The text of the articles of impeachment can be found at https://www.nps.gov/anjolearn/historyculture/the-articles-of-im- peachment.htm.*

Articles II through VIII were just different facets of the main charge. Article II accused Johnson of violating the Act by appointing General Thomas to replace Stanton when Johnson could not remove Stanton in the first place. Article III accused Johnson of appointing Thom- as without the advice and consent of the Senate. Arti- cle IV was based on an alleged conspiracy to replace Stanton with Thomas. Article V was another conspir- acy theory, this one to prevent Stanton from "holding" the office. Articles VI and VII alleged conspiracies with Thomas to improperly take the War Office property, which was rightfully in Stanton's custody. Article VIII alleged that Johnson had unlawfully sought to control the disbursements of ". . . the moneys appropriated for the military service and for the War Department."

Articles IX, X and XI did not relate to the Stanton re- moval. They were remarkably devoid of power. Article IX alleged that the President had wrongly told Gener- al William H. Emory, the Commander of the Depart- ment of Washington, that the provision in the Army Appropriations Act that required that all ". . . orders and instructions relating to military operations issued by the President or the Secretary of War shall be is- sued through the General of the army [Grant] . . ." was unconstitutional and that he induced General Emory to violate the statute by taking orders directly from the President.[294]

Article X was an act of petulance by the impeachers. It complained that the President had attempted to ". . . bring into disgrace, ridicule, hatred, contempt and re- proach the Congress of the United States" in various speeches he delivered from the hustings in the 1866 mid-term election campaign.

294 *In reality, this provision was a transparent attempt by Congress to make sure that General Grant, who generally opposed the President's Reconstruction program, would have the opportunity to disrupt it.*

> Article XI was a catchall. It claimed that the President had asserted that the Southern states were not repre- sented in the 39th Congress, and then used that assertion to argue that the Tenure of Office Act and the provision in the Army Appropriations Act requiring orders from Johnson to go through General Grant were invalid be- cause there was no properly constituted Congress.

With the charges in place, the House turned to selection of the "managers" who would present the House's case against the Presi- dent to the Senate. After some maneuvering, the House deputized a committee of seven, five Radicals and two Moderates. The Radicals were Benjamin Butler, Thaddeus Stevens, George Boutwell, John Lo- gan and Thomas Williams. Stevens and Butler would take the lead. Stevens was seemingly near the end of life. He had to be carried into the Senate chamber, was unable to stand once he got there, and would have to let someone else finish reading his closing argument at the end of the trial. Despite his physical ailments, he remained the soul of the Radical movement and was determined to rid the country of his archenemy. Butler was a flamboyant, controversial character and an experienced trial lawyer known for his courtroom antics.[295] Boutwell and Williams were persistent advocates for impeachment. The Mod- erates were John Bingham and James Wilson, who had changed his position since arguing against impeachment in December.

The public reaction to Johnson's removal of Stanton was captured in a Harper's Weekly editorial that appeared in early March.[296] The Tenure of Office Act ". . . was passed by Congress, vetoed by the Pres- ident, passed over his veto by the constitutional majority, and became the law." In firing Stanton over the Senate's opposition, according to the editorialist, Johnson

295 Trefousse, Andrew Johnson, 316. Butler was also an enemy of General Grant, who had insulted Butler in his final report for Butler's battlefield ineptitude during operations against Richmond in 1864. See Trefousse, Impeachment of a President, 49.

296 Harper's Weekly Editorial, "The President and the Law," March 7, 1968, http://www.andrewjohnson.com/09ImpeachmentAndAcquittal/ vi-2.htm.

had clearly violated theAct. "There could not be a more flagrant defiance of law or usurpation of authority." The ed- itorial ended with a confident prediction: "The President will not resist impeachment, and upon this simple point of deliberate violation of the law, the only point which should be raised, his trial, if ordered, need not last long."

That prophecy was wrong. The trial was not to be short and the result, although close, would not be what the Republicans and large segments of the population desired.

CHAPTER 12
JOHNSON'S IMPEACHMENT TRIAL

On Wednesday, March 4, 1868, the Senate gallery was packed and the atmosphere was one of excited anticipation. The press had followed every detail leading up to this historic day and huge crowds sought admission to the Senate.[297] Those who got in saw the House managers escorted by the Sergeant at Arms to their seats at a table on the floor of the Senate. They were then able to hear the Sergeant at Arms admonishing all those present: "Here ye! hear ye! hear ye! All persons are commanded to keep silence, on pain of imprisonment, while the House of Representatives is exhibiting to the Senate of the United States articles of impeachment against Andrew Johnson, Pres- ident of the United States." Manager Bingham read all eleven articles into the record.[298]

The next day, with the Chief Justice of the United States, Salmon P. Chase presiding, the court of impeachment was installed with the taking of the oath by the Senators who would sit as both judges and jurors in the trial:

> "I do solemnly swear that in all things pertaining to the trial of impeachment of Andrew Johnson, President of the United States, I will do impartial justice accord- ing to the

297 *Tresousse, Andrew Johnson, 316.*

298 *Trial of Andrew Johnson, President of the United States, before the Senate of the United States, on Impeachment by the House of Repre- sentatives, Vol. I. (Government Printing Office, 1868) (hereafter Trial of Andrew Johnson), 6.*

> Constitution and the laws, so help me God." A summons was issued to the President containing the articles of impeachment and directing him to file his answer by March. 23rd.299[299]

The President assembled a distinguished, able and politically di- verse team of lawyers to present his defense.[300] His Attorney General, Henry Stanbery, resigned from the Cabinet in order to take the nom- inal lead of the team. William Evarts and Benjamin Curtis pulled the laboring oars. Evarts was a distinguished member of the New York bar, a future Attorney General and Secretary of State, as well as a Republi- can who supported Grant for President, and who had also attackedthe President a few months earlier. He was described as the ablest lawyer on the President's side, who was ". . . lucid, precise, and cogent, sel- dom rhetorical or ornamental" in his courtroom delivery.[301] Curtis was a successful trial lawyer and Conservative Republican. He was also a former Supreme Court Justice who had distinguished himself by dis- senting from the horrific Dred Scott decision.[302] Another member was William Groesbeck, a renowned attorney and a Democrat who had be- come Johnson's friend during the war. Finally, A.R. Nelson, who was from Tennessee and trusted by Johnson, replaced Jeremiah Black who had a conflict of interest.

The President's lawyers took on a challenging assignment that required courage, perseverance and skillful advocacy. Their clienthad squandered whatever good will and support he had enjoyed when he was inaugurated

299 *Ibid., 16.*

300 *The description of the President's legal team is taken from Trefousse, Andrew Johnson, 317.*

301 *Harper's Weekly Article, "The Impeachment Trial," April 18, 1868, http//:www.impeach-andrewjohnson.com/09ImpeachmentAndAc- quittal/vi-46.htm.*

302 *Scott v. Sanford, 60 U.S. 393 (1857) (the "Dred Scott decision"). Widely recognized as one of the worst Supreme Court decisions ever, the case turned on whether the plaintiff, Dred Scott, a fugitive slave, was a "citizen of the United States." If not, he could not sue in federal court and his case should be dismissed. Chief Justice Roger Taney wrote for the majority, which ruled that ". . . neither . . . the class of persons who had been imported as slaves nor their descendants . . ." were intended by the Constitution to be citizens of the United States. In discussing the basis for the ruling, among other things, Taney wrote that "[t]hey [blacks] had for more than a century before been regarded as beings of inferiororder, and altogether unfit to associate with the white race either in social or political relations, and so far inferior that they had no rights which the white man was bound to respect, and that the negro might justly and lawfully be reduced to slavery for his benefit."*

just short of two years earlier. He was reviled and isolated. The Republican Party was lined up against him. He was the target of a conspiracy between the Radicals in the Senate and his Sec- retary of War to keep him from implementing what he sincerely be- lieved to be the proper policy for reconstructing the South. The North- ern press was almost unanimously against him. And now, their client was on the brink of an infamous removal from office. The stakes were enormous.[303]

The President's Answer .

The first task for the President's lawyers was to prepare his Answer to the articles of impeachment. It set out the defenses that would be detailed during the course of the trial.[304] The response toArticle I con- sumed the largest portion of the thirty page document. The first argu- ment was that the Tenure of Office Act was unconstitutional based on a reading of the founding instrument itself and the long-standing Con- gressional practice of deferring to the President on removals in order to facilitate his duty to run the executive department.[305] To bolster this argument and to underscore his benign intent in removing Stanton, the President's counsel pointed out that his Cabinet, including Stanton himself, had advised the President that the Act was unconstitutional and that he should veto it. While, as we have seen, the Supreme Court would vindicate Johnson on this point in 1926, it was an argument that fell on deaf ears in the Senate, which had passed the law and must have believed — or wanted to believe — it was constitutional.[306]

303 The renowned impeachment scholar, Professor Raoul Berger, has paid tribute to ". . . as valiant a group of advocates as can be found in the annals of the American bar. . ." See Berger, Impeachment, the Constitutional Problems, 286.

304 The Answer is at Trial of Andrew Johnson, Vol. I, 37-67.

305 Ibid., 38-39. Johnson's veto message on the Tenure of Office Act was attached as Exhibit A to the Answer. Ibid., 53-58.

306 During the trial, the President's lawyers attempted to present the powerful evidence that his Cabinet, including, Secretary Stanton, had advised him that the Tenure of Office Act was unconstitutional. Justice Chase ruled the evidence admissible, but the Senate overruled him. See Berger, Impeachment, the Constitutional Problems, 280-281.

The second argument was that, even assuming the Act was con- stitutional, it did not apply to Stanton under the "proviso" contained in Section 1:[307]

> "Provided, That the Secretaries of State, of the Trea- sury, of War, of the Navy, and of the Interior, the Post- master-General and the Attorney general, shall hold their offices respectively for and during the term of the President by whom they may have been appointed and for one month thereafter, subject to removal by and with the advice of the Senate."

The President's legal team argued that the language of the provi- so itself defeated the claim. Stanton's protection was limited to thirty days after the expiration of Lincoln's term, because Lincoln was the President "by whom" Stanton was appointed and Lincoln's term ex- pired upon his death. That being the case, after May 14, 1865, the pro- viso expired and Stanton was serving at the pleasure of Johnson who was not precluded from removing Stanton by the Act.[308] The sections of the Answer on Articles II through VIII were short, largely playing off the arguments made with respect to Article I.[309]

As to the accusations in Article IX relating to the President's con- versation with General Emory, the main argument was that he had merely expressed to the General that, having the constitutional power of the Commander-in-Chief his orders, ". . . whether issued through the War Department of through the General-in-Chief, or by any other channel of communication, are entitled to respect and obedience; and that such constitutional power cannot be taken from him by virtue of any act of Congress."[310]

307 *Trial of Andrew Johnson, Vol. I, 39-40.*

308 308 Although this argument wasn't advanced in the President's Answer, Professor Berger makes a well-supported argument that the Senate intended that the Act would not apply to Stanton. See Berger, Impeachment, the Constitutional Problems, 286-292; see also Trefousse, Impeach- ment of a President, 147.

309 *Trial of Andrew Johnson, Vol. I, 43-46.*

310 *Ibid., 47.*

Johnson's team first disputed the accuracy of the statements dis- paraging Congress attributed to him by Article X.[311] They then went on to argue that he, like all Americans, had a right to free speech and could not be convicted based on his exercise of that right. Finally, they stated that he had never intended to ". . . excite odium or resentment . . . of the good people of the United States against Congress," and had always ". . . recognized the authority of the several Congresses . . ." convened during his presidency. On the "catch all" Article XI, they referred to his defenses to the first and tenth articles, and denied the allegations against him.[312]

The Managers' Response .

The House managers responded to the President's Answer on March 24th. Consistent with the articles of impeachment, the thrust of their case at trial was to paint the President as a "usurper," who had violated a constitutional statute that had been passed by a two-thirds majority of Congress over the President's veto. They argued that, since Johnson was completing Lincoln's second term and that term would not expire until March 4, 1869, Stanton was protected until April 4, 1869, thirty days later.[313] Under these circumstances, the President had no choice but to comply with the law. To do otherwise would be a dereliction of his duty to "take care that the laws be faithfully executed." The President's "corrupt mind" was demonstrated by the fact that he had followed the provisions of the Tenure of Office Act by "suspending" Stanton in August 1867 and sending the Senate his reasons for sus- pending Stanton in December, as required by the Act. Then, the man- agers argued, Johnson reversed field in February 1868, when he dis- obeyed the Act by removing Stanton despite the Senate's opposition.[314] As to the non-Stanton articles, the House managers saw them as reflecting a consistent course of conduct in which the President sought to thwart the will of the people as reflected in the statutes passed by Congress, over the

311 *Article X is addressed at Ibid., 48-51.*

312 *Ibid., 51-53.*

313 *Benedict, Impeachment and Trial of Andrew Johnson, 149.*

314 *Ibid., 151.*

President's vetoes, to overturn the Reconstruction scheme that Johnson had implemented while the legislature was not in session in 1865.

The Presentation of the Case .

With the preliminaries out of the way, on Monday, March 28th shortly after noon, Chief Justice Chase entered the Senate chamber, the House managers were escorted in and the Chief Justice addressed them: "Gentlemen managers of the House of Representatives, you will now proceed in support of the articles of impeachment. Senators will please give their attention."

Benjamin Butler rose to give the opening statement. If the Sena- tors and the gallery were expecting an animated presentation from the courtroom star, they were to be disappointed. Instead, at least for this speech, Butler abandoned drama and elected to read a lengthy and dry tutorial on "high crimes and misdemeanors,"[315] arguing for the broad- est possible interpretation of the constitutional standard for the remov- al of a President:

> "We define, therefore, an impeachable high crime or misdemeanor to be one in its nature or consequences subversive of some fundamental essential principle of government, or highly prejudicial to the publicinterest, and this may consist of a violation of the Constitution, of law, of an official oath, or of duty, by an act commit- ted or omitted or, without violating a positive law, by abuse of discretionary powers from improper motives, or for any improper purpose."[316]

In case the Senators may have missed his point, Butler summa- rized by asserting that "You are a law unto yourselves, bound only by the natural principles of equity and justice, and that salus populi suprema est lex [let the welfare of the people be the supreme law]."[317] The argument for this standard was likely driven by the uncertainty the House managers had about

315 *Trefousse, Impeachment of a President, 153-154.*
316 *Trial of Andrew Johnson, Vol. I, 88.*
317 *Ibid., 90.*

their ability to win a conviction based upon a violation of the Tenure of Office Act. It was an invitation to convict the President for disagreeing with Congress.

In an attempt to ward that off, Evarts and Stanbery, arguing for the President, took a much narrower view. They asserted that conviction would require proof that the President had committed an indictable crime and that the crime was directly subversive of the government or the public interest.[318] This formula went beyond the standard that had staved off Johnson's impeachment in December 1867, which required only that the President had committed an indictable crime, with no further restriction. Groesbeck disagreed with his teammates andurged the December 1867 standard.[319] If enough Senators adopted either of these standards there could be an acquittal.

The trial unfolded over the next three weeks. The House managers over-played their hand, failing to support their bombast with hard evi- dence, and objecting repeatedly and unnecessarily. By several counts, the evidentiary squabbles consumed roughly one-third of the trial.[320] Not only did this break up the flow of the evidence, it also distracted the Senators – and the public – from the importance and historical significance of the charges against the President, and bled off the power of the prosecution's case.

In his opening statement, Butler warned that Johnson emulated usurpers like Oliver Cromwell and Napoleon Bonaparte and de- rided Johnson's accidental Presidency: "By murder most foul he succeeded to this Presidency, and is the elect of an assassin to that high office."[321] As a bookend of rhetorical venom, in his closing, Thaddeus Stevens exhorted the Senators in typically picturesque and inflammatory words:

---

318 *Benedict, Impeachment and Trial of Andrew Johnson, 145.*
319 *Ibid.*
320 *Stewart, Impeached, 217.*
321 *Trefousse, Impeachment of a President, 54.*

> "Wretched man [this off-spring of assassination], standing at bay, surrounded by a cordon of living men, each with an ax of an executioner uplifted for his just punishment. Every Senator now trying him . . . voted for this same resolution [the Tenure of Office Act], pro- nouncing his solemn doom. Will any of them vote for his acquittal on the ground of its unconstitutionality."[322]

Despite these dramatic entreaties, the heart of the case boiled down to the undisputed facts surrounding Johnson's removal of Stan- ton, many of which were contained in documents that were entered into evidence, and the interpretation of the obtuse Tenure of Office Act. The rest was fluff. One big fact hung over the trial: Stanton himself, the man who stood at the center of the dispute, had advised the President that the Act was unconstitutional and had assisted in drafting the Presi- dent's veto message based on that advice. The House managers' objec- tion to the admission of this evidence was ill-advised and it backfired on them.[323] Although the Republican majority reversed Chief Justice Chase's ruling to admit it, there was plenty of evidence on this score in the President's Answer that was already in the record. That bell could not be "unrung." All the managers succeeded in doing was to remind the impeachment court that Johnson acted with the well-supported be- lief that he was on solid constitutional ground.

The closing arguments began on April 22nd and concluded on May 6th.[324] The vote was originally scheduled for May 12th, but was postponed to May 16th, due to the illness of Senator Jacob Howard of Michigan, a stalwart Radical whose vote the impeachers did not want to lose.[325]

---

322 *Quoted in Berger, Impeachment, the Constitutional Problems, 278.*

323 *By a vote of 20 to 29, the Senate refused to hear Secretary of the Navy Welles testify about the Cabinet Secretaries' views on the Tenure of Office Act, and also rejected evidence of the Cabinet's wish for a court challenge of the law. See Stewart, Impeached, 217.*

324 *For a synopsis of the closing arguments see Stewart, Impeached, 229-239; Trefousse, Impeachment of a President, 162-163.*

325 *Stewart, Impeached, 258.*

The Verdict .

On Saturday, May 16, 1868, the Chief Justice of the United States took the chair in the Senate at noon. The first order of business was to decide which of the articles of impeachment would be offered first for vote by the Senate. A motion had been offered by Senator George H. Williams of Oregon to take up Article XI first. This mo- tion was prompted by the Senate leadership's concern that Article I might not result in a conviction, because Senators Sherman and Henderson doubted that the Tenure of Office Act applied to Stan- ton. Since Articles II to VIII were based on Article I that left Arti- cles IX, X and XI as candidates to go first. They picked Article XI has having the best chance of success.[326] The motion passed by a vote of 34 to 19.[327]

The Clerk was then instructed to read Article XI aloud, after which the roll was called for vote. Everyone knew that it would take 36 votes to convict. The vote was taken in alphabetical order, starting with Sen- ator Anthony, who rose in his place when the chief clerk called his name.[328] The following exchange occurred:

> "THE CHIEF JUSTICE. Mr. Senator Anthony, how say you? Is the respondent, Andrew Johnson, President of the United States, guilty or not guilty of a high mis- demeanor, as charged in this article.

MR. ANTHONY. Guilty."

The roll call unfolded in a steady and repetitive series of mini- dramas. Virtually everyone was keeping the vote count and the tension mounted

326 *Stewart, Impeached, 256.*

327 *The split on the vote could not have been good news for those who favored conviction. The record of the "yeas" and "nays" shows that Senator Grimes, who was not present, did not vote on the motion, although he made it to the Senate chamber to cast his vote for acquittal. Other- wise, all those who voted to acquit also opposed considering Article XI first, rather than Article I. See The Trial of Andrew Johnson, Vol. II, 485.*

328 *Senator Grimes, "he being very feeble," was permitted to remain seated. Ibid., 486.*

as the vote progressed. A Senator's name was called, the Senator rose, the Senator was asked by the Chief Justice to respond "guilty" or "not guilty," and each Senator responded. When the Chief Justice got to Ross, all eyes were fixed on him. To this point, Fessenden, Fowler, Grimes and Henderson had voted "not guilty." Trumbull was solid for acquittal and it was thought that Peter Van Winkle of West Virginia would also vote "not guilty." Other than Trumbull and Van Winkle, the remaining Senators were committed to conviction.[329] Sitting at his desk, Ross shredded paper into smaller and smaller bits. Ross rose for the Chief Justice's ques- tion, paper bits on his fingertips, his face white. Aware that every eye was trained on him, Ross felt as if he "looked down into my open grave." Without hesitation, he answered, "not guilty."[330] After Ross, Trumbull and Van Winkle voted to acquit, but all the other remaining Senators voted to convict. The final tally was 35 guilty and 19 not guilty, one vote short of conviction.

This left the Republican leadership in disarray. Under the motion that was approved, the next vote would be on Article I,[331] which they did not want to happen. There was a motion to postpone the votes on the remaining articles, and a motion to recess the trial until May 26th, both of which were approved.[332] Between May 16th and 26th, the Republicans met in convention and nominated General Grant as their candidate for President in the forthcoming election in the fall.

When the Senate reconvened to vote on the remaining articles, the leadership still shied away from a vote on Article I, offering instead Articles II and III, both of which were defeated by the same thirty-five to nineteen

---

329 Professor Hans Trefousse argues that Ross's reputed pivotal role in the vote overlooks the fact that, when Ross rose, it was not ". . . entirely certain how either Van Winkle or his colleague, Willey (who finally opted for conviction) would vote." See Trefousse, Impeachment of a President, 168. If this is true, then Ross's vote did not end the drama, although at least some of the contemporaneous accounts seem to show that those present saw Ross's vote as being decisive. See, e.g., Stewart, Impeached, 277.

330 The description of Ross's conduct during the vote is taken from Stewart, Impeached, 277.

331 The Trial of Andrew Johnson, Vol. II, 484.

332 Ibid., 488-489.

count that defeated Article XI.[333] Having suf- fered the three consecutive losses, the majority gave up and a mo- tion to adjourn the Senate sitting as a court of impeachment was made and passed.[334] The first impeachment trial of a President of the United States was over. President Johnson was acquitted.

The Opinions of the Senators.

Thirty Senators took advantage of the rule allowing separate opinions explaining the reasons for their votes.[335] That was a little more than half of the 54 Senators who voted on the impeachment charges against the President. Of the 30, 24 were Republicans, five were Democrats and one was a "Johnson Conservative." Six of the seven Republicans who voted for acquittal lodged opinions, all but Edmund Ross of Kan- sas. The other 18 Republicans who recorded their opinions voted to convict the President.

Senator Charles Sumner of Massachusetts led the pack in favor of conviction. He was Thaddeus Stevens's Radical counterpart in the Senate. Like Stevens, Sumner hated Johnson and all that he stood for. Sumner's mission was to get rid of the President and he voted proud- ly to convict him. He believed that, once the President had been im- peached, the Senate had an unfettered right to decide his fate. Sumner saw Johnson's impeachment as another battle against slavery:

> "This is one of the last great battles of slavery. Driven from these legislative chambers, driven from the field of war, this monstrous power has found a refuge in the Executive Mansion, where, in utter disregard of the Constitution and laws, it seeks to exercise its ancient far-reaching sway. All this is very plain. Nobody can question it. Andrew Johnson is the impersonation of the tyrannical slave power. In him it lives. . . . With the

333 *Ibid., 496-497.*

334 *Ibid., 497-498.*

335 *The opinions are all contained in Volume III of the Trial of Andrew Johnson. They fill 353 pages in the official record of the trial.*

> President at [the head of the partisans of slavery], they are now entrenched in the Executive Mansion. Not to dislodge them is to leave the country a prey to one of the most hateful tyrannies of history."[336]

In pursuit of his end, Sumner avowed that the "trial" in the Sen- ate was nothing of the sort. It was a political inquisition and Sumner would have stripped the proceedings of all pretensions of judicial de- cision- making. "Call it senatorial or political, it is a power by itself and subject to its own conditions."[337] That being the case, the only guardrails on the Senate's discretion were political:

> "As we discern the true character of impeachment un- der our Constitution we shall be constrained to confess that it is a political proceeding before a political body, with political purposes; that it is founded on political offenses, proper for the consideration of a political body and subject to political judgment only."[338]

Taken to its logical extreme, Sumner's argument cedes to the Senate an unrestrained right to remove a President for whatever polit- ical purpose can capture two-thirds of that body. We have no concrete way of determining how many of those Senators who voted to convict the President ascribed to this extreme view. Twenty-four Senators, in- cluding both Republicans and Democrats, did not write opinions. Of the 23Republican Senators who voted to convict and also issued opin- ions, nine expressed no view on the impeachment standard.[339] Howev- er, it is safe to say that none of those voting to convict the President believed it was necessary to charge him with an indictable crime, since no such crime appeared in the articles of impeachment.

336 Trial of Andrew Johnson, Vol. III, 247.

337 Ibid., 248.

338 Ibid., 249.

339 Those nine Republicans were Senators Cattell, Ferry, Harlan, Howard, Merrill of Maine, Patterson of New Hampshire, Pomeroy, Stewart and Tipton.

In addition to Sumner, there were eight Republicans who expressed a view on the impeachment standard. Of those eight, three seemed to agree with Sumner on the open-ended discretion given to the Senate by the Constitution: Edmunds,[340] Frelinghuysen,[341] and Sherman.[342] Three of the remaining five (Howe, Morrill of Vermont and Williams) endorsed the notion that impeachment did not require proof of an indictable crime. Wilson[343] and Yates[344] fashioned their own more specific tests.

Only four Democrats and one "Johnson Conservative," all of whom voted to acquit, submitted written opinions. Democrats Buck- alew and Vickers and Johnson Conservative Doolittle expressed no view on what constituted impeachable conduct. Democrats Davis[345] and Johnson[346] said proof of an indictable crime was required for im- peachment. Since no Democrats voted to convict the President, oneof two things, and perhaps both, can be inferred: they required proof of an indictable crime, or they found the charges, even if non-indictable, were not proved.

340 *See Trial of Andrew Johnson, Vol. III, 94: ". . . the Constitution did not establish this procedure for the punishment of a crime, but for the secure and faithful administration of the law, it was not intended to cramp it by any specific definition of high crimes and misdemeanors, but to leave each case to be defined by law, or, when not defined, to be decided on its own circumstances, in the patriotic and judicial sense of the representatives of the States."*

341 *Ibid., 208: "The Senate, while trying the President, are [sic] not only invested with the function of a court and jury but also retain their official characters as senators intrusted [sic] with the interests of the nation. . . if those charges are proven, we may, for the well-being of the republic, abstain from the exercise of that clemency which in other judicial proceedings is reposed in the court and in the pardoning power, but which in the matter of impeachment is involved in the verdict of the Senate.*

342 *Ibid., 3: "[We] are not bound by the technical definitions of crimes and misdemeanors. A willful violation of the law, a gross and palpable breach of moral obligations tending to unfit an officer for the proper discharge of his office or to bring the office into public contempt and derision is, when charged and proven, an impeachable offense."*

343 *Ibid., 215: Conviction could be based on ". . . misbehavior in office detrimental to the interests of the nation, dangerous to the rights of the people, or dishonoring to government."*

344 *Ibid., 104: ". . . wanton removal of meritorious officers is impeachable."*

345 *Ibid., 158.*

346 *Ibid., 51.*

The "Recusants ."

Had the Republicans held firm to the party line, Johnson's removal would have been assured. But that did not happen. Seven Republicans broke ranks and saved Johnson's Presidency by a single vote. The sev- en Republican Senators who voted to acquit the President have gone down in history collectively as the "recusants," or dissenters. They have been called that because they dissented from the Republican Congressional monolith that was committed to clearing Johnson out of the path to Congressional Reconstruction. If any one of these dissent- ers had voted guilty, Andrew Johnson would have been removed from office, Senator Benjamin Wade would have become President and the course of history would have changed. It should also be said that the loss of one Democrat from the acquittal column would have yield- ed the same result. The point is that these seven men stepped away from the partisan warfare that drove the Johnson impeachment and trial from start to finish. Given the high passions in Congress and in the public arena clamoring for Johnson's removal, it was an act of the highest political courage. After they served out their terms, none of them would ever return to Congress.

Six of the seven chose to record their views in written opinions: Fes- senden, Fowler, Grimes, Henderson, Trumbull, and Van Winkle. Thesev- enth, Edmund Ross, elected not to do so, even though he is often portrayed heroically as having cast the deciding vote.[347] Not surprisingly, all the Senators who wrote opinions assumed that the Tenure of Office Act was constitutional. After all, they voted for it. Although there are differences in emphasis and analysis, Fessenden, Grimes and Henderson all found that the Act did not apply to Stanton and, therefore, Johnson was free to remove him without the consent of the Senate.[348]

347 Ross's heroic stature likely stems in the modern age from the essay about his role in the Johnson impeachment trial contained in John F. Kennedy's Profiles in Courage, first published in 1956. For a contrary view of Edmund Ross see Stewart, Impeached. For instance at 228, Stewart quotes the following assessment of Ross from a contemporary: "A great and insidious influence is operating upon Ross, who is a weak man and may be artfully operated on without apprehension of fact." In that regard, it may be significant that, within a few weeks of the President's acquittal, Ross received access to the President's patronage. See Trefousse, Impeachment of a President, 168.

348 Fessenden opinion, Trial of Andrew Johnson, Vol. III, 16-31; Grimes opinion, Ibid., 328-

Trumbull took a somewhat different approach. He began by nar- rowing the issue to be decided and implicitly scolding Sumner for his claim of unrestricted discretion in deciding the President's fate:

> "The question to be decided is not whether Andrew Johnson is a proper person to fill the presidential office, nor whether it is fit that he should remain in it, nor, in- deed, whether he has violated the Constitution and laws in other respects than those alleged against him. As well might any other 54 persons take upon themselves by vi- olence to rid the country of Andrew Johnson, because they believe him a bad man, as to call upon 54 senators, in violation of their sworn duty, to convict and depose him for any other cause than those alleged in the arti- cles of impeachment."[349]

Trumbull claimed that only an "intent to remove" Stanton was alleged, which was not proved. As to the Tenure of Office Act, he de- clared that he could not vote to convict based on "what must be admit- ted to be a doubtful statute, and particularly when the misconstruction was the same put upon it by the authors of the law at the time of its passage."[350] He closed with this admonition:

> "In view of the consequences likely to flow from to- day's proceedings, should they result in a conviction on what my judgment tells me are insufficient charges and proofs, I tremble for the future of my country. I cannot be an instrument to produce such a result; and at the hazard of the ties even of friendship and affection, till calmer times shall do justice to my motives, no alterna- tive is left but the inflexible discharge of myduty."[351]

340; Henderson opinion, Ibid., 295-309.

349 Ibid., 319.

350 Ibid., 323. Trumbull is referring to the legislative history of the Act showing that the Senate did not intend it to apply to Stanton.

351 Ibid., 328.

Like Trumbull, Fowler began by noting that the President was ". . . not on trial for his political opinions, nor for his general character, nor for every act of his life or administration, but for eleven specific charges."[352] Fowler discussed his understanding of the impeachment standard, albeit in fuzzy terms. He defined a crime as "an offense against a public law." In this case that would be the Tenure of Office Act. Fowler also wrote that "[i]t is a principle of natural justice and of our law that the intent and the act must both concur to constitute a crime."[353] In this case, Fowler concluded that the Tenure of Office Act did not preclude the President from removing Stanton, and, therefore, no "crime" was committed.[354]

Van Winkle allowed that ". . . there is no doubt that an actualpre-vention of the execution of a law by one whose duty is to take care that the laws be faithfully executed is a misdemeanor, . . ."[355] He finessed the issue by proclaiming that "no removal or attempt to remove is charged, and consequently the [President] could not have been guilty of a 'high misdemeanor,' " as charged in this (first) article."[356]

Fessenden took the bull of the impeachment standard by the horns. Granting the view that an indictable crime was not necessary for impeachment, he went on to say:

> ". . . it must be conceded that the power thus conferred might be liable to very great abuse, especially in times of high party excitement, when the passions of the people are inflamed against a perverse and obnoxious public officer. . . . It is evident, then, as it seems to me that the offence for which a Chief Magistrate is removed from office . . . should be of such a character as to commend itself at once to the minds of all right thinking men as, beyond all question, an adequate cause

352 *Ibid., 193.*
353 *Ibid., 194.*
354 *Ibid., 194-198.*
355 *Ibid., 151-152.*
356 *Ibid., 148.*

> . It should be free from the taint of party. . . ."[357] (emphasis added)

These were words of wisdom for the ages. They were, how- ever, largely ignored at the time by Fessenden's fellow Senators, who generally arrayed themselves at two extreme poles. At one extreme were those who would require proof of an indictable crime, at the op- posite pole were those who would follow Stevens and Sumner down the road of political removal. Neither view honored the intent of the framers of the Constitution.

357 *Ibid., 29-30.*

CHAPTER 13
SHOULD JOHNSON HAVE BEENIMPEACHED?

Alexander Hamilton's Federalist 65 prophecy about the role of "passion" in the impeachment process rang true in Andrew Johnson's case. The Civil War had just ended and the wounds were still very much unhealed. An estimated total of 620,000 menhad been killed.[358] The economy of the South had been devastated. Amidst this devastation, 4,000,000 people had been freed from slavery. There was a desperate need to deal with the governmental, cultural, legal and economic changes that came with that freedom, for the former slaves as well as their masters. Short of refighting the war, no greater national challenge could be imagined. President Andrew Johnson's impeach- ment cannot be divorced from the crisis that still faced the nation. At bottom, his impeachment was the major skirmish in a heated battle between the President and the Congress over who got to decide what the Reconstruction policy would be.

The passions were hot on both sides. It was passion that drove Thaddeus Stevens and Charles Sumner to adopt their extreme, and unconstitutional, view of the Senate's unfettered discretion in judg- ing the impeachment case against the President. Their view that the Senate "was a law unto itself" was fundamentally incompatible with the founders' intent as expressed at the

---

358 That represented approximately 2% of the population in the 1860's. That would equate to about six million deaths given the current population of the United States.

Constitutional Convention and the ratification conventions that followed. If adopted, it would have altered the balance of power between the Congress and the Presidency, leaving the President at the mercy of Congress, at least when the party opposing him has at least a simple majority in the House and a two- thirds majority in the Senate. Yet, this view almost carried the day.

Andrew Johnson brought much of this on himself and he must bear his share of the responsibility for what happened. He acted as if he had a mandate when he didn't. Ironically, he was included on the "Republican Union Party" ticket to help support Lincoln's effort to unite the country in the aftermath of the Civil War. The 1864 election was run on Lincoln's platform; Johnson was just along for the ride. The Republicans did not win the election in order to return the South to the Confederates, but that's exactly what Johnson's Reconstruction policy was doing. Remarkably, he was able to stave off impeachment for almost two years. Had Johnson been willing to compromiseon the dispute over his Secretary of War, he would have avoided it altogether.

The judgment of most historians and constitutional scholars is that Johnson should not have been impeached and that his conviction would have fundamentally shifted the balance of power between Con- gress and the President, resulting in what would amount to a vote-of- no confidence view of impeachment. This would have made our gov- ernment more akin to the British parliamentary system. For instance, Professor Raoul Berger, both a lawyer and a constitutional historian and one of the most renowned impeachment scholars, has said in no uncertain terms, "[t]he impeachment and trial of Andrew Johnson . . . represent a gross abuse of the impeachment process, an attempt to punish the President for differing with and obstructing the policy of Congress."[359] In Berger's view, had the effort succeeded, it would have ". . . undermined the separation of powers and constituted a long stride toward the very 'legislative tyranny' feared and fenced in by

359 Berger, Impeachment, the Constitutional Problems, 308; Turley, "Senate Trials and Factional Disputes," 87.

the Founders."[360] He credits the seven Republican recusants with hav- ing preserved the constitutional separation of powers, saying, '[i]n the midst of the storm that beat upon them they stood upright."[361]

Historian Michael Les Benedict takes a somewhat different view. While acknowledging that most historians view the attempt to remove Andrew Johnson as a "blatant political move" by the Republicans, he argues that political considerations also secured his acquittal.[362] For instance, Benedict notes that ". . . men like Fessenden, Trumbull, and Grimes disliked the Radicals nearly as much or more than they dis- liked Andrew Johnson, and it was the Radicals who stood to gain most by Johnson's removal."[363] Likewise, there were powerful interests ar- rayed against Senator Benjamin Wade, who would have become Pres- ident had Johnson been removed.[364]

Undoubtedly, politics did play a role, but, in the end, we know that the six Republicans who voted to acquit and also wrote opinions were also motivated by the long view of history and what conviction would have meant for the constitutional checks and balances structure created by the founders.[365] Ironically, at least one of the recusants and like- ly most of the Democrats, applied the improperly narrow, "indictable crimes" view of impeachment, which means that the Johnson acquittal was right, but for the wrong reason. William Fessenden eloquently captured the essence of the founder's understanding of "high crimes and misdemeanors" as not limited to indictable crimes, but also not without limit. And he used it to conclude that Johnson was not guilty of impeachable conduct. No matter what standard was used, as Chief Justice Rehnquist has noted, Johnson's acquittal meant that impeach- ment would not be a ". . . referendum on the [President's] performance in office."[366]

360 *Ibid., 308-309; Rehnquist, Grand Inquests, 268.*
361 *Ibid., 309.*
362 *Benedict, The Impeachment and Trial of Andrew Johnson, 126.*
363 *Ibid., 132.*
364 *Ibid., 133-135.*
365 *Ibid., 178-179.*
366 *Rehnquist, Grand Inquest, 271.*

PART 3

PRESIDENT RICHARD M .NIXON

CHAPTER 14
THE INSECUREPRO

"Of course I knew Jerry Voorhis wasn't a Communist. I had to win. That's something you don't understand. The important thing was to win."[367]

Richard Milhous Nixon was the first and only President to resign his office. He did so in the face of certain impeachment in the House of Representatives and conviction in the Senate. By the time of his resignation on August 9, 1974, he had lost the support of almost the entire Congress, virtually all of his staff, the media and the majority of Americans. President Nixon's political demise did not happen overnight. It took over two years from beginning to end. Most of his party and many Americans backed him for much of those two years. The support eroded as a function of the ever-increasing evidence that, despite his protestations to the contrary, the President was a crook. It was Nixon himself, a consummatepolitician and able executive, who caused his unprecedented political collapse. The seeds of his own destruction were sown all along the path of his journey from a backwater California town to the leader of the free world.[368]

---

367 Richard Nixon's statement to Stanley Lake, Jerry Voorhis's adviser, about his attacks on Voorhis, Nixon's Democratic opponent in the 1946 Congressional election, as quoted in Farrell, John A., Nixon, The Life, (Doubleday, New York, 2017) (hereafter Farrell, Nixon), 41.

368 For more detailed treatments of Nixon's formative years, see Farrell, Nixon, 3-8, 42-59; Wills, Gary, Nixon Agonistes, the Crisis of the Self-Made Man (Houghton Mifflin Company, Boston, 2002) (hereafter Wills, Nixon Agonistes), 150-186; Mazo, Earl and Hess, Stephen, Nixon, A Political Portrait, (Harper & Row, New York, 1967), (hereafter Mazo and Hess, Nixon, A Political Portrait), 9-33.

The Years Before Politics .

Richard Nixon was born in a Yorba Linda, California farmhouse on January 9, 1913. The doctor came in a horse and buggy.[369] When Nixon was nine, the family moved to Whittier, larger than Yorba Linda, but still small by most standards. Whittier had a substantial Quaker population, a religion the Nixon family shared though their mother's side of the family. There were five children, all boys, two of whom died of tuberculosis. Nixon had a difficult father and a conciliatory, yet unemotional mother. The household was noted for its physical and emotional severity.[370]

Nixon was socially awkward and not easy to like. He was keenly aware that, in contrast to his popular brother, Don, he was known in town as a "sour puss."[371] One of his neighbors described him in high school as "always so serious that we always thought he never had any fun. I think he was more or less a loner."[372] More than a few of his classmates thought he was "sanctimonious, priggish and a teacher's pet."[373]

Nixon's defining feature was his mind, which was sharp and ana- lytical, coupled with a remarkable memory.[374] He was also self-disci- plined and a hard worker. Not surprisingly, he excelled in high school, where he became an excellent debater and a good actor, skills that were to serve him well in his political career. He was offered an opportunity to attend Yale or Harvard, an opportunity the family could not afford. So, he attended Whittier College in his hometown, where he could live at home and continue to work at his father's grocery store. He did well enough to be accepted with a scholarship to Duke Law School in 1934, from which he graduated third in his class three years later.[375]

---

369 *Farrell, Nixon, 42.*
370 *Ibid., 47.*
371 *Ibid., 3.*
372 *Ibid., 58.*
373 *Ibid.*
374 *Ibid., 3.*
375 *Ibid., 69.*

Nixon was hoping to use his Duke law degree as a ticket out of his small town. However, even with his stellar record and recommen- dations from his professors, he was unable to land the job he wanted with a Wall Street law firm. His back-up plan was to join the FBI in Washington, D.C., but that also failed to pan out. He suffered the in- dignity of returning to Whittier where his mother was able to get him a job with a family friend who had a law practice in town.[376] The bright spot in this picture was that Nixon met Thelma Catharine (Pat) Ryan, whom he married in June, 1940.

World War II gave Nixon the chance he needed to escape the small world of Whittier. Before the Japanese attacked Pearl Harbor on De- cember 7, 1941, one of Nixon's law professors recommended him to become a staff attorney with the Office of Price Administration (OPA) in Washington, D.C., a job that he accepted. The Japanese attack on Pearl Harbor occurred just before he and Pat moved east. Nixon did not like his bureaucratic duties with the OPA. Although he was exempt from the draft, he joined the Navy and entered officer training school in August 1942. By May 1943 he was at New Caledonia in the Solo- mon Islands, northeast of Australia in the South Pacific, working as a supply officer. While Nixon was never on the front line, his camp came under enemy artillery fire from time to time. He served honorablyand earned a reputation as an effective leader. After his overseas duty, Nix- on was transferred back to the States and, in the summer of 1945, was a contract officer representing the Navy at a huge manufacturingplant near Baltimore.

He and Pat were considering their options: staying in the Navy, something in New York City, or maybe returning to the law practice in Whittier. Then, the unexpected occurred. Nixon received a letter from a group of Whittier-based businessmen who were looking for a promising young Republican to oppose Jerry Voorhis, the four-term Democratic incumbent as the U.S. Representative for the Twelfth Con- gressional District, which included

376 Ibid., 4.

Whittier. Voorhis was a popular Congressman. It was a risky venture, especially for a virtual unknown like Dick Nixon. They decided to take the risk.[377]

The 1946 Congressional Election .[378]

Nixon flew back to California to be interviewed by his would-be political sponsors. He passed with flying colors and returned to Washington to await, with Pat, word of his nomination, which was secured a few days later.[379] While still on the East Coast, he began preparations for the campaign. As was his habit, Nixon made a lengthy "to do" list on yellow pads, which eventually found their way into the archives at the Richard Nixon Library.[380] The list included such pedestrian items as setting up a budget, procuring office furniture, and calling on news- papers.[381] But it also included this startling item, apparently listed on the candidate's own initiative, in Nixon's very first political campaign: "Set up . . . spies in V. camp." (emphasis added)[382]

Nixon entered politics at the dawn of the Cold War. In a speech delivered at Westminster College in Fulton, Missouri on March 5, 1946, former British Prime Minister Winston Churchill, with President Harry Truman looking on, uttered these famous words that would help to define an era: "From Stettin in the Baltic to Trieste in the Adriatic, an iron curtain has descended across the continent."The Soviet Union exploded its first atomic bomb in August 1949. On June 25, 1950, the North Koreans invaded the South and the United States joined the war two days later. By October 1950, the Chinese had entered the war. Communism was on the march, with a declared intention to consign our way of life to the dustbin of history. Americans were understand- ably worried about this threat.

---

377 Ibid., 11-12.

378 More extensive accounts of Nixon's 1946 campaign can be found in Farrell, Nixon, 1-41 and Mazo and Hess, Nixon, A Political Portrait, 34-43.

379 Farrell, Nixon, 16.

380 Ibid., 569 (note supporting 17 of text).

381 Ibid., 16-17.

382 Ibid., 17. There is no evidence that Nixon was successful in placing a "spy" in the Voorhis campaign organization.

The year 1946 was also the beginning of what came to be known as the McCarthy Era, which lasted until 1954. This sad chapter of American history is named after Wisconsin Senator Joseph McCarthy who, for eight years, led a series of investigations designed to ferret out members of the Communist Party and its so-called "fellow travelers." Before McCarthy's official censure by the Senate in December 1954, "red-baiting" haunted America's political landscape. Membership in, or any association with, the Communist Party or its fellow travelers was anathema to McCarthy and many Americans.

Richard Nixon was to become the advanced guard of the red-baiting movement. His strategy was to attack his opponent, Jerry Voorhis, a liberal Democrat, for his alleged affiliation with the Communist Party.[383] It would be guilt by association. Voorhis was not and had nev- er been a member of the Communist Party. However, his left leaning stance on many issues earned him the support of organizations that were identified with the Communist Party. Nixon and his campaign strategists decided to focus their attack on support given toVoorhis by the CIO's[384] Political Action Committee (PAC), which Voorhis him- self admitted was Communist-directed. Nixon's campaign literature branded Voorhis as a PAC puppet and Nixon hammered on this theme throughout the campaign, including at the five debates the two candi- dates held.[385] Nixon's relentless and false attacks kept Voorhis, whose campaign was underfunded and uncertain, back on his heels.[386] Nixon defeated the popular incumbent by a wide margin (56% - 42%).

Nixon's first political campaign displayed both his talents andhis dark underside. He was a brilliant political strategist, an able cam- paigner, an excellent public speaker, and he was ruthless in pursuit of victory. As Nixon

---

383 Wills, Nixon Agonistes, 82-83.

384 CIO stands for Congress of Industrial Organizations, one of the largest and most influential labor organizations in the 1950s

385 Wills, Nixon Agonistes, 82-83; Farrell, Nixon, 29-41.

386 Nixon, p. 39.

said to one of Voorhis's advisers after the election: "Of course I knew that Jerry Voorhis wasn't a Communist . . . But you're just being naïve. I had to win. That's something you don't un- derstand. The important thing was to win."[387]

From the House of Representatives to Exile (1946-1967) .

Richard Nixon entered the House of Representatives at the age of thirty-three. Within six years, he went from Representative to Senator to Vice President. He skated to re-election to the House in 1948, earn- ing a whopping 86% of the vote. During the four years he served in the House, Nixon established himself as a "comer" in the Republican Party, largely through his service on the House Un-American Activi- ties Committee (HUAC), where he earned national renown for his de- termined and controversial investigation that resulted in a charge that Alger Hiss, a former State Department employee, was a Soviet spy.[388] In 1950, Nixon took another risk and ran for the Senate against Helen Gahagan Douglas, a movie star and liberal Democratic U.S. Representative, who defeated the Democratic incumbent in the pri- mary election. Nixon reprised his Voorhis red-baiting strategy against Douglas, who had already been dubbed the "Pink Lady" in the primary election. Nixon's anti-Communism strategy got a boost from North Korea's invasion of South Korea on June 25th, which precipitated the Korean War. Although Douglas fought back more vigorously than Voorhis, she too lost by a wide margin, making Nixon a United States Senator at the age of thirty-seven.[389]

---

387 Ibid., 41.

388 For a detailed account of the Alger Hiss investigation see Farrell, Nixon, 93-128; Mazo and Hess, Nixon, A Political Portrait, 44-63. For Nixon's account of the investigation, see his autobiography, Six Crises, (Doubleday & Company, Inc., New York, 1962) (hereafter Nixon, Six Crises), 1-71. Ironically, Hiss was never convicted of espionage. He was tried twice on charges of perjury. The first trial ended with a hung jury. He was found guilty in his second trial and served three and a half years in prison.

389 For a detailed account of the Nixon-Douglas campaign see Farrell, Nixon, 129-157; Mazo and Hess, Nixon, A Political Portrait, 64-75.

Just two years later, Nixon maneuvered himself into position as Gener Dwight Eisenhower's running mate.[390] The two were elected in 1952 and re-elected in 1956. Nixon idolized the war hero, but was never able to win Eisenhower's respect.[391] In fact, Eisenhower seri- ously considered dropping Nixon from the Republican ticket in both 1952 and 1956. The 1952 episode, which featured Nixon's celebrated "Checkers" speech, was especially searing to Nixon, so much so that it became one of his "six crises" described in his 1962 autobiography of that name.[392]

The controversy centered on Nixon's use of financial contribu- tions by wealthy donors to a political fund of about $18,000 that was used to cover such political costs as airfare, postage, long distance phone calls, and advertising. Nixon wasn't the only politician of the time who used such a fund, but his became the subject of attacks ear- ly in the 1952 presidential campaign. Ike's advisors were divided on whether or not to drop Nixon. In the end, Ike agreed to allow Nixon to attempt to save himself by making a direct appeal to voters in a tele- vised speech from Los Angeles on September 23, 1952.

Television was in its infancy in 1952. The broadcasts were in black and white, the sound was poor and the screens were tiny. Yet, three out of five families owned a television, accounting for about 17 million units, with nearly half located in the largest ten cities. While there had been live coverage of political conventions in 1948 and 1952, Nixon's speech was the first time that a major political figure had communicat- ed one-on-one with the American people by television. Nine million televisions were tuned into Nixon's speech, the largest TV audience to that time.[393]

---

390 This event is described in Farrell, Nixon, 158-176.

391 Ibid., 210-212.

392 Nixon did not like the "Checkers" catch line for his speech. He always referred to it as the "fund" crisis/speech. Writing in 1962, Nixon said that "[t]he crisis of the fund was the hardest, the sharpest, and the briefest of my public life. . . . it left a deep scar which was never to heal completely." See Nixon, Six Crises, 128.

393 Farrell, Nixon, 195.

not had as much time to prepare for the speech as he normally result, he decided to read his remarks, which was unusual for to Nixon's already high level of stress, just before he went on is told by an Eisenhower representative that the General wanted Nixon to end the speech with a withdrawal from the Republican ticket.[394] Although Nixon did not say so, he had no intention of withdrawing. The end of his speech came as a surprise to Eisenhower and his advisors.

While under extreme pressure, Nixon delivered what is widely recognized as a career-saving speech, one that captured the admiration of the millions of average Americans who tuned in.[395] It was to them that he spoke. Sitting behind a small desk on a sparse set, with his wife sitting in a chair off to his left, he started by explaining what the $18,000 fund was and how it was used.[396] He stressed that the money was used only to fund political activities such as travel, mailings and advertising, so that the American taxpayer wouldn't have to pay for them. None of the money was paid to him or his family. He held up for the audience to see the accounting and legal "audits" that supported the propriety of what he had done. He quoted the legal audit's conclusion that he had done nothing illegal.

Then he got to the heart of the speech. He played up his humble beginnings and the modest lifestyle that he and his family were lead- ing, despite his political success. He provided a detailed run-down of what he and his wife had earned over the years and what they now owned. To summarize his financial status, he smiled at the camera, which panned out to show Mrs. Nixon sitting just a few feet from her husband, and said: "Pat doesn't have a mink coat. But she does havea respectable Republican cloth coat. And I always tell her that she'd look good in anything."

---

394 Farrell, Nixon, 189-190.

395 A text of the speech can be found at http://watergate.info/1952/09/23/nixon-checkers-speech.html.

396 Even after adjusting for inflation, this is a stunningly meager amount of money compared to the millions of dollars that are donated to political campaigns today.

If that wasn't schmaltz enough, he then turned to the dog that had been a gift to his two young girls from a supporter in Texas, who had heard Pat say on the radio that they would like to have a dog. The black and white spotted cocker spaniel was dubbed "Checkers" by his daughter Tricia. Then he looked down, dropped his voice and said: "And you know, the kids, like all kids, love the dog and I just want to say right now, that regardless of what they say about it, we're gonna keep it." He wrapped up this part of the speech by saying that he felt it was essential that a man of modest means like himself could also run for Vice President because ". . . you remember what Abraham Lincoln said: "God must have loved the common people – he made so many of them."

At the close of his speech, Nixon took two huge risks. First, he did not withdraw, as he had been told he was supposed to do. Sec- ond, rather than leaving the decision on his future to Ike, he urged the television audience to ". . . [l]et [the Republican National Committee] decide whether my position on the ticket will help or hurt. And I am going to ask you to help them decide. Wire and write the Republican National Committee whether you think I should stay on or whether I should get off."[397] And wire and write they did. People wrote hundreds of thousands of telegrams and letters in Nixon's support.[398]

Nixon kept his place on the ticket. Due to Eisenhower's popu- larity, they won the election in a landslide, capturing 442 of the 531 electoral votes. Nixon became Vice President of the United States at the age of 39. After flirting briefly with dropping Nixon from the 1956 Republican ticket, Ike decided to keep him on for another run. Once again, they prevailed in a rematch against Adlai Stevenson by another landslide (457 of the 531 electoral votes).

---

397 Although General Eisenhower was pleased with the overwhelmingly positive response to Nixon's speech, he was unhappy with Nixon for disobeying his orders. In a statement to the nation's Republicans, Eisenhower made it clear that Nixon's future was his decision, not theirs. See Farrell, Nixon, 195. In a separate telegram, Ike told Nixon they could resume the campaign after Nixon had reported to him and Ike had made his "personal decision." Ibid.

398 Ibid.

By 1960, Nixon had served at the highest levels of government for fourteen years. Having lived in Ike's shadow for eight of those fourteen years, it was now time for Nixon to seek the top spot on his own merits. The Democrats nominated John F. Kennedy, to bring new blood into the presidential fray. He had his southern flank covered by his running mate, Senator Lyndon B. Johnson from Texas.

After first beating out Nelson Rockefeller for the Republican presidential nomination, Nixon got off to a strong start with what Ted Sorenson, JFK's speechwriter, described as a "brilliant" acceptance speech at the Republican National Convention.[399] But shortly thereaf- ter, his boss and sometime nemesis delivered an unkind public blow to Nixon. When asked at a press conference for an important contri- bution that Nixon had made to one of Ike's presidential decisions, the President quipped: "If you give me a week, I might think of one."[400] Although Ike would later campaign for Nixon, the President's slam against his faithful Vice President was unfortunate and a personal blow to Nixon. In the end, Nixon lost to Kennedy by only 113,000 votes, the closest presidential election in history.[401]

Two years later, he was defeated by the incumbent Democrat, Pat Brown, father of the current California Governor Jerry Brown, in his one and only bid to become Governor of California. In typical Nixo- nian fashion, in his concession speech, he complained about the treat- ment he had received from the press and vowed that "you won't have Dick Nixon to kick around anymore."

---

399 Farrell, Nixon, 274; Mazo and Hess, Nixon, A Political Portrait, 228-229.

400 arrell, Nixon, 274-275; see also Mazo and Hess, Nixon, A Political Portrait, 238-239, where the authors argue that Ike's comments were misunderstood. These and other slights delivered by Eisenhower to Nixon over the eight years they worked together must have been difficult for Nixon's fragile ego to overcome. The degree to which Nixon suffered under Eisenhower is revealed by this anecdote told by John Farrell in his biography of Nixon. On an airplane ride with reporters and staffers in the run up to the 1960 presidential election, after downing two stiff drinks, Nixon launched into a tirade against Eisenhower, calling him an idiot, cruel and ungenerous, who subjected him to gross indignities. He called the President a tin god who had duped the American people. See Farrell, Nixon, 263.

401 Nixon received 34,108,157 votes (49.55%) to Kennedy's 34,220,984 votes (49.72%). Kennedy received 303 electoral votes to Nixon's 219.

The 1968 Presidential Campaign .

Six years after Nixon supposedly bowed out of politics, he was back. He earned the Republican nomination for president with a "southern strategy" that recognized the key to the Republican nomination was to play to the Southern delegations. Nixon's choice of SpiroAgnew over Nelson Rockefeller as his running mate placated the Southern delega- tions and won him the nomination.[402] Once Lyndon Johnson withdrew from politics after being crushed by the weight of the Vietnam War, Nixon was up against Johnson's Vice President, Hubert Humphrey, and third party candidate, Alabama Governor George Wallace, who captured 9,901,118 popular votes (46 electoral votes). Nixon won a plurality of the popular vote (31,783,783), which gave him 301 elec- toral votes. Humphrey received 31,271,839 popular votes, yielding 191 electoral votes.

Nixon was the law and order candidate who spoke on behalf of what he later termed the "silent majority" and aggressively sought sup- port from Southern conservatives who were historically part of the successful coalition which Franklin Roosevelt built during the New Deal and which lasted for over three decades. The big issue was the Vietnam War. The country was war weary and torn apart. Nixon said he would do what the Democrats had not done – get America out of the war. Much as President Johnson had promised to do, Nixon devoted the last months of his presidency to a determined effort to end the war. The race between Nixon and Humphrey was getting tighter as the November 4th election day approached. At the same time, President Johnson was working on a secret deal to end the war. If Johnson would stop the bombing of North Vietnam, the Soviet Union pledged it would get the North to engage in talks to end the war.[403] If those

402 *Wills, Nixon Agonistes, 258-275.*

403 *New York Times, Op Ed, John A. Farrell, "Nixon's Vietnam Treachery," December 31, 2016, https://nytimes.com/2016/12/31/opinion/ sundays/nixons-vietnam-treachery.html; see also New York Times, Article, Peter Baker, "Nixon Tried to Spoil Johnson's Vietnam Peace Talks in '68, Notes Show," January 2, 2017, https://www.nytimes.com/2017/01/02/us/politics/nixon-tried-to-spooil-johnsons-vietnam-peace-talks ; Farrell, Nixon, 342-344.*

negotiations succeeded, Nixon would lose the edge on the biggest issue in the cam- paign. Henry Kissinger, who was an outside Republican adviser, got wind of the pending deal and alerted Nixon to it.

Based on documents that were not publicly available until 2007, author John A. Farrell has documented back-channel efforts initiated by Nixon to persuade South Vietnamese President Nguyen Van Thieu to stall the peace talks until after the election. Those documents includ- ed a hand-written memo by Nixon's campaign aid, H.R. Haldeman, dated October 22, 1968, in which Nixon directed his staff to "monkey wrench" Johnson's peace negotiations.[404]

On October 31st, President Johnson announced a halt to bombing of the North. Two days later, President Thieu announced his govern- ment would not take part in any peace talks. On November 4th, Richard Nixon was elected President.[405]

During his life, Nixon steadfastly maintained that he had not in- terfered with the negotiations. It is now known that was a lie. Although there is no evidence that he actually influenced Thieu, this episode shows that Nixon, who was a private citizen at the time, was willing to break the law by interfering with ongoing efforts by the President of the United States to end a war that had already cost more than 30,000 American lives and hundreds of thousands of Vietnamese deaths. It was this "win at any cost" mentality that Richard Nixon and his team brought to his presidency.

Nixon the Insecure Pro .

Richard Nixon was one of the most successful politicians in our histo- ry. He had a keen mind. He was a great political strategist, an effective

404 *Ibid. The conduit was Anna Chennault, who was a Nixon fund raiser with connections throughout Asia. She was a widow of WW II war hero, Claire Chennault who, among other duties, commanded the Flying Tigers, a group of volunteer American aviators who flew against the Japanese from bases in China before the United States entered the war.*

405 *The Guardian, Martin Kettle, "Nixon Wrecked Early Peace in Vietnam," August 8, 2000, https://www.theguardian.com/world/2000/ aug/09/martinkettle.*

campaigner and excellent public speaker. He was also willing to take risks and had the ability to rebound when the risks did not pay off. His political star rose fast, dimmed for a while and then blazed upon his 1968 election as President of the United States. However, hispolitical victories were tarnished by his win at any cost mentality. That men- tality was evident in his very first political campaign and remained a central feature of his politics until it cost him his Presidency.

Perhaps it was his insecurity that drove him to extreme measures to ensure political success. His close associates saw the various mani- festations of that insecurity. For example, his speechwriter, Raymond

K. Price, Jr., "never deluded himself about Nixon's darker instincts, his paranoia, the capacity for hatred, the need for revenge, the will to crush anyone perceived as an enemy."[406] Henry Kissinger, who was Richard Nixon's foreign policy alter ego, had a well-kept secret "loath- ing and contempt" for his boss.[407] He thought Nixon was "a man con- sumed by memories of his past failures" and was "isolated, secretive, paranoid."[408]

The President revealed much about himself when he made this comment to one of his presidential staffers: "People react to fear, not love. They don't teach that in Sunday school, but it's true."[409] Or, as he said in another moment of self-reflection: "Balzac once wrote that politicians are 'monsters of self-possession.' Yet while we may show this veneer on the outside, inside the turmoil becomes almost unbear- able."[410] And finally, as we shall see, the secret tape recordings Nixon ordered speak graphically, in the President's own words, to his basest, even criminal, instincts.

---

406 Bernstein, Carl and Woodward, Bob, The Final Days (Simon and Schuster, New York, 1976) (hereafter Bernstein and Woodward, The Final Days), 329.

407 Ibid., 186.

408 Ibid., 36.

409 Farrell, Nixon, 51.

410 Ibid., 161.

CHAPTER 15
THEWATERGATE SAGA

"Most men, however, are inclined to forget justice altogether, when once craving for military power or political honors and glory has taken possession of them. Remember the saying of Ennius, 'When crowns are at stake, no friendship is sacred, no faith shall be kept.'"[411]

The Watergate saga began with a break-in at the headquarters of the Democratic National Committee (DNC) in the early morning hours of June 17, 1972.[412] It ended 26 months later with the resigna- tion of President Richard M. Nixon on August 9, 1974. Over those 26 months, the President of the United States orchestrated an elaborate cover-up in a determined attempt to prevent the American people from learning that he sat atop a secret organization designed to subvert the integrity of our electoral system and to highjack the organs of govern- ment for his political benefit.

411 Cicero quoted by Senator Sam Ervin in his Individual Statement accompanying the Final Senate Watergate Report. See The Senate Watergate Report (Abridged Edition) (Carroll & Graf, New York, 2005) (hereafter The Senate Watergate Report), 14.

412 What became known as "Watergate" was the subject of two Congressional investigations, one by the Senate Select Committee on Cam- paign Activities (the "Senate Watergate Committee") and the other by the House Judiciary Committee, which conducted an impeachment in- vestigation of the President. Two special prosecutors, Archibald Cox and Leon Jaworski also investigated the same issues. A veritable mountain of evidence was gathered and preserved during these investigations. The account here is a summary sufficient to understand the basis for the articles of impeachment the House Judiciary Committee approved against President Nixon. This summary account is drawn heavily from two sources: The Senate Watergate Report and House Calendar No. 426, Impeachment of Richard Nixon, President of the United States, Report of the Committee on the Judiciary, House of Representatives, August 20, 1974, U.S. Government Printing Office (hereafter The 1974 Judiciary Committee Impeachment Report).

The ultimate purpose of the cover-up was to protect the Pres- ident. The strategy was one of "containment and concealment." For almost a year, the goal was to confine the damage to the seven men who had planned and conducted the break-in, to make it appear to have been "a third rate burglary" without ties to Nixon's presidential cam- paign or the White House. In March, 1973, when the unfolding facts exposed Nixon's most senior and trusted advisers in the campaignand the White House, these advisers were jettisoned and the goal became to hide the damning evidence against Nixon contained in the secret tapes of White House conversations.

This last desperate campaign featured the firing of Archibald Cox, the Watergate Special Prosecutor with whom Nixon had vowed to cooperate, the bogus assertion of executive privilege to keep the tapes from being turned over, and finally, the erasure of key portions of at least one tape that likely contained proof of the President's guilt. In the end, Nixon lost virtually all political support and he resigned in the face of what was sure to be impeachment and likely removal from office.

The White House Tapes.

Much of the narrative that follows is based on audio tapes ofmeetings held by President Nixon in the Oval Office and in his office in the Executive Office Building at the times of the events described. It is important to keep in mind that the existence of the taping system was a closely guarded secret. Only a handful of people beside the Presi- dent knew about it. The public first learned of it in July 1973, when a White House official, Alexander P. Butterfield, revealed it in testimony before the Senate Watergate Committee. This revelation touched off a determined campaign by the SenateWatergate Committee and Special Prosecutors Archibald Cox and Leon Jaworski to obtain the tapes, re- sulting in a July 24, 1974 unanimous Supreme Court decision ordering Nixon to provide the relevant tapes to the Special Prosecutor. This order ended the President's desperate efforts to hide his gross abuses of power and cratered whatever support he had in Congress at the time, leading directly to his resignation on August 9th.

Pre-Watergate Abuses of Power .

By the summer of 1972, the Nixon White House had become committed to retaining political power at all costs. While we tend to see Pres- ident Nixon's abuse of his presidential powers as beginning with the Watergate break-in on June 17, 1972, that was actually just the latest in a string of secret activities in which Nixon and his cadre of Con- stitution breakers had engaged.[413] There was the Huston Plan, under which, in 1970, President Nixon approved the use of illegal wiretap- ping, illegal break-ins and illegal mail covers for domestic intelligence purposes, even though he had been advised of their illegality. This plan was prompted by the White House's fear of demonstrations and dis- sent, including, according to John Dean, peaceful protests. The Huston Plan was followed in August 1971 by the establishment of an "enemies list." According to a John Dean memorandum dated August 16, 1971, the purpose of the list was to:

> ". . . maximize the fact of our incumbency in dealing with persons known to be active in their opposition to our Administration. Stated a bit more bluntly – how can we use the available federal machinery to screw our political enemies." (emphasis added in The Senate Watergate Report)[414]

The leak of the Pentagon Papers in June 1971 prompted the formation of a special investigation unit, led by G. Gordon Liddy and E. Howard Hunt, which came to be known as the "Plumbers."[415] Liddy was a lawyer and former FBI agent. Hunt was a former CIA agent and author of more than seventy books. This group planned and carried out the burglary of the office

---

413 The description of the pre-Watergate illegal activities in the text is taken from The Senate Watergate Report, 53-72 and The 1974 House Judiciary Committee Impeachment Report, 35-39.

414 The Senate Watergate Report, 59. Committing something like this to writing both epitomiz- es the arrogance of power and is testimony to the stupidity of even the most sophisticated people.

415 The Pentagon Papers were a collection of secret government documents that recorded the history of the Vietnam War. They contained substantial evidence that, despite the government's knowl- edge that the war was not being won, and likely could not be won, a string of presidents had lied to the American people about the progress of the war. They were leaked to the press by Daniel Ellsberg, a Defense Department employee.

of Daniel Ellsworth's psychiatrist, Dr. Lewis Fielding, to obtain Ellsworth's psychiatric records, with the obvious hope of obtaining "dirt" on Ellsworth, who had disclosed the Pentagon Papers to the media. The Plumbers became a bridge to the Watergate break-in. Liddy and Hunt led the Ellsworth and Watergate break-ins. Two of Hunt's recruits participated in both escapades.

As the White House began gearing up for the 1972 presiden- tial campaign, the so-called Committee to Re-elect the President, or "CRP," considered establishing its own program of political espio- nage that was given the code word "Project Sandwedge." In addition to traditional investigative activities, the proposal included the use of bagmen and other covert intelligence gathering operations. The project was not approved. Instead, John Dean recruited Lid- dy, a lawyer, to be the CRP General Counsel and direct the White House's own intelligence gathering program in support of the cam- paign.

The implementation of the plan to gather political intelligence for use in the President's re-election campaign began in April 1972, with the disbursement of $199,000 in cash to Liddy, about $65,000 of which James McCord used to buy electronic monitoring equip- ment.[416] This equipment was used in the first, undetected break-in at the Democratic National Committee office on May 27th. Appar- ently, a bug was planted because, in early June, transcripts of the intercepts, labeled "Gemstone," were being reviewed by campaign officials.[417]

The June 17, 1972 Watergate Break-in .

"Watergate" quickly became, and has remained, the single-word iden- tifier for the most egregious political scandal in America's history. But on June 17, 1972, Watergate was just a place, a new ten acre high-end real estate complex with a tony address in the Foggy Bottom area of the nation's capital on the banks of the Potomac River, sharing the neigh- borhood with the

---

416 *The 1974 House Judiciary Committee Impeachment Report, 40.*
417 *Ibid.*

State Department and the John F. Kennedy Center for the Performing Arts. The complex consisted of several buildings, containing co-op apartments, a hotel and an office building. The DNC headquarters occupied the entire sixth floor of the office building. The DNC had some real problems to deal with. In the middle of June, less than a month before the Democratic convention, Nixon bested all the announced Democratic candidates by a minimum of 19 points, and it was looking as if South Dakota Senator George McGovern, Nixon's weakest opponent, would get the nomination.[418]

In the early morning hours of June 17th, a team of plainclothes policemen arrested, at gun-point, five men who were burglarizing the DNC's offices.[419] They had been called to the Watergate office build- ing by a security guard, Frank Willis, whose vigilance ultimately led to the resignation of the President of the United States. In making his rounds, Willis had noticed masking tape holding back the lock on the door between the parking garage and the building. He became suspi- cious because he had seen masking tape in the same place on an earlier inspection. Thinking that it had been left in place inadvertently by the maintenance crew, he removed it. When it reappeared, he called the police. Like John Wilkes Booth's impact on the events that led inexo- rably to Andrew Johnson's impeachment, Willis inserted the element of caprice into history. But for his alertness, the break-in would have gone undetected and Nixon's illegal, clandestine political intelligence operations might never have been uncovered.

Five of the burglars were arrested at the scene. Four of them, Ber- nard L. Barker, Frank A. Sturgis, Virgilio R. Gonzales and Eugenio R. Martinez, were from Miami. They were involved in anti-Castro activ- ities and were said to have CIA connections.[420] The fifth was James A. McCord, who turned out to be a key player in unearthing the Water- gate cover-up. He

---

418 Bernstein, Carl and Woodward, Bob, All the President's Men(Simon & Schuster Paper-backs, New York, 2014) (hereafter Bernstein and Woodward, All the President's Men), 19.

419 The description of the break-in is based on The Senate Watergate Report, 51-53 and The 1974 House Judiciary Committee Impeachment Report, 42.

420 Bernstein and Woodward, All The President's Men, 19-20. 421

was the security coordinator of CRP. McCord was a deeply religious, ex-FBI agent, military reservist, former chief of physical security for the CIA and the father of an Air Force Academy cadet.[421] Liddy and Hunt were in the Watergate building, but escaped unnoticed.[422]

These were not your typical burglars. All five who were arrested were dressed in suits and wearing rubber surgical gloves. They had at least two sophisticated devices capable of picking up and transmit- ting conversations, a walkie-talkie, a short wave receiver capable of picking up police communications, forty rolls of unexposed film, two 35 millimeter cameras and three pen-sized tear gas guns. They also brought plenty of cash, having among them fifteen $100 bills. A search of their hotel rooms uncovered additional $100 bills, a check drawn by Hunt and a notebook that contained Hunt's White House telephone number.[423] This was hardly a "third rate burglary."

High-level CRP and White House officials were immediately in- formed of the risk that the break-in could be linked to CRP and the White House. The cover-up began right there. John Mitchell, Nixon's Attorney General who had resigned to become the President's cam- paign manager, authorized a false press release to be issued:

> "We have just learned from news reports that a man identified as employed by our campaign committee [James McCord] was one of five persons arrested at the Democratic National Committee headquarters in Washington, D.C. early Saturday morning. The person involved is the proprietor of a private security agency who was employed by our Committee months

421 *Ibid., 20-21.*

422 *The Senate Watergate Report, 52.*

423 *The 1974 House Judiciary Committee Impeachment Report, 42; Washington Post Article, "5 Held in Plot to Bug Democrats' Office Here," June 18, 1972, http://www.washingtonpost.com/wp-dyn/content/article. This newspaper article was the first in a long series of investigative articles for which Carl Bernstein and Robert Woodward became famous. Their story is described by them in detail in All The President's Men, which also became the basis for a popular 1976 movie starring Dustin Hoffman and Robert Redford.*

> ago to assist with the installation of our security system. He has, as we understand it, a number of business clients and interests and we have no knowledge of those rela- tionships. We want to emphasize that this man and the other people involved were not operating in our behalf or with our consent. I am surprised and dismayed at these reports . . . There is no place in our campaign or in the electoral process for this type of activity and we will not permit nor condone it."[424] (emphasis added)

All of the underlined language of the press release was false and known by Mitchell to be false. He was covering himself and the other CRP and White House personnel who had participated in the funding and planning of the break-in. This false press release became part of the initial cover-up plan, which was to hang the Watergatebur- glars out to dry, making it seem like a break-in that Liddy had master- minded without CRP or White House involvement.[425] Its purpose was to prevent disclosures that could lead to indictments of high-ranking CRP and White House officials, that could expose Hunt's and Liddy's prior illegal covert activities, and, therefore, that might jeopardize the President's re-election in November.[426]

The first threat to this plan came from the FBI, which was hot on the trail of those $100 bills that the "burglars" had in their possession when they were arrested. It was standard practice for banks to record serial numbers of cash paid out in large transactions. Thus, the FBI could probably trace the $100 bills back to the bank that supplied the cash and where Bernard Barker had an account. In fact, the FBI had already begun to do so.[427] The President and his senior staffers were especially concerned about the FBI getting to Hunt, who, as the President expressed it, "knows too damn much."[428]

424 *The 1974 House Judiciary Committee Impeachment Report, 42-43.*
425 *The Senate Watergate Report, 42.*
426 *The 1974 House Judiciary Committee Impeachment Report, 53.*
427 *Ibid., 48.*
428 *Ibid., 53, quoting from an audio tape of the June 23, 1972 meeting with Haldeman and*

On the morning of June 23rd, the President met with his Chief of Staff, H.R. Haldeman to discuss stopping the FBI investigation.[429] As the tape of that meeting reveals, the President ordered Haldeman to direct the CIA to impede the FBI investigation. Not wasting any time, that very afternoon, Haldeman and John Ehrlichman,[430] a senior advisor and close confidante of the President, met with CIA Director Richard Helms and his Deputy Director, Lieutenant General Vernon Walters. Haldeman and Ehrlichman relayed the President's concern that the FBI investigation was leading to important people and sug- gested that Walters tell FBI Acting Director, L. Patrick Gray, that it was not desirable to pursue the investigation.[431] In the face of push- back from Walters, John Dean took up the task and urged Gray to call off the FBI's investigation, "for national security reasons." Gray honored the request.[432]

If keeping the problem from spreading beyond those direct- ly involved in the burglary was to succeed, the cooperation of the Watergate burglars and their two leaders, Liddy and Hunt — all of whom were eventually indicted — was essential. To begin with, that required getting money to them, initially to fund their defense, but also to demonstrate that they would be taken care of. By the middle of September, approximately $190,000 in cash was paid clandestinely to the defendants. The cash was raised and delivered by Herbert Kal- mbach, Nixon's personal attorney, with the knowledge of Haldeman, Ehrlichman and Dean.[433]

The plan worked through the election. The Watergateburglars, who were indicted in September, kept their mouths shut andhunkered down for their trial, which was set for January 1973. However,Water- gate remained

---

Ehrlichman.

429 Haldeman was ultimately tried on counts of perjury, conspiracy and obstruction of justice. He was found guilty and served 18 months in prison.

430 Ehrlichman was tried and convicted of the same suite of crimes as Haldeman and also served 18 months in prison for his role in the Watergate cover-up.

431 The 1974 House Judiciary Committee Impeachment Report, 49.

432 Ibid., 48-50.

433 Ibid., 56-57.

prominent in the news. At the time of the election, the Washington Post's reporting alone had tied Nixon's campaign to the burglars, and had alerted the public to a secret fund, controlled by cam- paign manager and former Attorney General Mitchell, that was used to gather information about the Democrats.[434] In an article published on October 10, 1972, Carl Bernstein and Robert Woodward reported that FBI agents had ". . . established that the Watergate bugging incident stemmed from a massive campaign of political spying and sabotage conducted on behalf of President Nixon's re-election and directed by officials of the White House and the Committee for Re-election of the President."[435]

However, none of the reporting had yet directly implicated the President, and allegations of campaign and White House wrong-doing were denied by CRP and the White House. In any event, President Nixon drubbed Senator George McGovern. When the final count was in, Nixon had won 520 of the 538 electoral votes. Despite the Presi- dent's landslide victory, the Democrats still had majorities in both the House and the Senate.

The Trial of the Five Watergate Burglars, Liddy and Hunt.

The Watergate burglars, plus Liddy and Hunt, were indicted by the grand jury on September 15, 1972, on eight counts each, all related to conspiracy, burglary and the federal wiretapping statute prohibit- ing electronic interception of oral communications.[436] Their trial began on January 8, 1973, in federal court in Washington, D.C., with Chief Judge John R. Sirica presiding. Judge Sirica, who was 69 when the trial began, was literally a fighter. Before committing to a career as a lawyer, he had

---

434 Washington Post Article, "GOP Security Aide Among Five Arrested in Bugging Affair," June 19, 1972, https://www.washingtonpost.com/ politics/gop-security-aide-among-five-arrested-in-bugging-affair; Washington Post Article, "Bug Suspect Got Campaign Funds," August 1, 1972, https:// www.washingtonpost.com/politics/bug-suspect-got-campaign-funds; Washington Post Article, "Mitchell Controlled Secret GOP Fund," September 29, 1972, https://www.washingtonpost.com/politics/ mitchee-controlled-secret-gop-fund.

435 Washington Post Article, "FBI Finds Nixon Aides Sabotaged Democrats," October 10, 1972, https://www.washingtonpost.com/politics/ fbi-finds-nixon-aides-sabotaged-democrats.

436 Bernstein and Woodward, All The President's Men, 69.

boxed professionally in Miami and Washington, count- ing Jack Dempsey as a friend. He practiced law in Washington, including service as a federal prosecutor. Judge Sirica was a Republicanand was appointed to the federal bench by President Eisenhower in 1957. He brought his courtroom experience with him to the bench and was known as a no-nonsense trial judge. As his questioning showed during the course of the trial, he never bought the theory that Liddy and Hunt had acted on their own. As he was frank to say, the trial of in his court had not gotten to the bottom of the case.[437]

Within three days, Hunt pleaded guilty. A week after the trial started, Barker, Gonzales, Martinez and Sturgis also pleaded guilty. On January 30th, Liddy and McCord were convicted of conspiracy, burglary and wiretapping. Thus far, all seven had played along with the White House plan to confine the Watergate scandal to their conduct. That was about to change.

On March 23, 1973, Judge Sirica unsealed and read a letter in open court that had been sent to him by McCord on March 19th.[438] It was a bombshell. McCord offered the information in the letter ". . . in the interests of justice, and in the interests of restoring faith in the criminal justice system, which faith has been severely damaged in this case . . . ." Among other things, he said that "political pressure" had been applied to the defendants to plead guilty and remain silent;" that "[p]erjury occurred during the trial;" and that "[o]thers involved in the Watergate operation were not identified during the trial, when they could have been by those testifying." This startling series of ad- missions ratified what the press had already uncovered – that all those responsible for the Watergate break-in had not yet been brought to justice and that the trail led directly to the White House.

Meanwhile, on March 21st, the President held two significant meet- ings in the White House regarding modifications to the cover-up plan. The first

437 *The Senate Watergate Report, xv.*

438 *The text of the letter can be found at http://watergate.info/1973/03/19/mccord-letter-to-judge-sirica.html.*

one began at about 10 a.m. and lasted until almost noon.[439] It began with the President and John Dean, who got quickly to the point:

> "I think there is no doubt about the seriousness of the problem we've got. We have a cancer within, close to the Presidency, that is growing. It is growing daily. It's compounded, growing geometrically now, because it compounds itself. That will be clear if I, you know, explain some of the details of why it is. Basically it is be- cause (1) we are being blackmailed; (2) People are go- ing to start perjuring themselves very quickly that have not had to perjure themselves to protect other people in the line. And there is no assurance - that that won't bust . . ."[440]

Dean went on to say that he, Haldeman, Ehrlichman and Mitch- ell were involved in payments to the Watergate defendants and "that's an obstruction of justice." Dean was especially concerned because the grand jury would be reconvening in the near future and some or all of them would likely be called to testify. Another problem they faced was "continued blackmail," particularly by Hunt, who was now demanding $120,000 and had threatened to put Ehrlichman in jail for his involve- ment in the Ellsberg break-in.

The President suggested that it could come down to a criminal case against Haldeman, Dean, Mitchell and Ehrlichman. After discuss- ing the potential for criminal liability, the President instructed Dean to "stabilize Hunt for the short term and get Mitchell down to meet with Haldeman, Ehrlichman and Dean, to discuss the most dangerous problems for the President, e.g., criminal liability of his close subor- dinates."[441] The President called Haldeman into the room and directed him to set up a meeting with Mitchell, Ehrlichman and Dean to discuss ways to avoid criminal liability.

439 A transcript of the tape recording of this meeting can be found in The White House Transcripts (The Viking Press, New York, 1974), (here- after The White House Transcripts), 132-180. The meeting is summarized in The 1974 House Judiciary Committee Impeachment Report, 98-100.

440 The White House Transcripts, 134.

441 The 1974 Judiciary Committee Impeachment Report, 99.

On the afternoon of March 21st, Nixon met again with Haldeman and Dean and they were joined by Ehrlichman.[442] In this meeting, the President decided on a strategy of continued concealment. In the Pres- ident's own words, "I want you all to stonewall it, let them plead the Fifth Amendment, cover-up, or anything else, if it'll save it – save the plan."[443] Based on its impeachment investigation, the Judiciary Committee concluded that, "[d] uring the rest of March and through- out April, the President assumed active command of the cover-up. He, himself, acted time and time again to protect his principal assistants who were the subject of criminal and congressional Watergate inves- tigations."

The President's new plan ultimately did not work. On April 30th, Haldeman, Ehrlichman, and Dean, who had already begun cooperating with the prosecutors and was eventually given immunity as part ofthe Senate investigation, resigned from the White House. Mitchell, Halde- man and Ehrlichman were all subsequently indicted, tried, convicted and spent time in prison. As of April 30, 1973, the President was the last man standing. It took more than a year of investigations by the Senate, two special prosecutors, and the House Judiciary Committee, as well as a Supreme Court decision, to topple him.

---

442 *The transcript of the tape of this meeting is in The White House Transcripts, 180-265. The meeting is summarized in The July 1974 Judiciary Committee Impeachment Report, 100-101..*

443 *Ibid., 101*

CHAPTER 16 THE SENATE INVESTIGATIONS AND THESPECIAL PROSECUTORS

'The smell of cover-up was in the air.'[444]

In the wake of the trial of the Watergate burglars, the departures of Nixon's senior White House advisors at the end of April, and in the face of aggressive investigative reporting since the Watergate break-in, two Watergate inquiries were launched in the first four months of 1973. The first to get underway was the Senate Select Com- mittee on Presidential Campaign Activities, which came to be known as "The Senate Watergate Committee." The second investigation was conducted by a special prosecutor operating under the aegis of the Department of Justice, who was nominated by the Attorney General and approved by the President. Each of these investigations, in its own way, helped to pave the way to the impeachment investigation undertaken by the House Judiciary Committee beginning in February, 1974.

---

444 *The Senate Watergate Report, 43.*

The Senate Watergate Committee .

On February 5, 1973, North Carolina Democratic Senator Sam Ervin, for himself and Democratic Senator Mike Mansfield of Montana, in- troduced Senate Resolution 60, the purpose of which was:

> "To establish a select committee of the Senate to con- duct an investigation and study of the extent, if any, to which illegal, improper, or unethical activities were engaged in by any persons, acting individually or in combination with others, in the Presidential election of 1972, or any campaign, canvas, or other activity related to it."

On February 7th, the Senate voted 77-0 to adopt Resolution 60, with Senator Ervin as its Chair and Republican Senator Howard Baker from Tennessee as Vice Chair.[445]

The overwhelming support for Resolution 60 reflected the widespread belief that criminal liability for the Watergate break-in did not stop at G. Gordon Liddy. Judge Sirica's questioning of witnesses and comments during the trial of the Watergate burglars revealed his belief that culpability likely extended upstream of Liddy. Likewise, aggressive reporting, led by Bernstein and Woodward of The Washing- ton Post, corroborated Judge Sirica's skepticism.[446] McCord's March 19thletter had not yet been written at the time of the vote on Resolution 60, but his candid statements in that letter, once they became public, fortified those suspicions.As the Committee said in its final report:

> "The smell of coverup [sic] was in the air. S. Res. 60, passed after the Watergate trial concluded, evinces the Senate's belief that the Department of Justice could not be trusted fully to

---

445 There were three other Democrats on the Committee: Daniel Inouye of Hawaii, Joseph Montoya of New Mexico and Herman Talmadge of Georgia. The Republican members aside from the Vice Chair were Edward Gurney of Florida and Lowell Weicker, Jr. of Connecticut.

446 The Senate Watergate Report, 42-43.

igate and uncover the true story of Watergate. But no antial indication of the mag- nitude of the Watergate r had yet emerged."[447]

The Committee started its hearings on May 17th, and "gavel to gavel" television coverage of the 53 days of hearings over several months began the next day. The Senate Watergate Committee's in- vestigation was a fact-finding venture. It could not indict anyone. It could not recommend impeachment of the President.[448] Nonetheless, it played a key role in the process that resulted in President Nixon's resignation. It gathered thousands of documents and took the sworn testimony of scores of witnesses, including John Dean, who was the star witness. Having been granted immunity by the Committee, Dean was the first high-level presidential advisor to point the cover-up finger at the President. Among other damaging testimony, he asserted that Nixon was involved in the cover-up within days after the break-inand that, in the "cancer on the Presidency" meeting on March 21st 1973, the President had discussed and then authorized payoffs to the Watergate defendants. The Committee issued its final report in June 1974.

The Special Prosecutor .

On April 17th, in a press briefing, the President said that, ". . . on March 21st, as a result of serious charges which came to my attention, . . . I began intensive new inquiries into this whole matter" and he con- demned any cover-up attempts.[449] He followed that up with a televised address to the nation on April 30th, during which he maintained that, "[u]ntil March of this year, I remained convinced that the denials [of wrongdoing by my staff] were true and that the charges of involve- ment by members of the White House staff were false." This was an outright lie. In fact, as we have seen, the President himself was directly involved in the cover-up within a week of

---

447 Ibid., 43.

448 The Committee made a number of recommendations for legislative and other reforms to rectify the shortcomings revealed by the investi- gation of the Watergate scandal. See The Senate Watergate Report, 17-28.

449 The 1974 House Judiciary Committee Impeachment Report, 28.

the break-in.[450]

On April 30th, the White House also announced the departuresof Haldeman, Ehrlichman, Dean and Attorney General Richard G. Klein- dienst. President Nixon first offered Kleindienst's job to Secretary of State William P. Rogers, who declined.[451] Nixon's second choice was Secretary of Defense Elliot L. Richardson, a Harvard educated lawyer. As part of the President's efforts to demonstrate his supposed desire fully to investigate Watergate, Nixon agreed that a special prosecutor, acting under the supervision of the Attorney General, should be ap- pointed. Nixon also agreed to Richardson's nomination of Archibald Cox, a Harvard Law professor and President John F. Kennedy's So- licitor General, as the Special Prosecutor. Cox had strong ties to the Kennedy family, as his service in JFK's Administration indicated.

Both Edward Kennedy and his brother Robert's widow, Ethel, attend- ed Cox's swearing-in.[452] This must have galled Nixon, who viewed the Kennedy family as some of his most prominent enemies. Plus, Cox's Harvard connection certainly stung Nixon, since he viewed that Ivy League institution as the seat of the Eastern elite who had opposed him since the days of the Hiss investigation.

Finally, in order to isolate himself from the investigation, Nixon said he had given Richardson absolute authority to make all decisions relating to the prosecution of the Watergate case.[453] Richardson and Cox both appeared before the Senate Judiciary Committee on May 21st. In response to requests from Senators on the Committee, Rich- ardson submitted a statement of guidelines that were eventually pub- lished as a formal Department of Justice regulation. The guidelines gave the Special Prosecutor jurisdiction over

450 *Most dramatically, the tape of a June 23, 1972 meeting between Haldeman and the President shows that he knew of efforts to cover up the break-in and discussed with Haldeman how to get the CIA to stop the FBI investigation into it. See Ibid., 52-53. This tape was not released by the President until after he had been ordered to do so by the Supreme Court on July 24, 1974.*

451 *Bernstein and Woodward, The Final Days, 60.*

452 *Farrell, Nixon, 514.*

453 *Ibid.*

"offenses arising out of the unauthorized entry into the DNC Headquarters at the Watergate, offenses arising out of the 1972 Presidential election, allegations in- volving the President, members of the White House staff and other matters which the Special Prosecutor consented to have assigned by the Attorney General."[454] Cox was also given full authority to contest all testimonial privileges that might be asserted and to prosecute objections to assertion of executive privilege. The Special Prosecutor could not be removed except for "extraordinary improprieties."[455] Despite these protections, seven months later, Archibald Cox would be fired by order of the President.

The Secret White House Taping System .

The Senate Watergate Committee's greatest contribution to the events that led to the President's resignation was to unearth the existence of the secret White House voice activated audio taping system.[456] At the time the Senate Watergate Committee began its hearings, only ahand- ful of people knew that the President's conversations were being taped. One of them was Alexander P. Butterfield, an Air Force colonel who resigned his commission to work as Chief of Staff H.R. Haldeman's assistant.[457] Butterfield was interviewed by the Committee staff solely because he had been identified as a "satellite" of Haldeman, one of the main targets of the investigation.[458]

During the course of an interview on July 13th, Butterfield was questioned by the staffers regarding a statement made by John Dean to them that Dean had the feeling that one of his conversations with the President was taped. Butterfield responded, "No, Dean didn't know about it. . . . There is a tape in each of the President's offices. It is kept by the Secret Service and only

454 *Ibid.*

455 *Ibid.*

456 *Nixon was not the first president to tape White House meetings. Both Presidents Kennedy and Johnson did so, but on a selective basis. Nixon's innovation was to voice-activate the system.*

457 *In addition to Butterfield, the following knew about the system: the President, Haldeman, Lawrence Higby, Stephen Bull, Ron Zeigler, Butterfield's secretary and the Secret Service technicians who maintained the system. See Bernstein and Woodward, The Final Days, 43.*

458 *The Senate Watergate Report, 47.*

four other men know about it. Dean had no way of knowing about it."[459] With that offhand comment, But- terfield became an important witness. He testified publicly about the taping system before the Committee on the following Monday, July 16th.[460]

Having been alerted to the existence of a taping system, on July 18th, Special Prosecutor Cox requested from the White House copies of tapes of eight presidential meetings, which was denied. On July 23rd, Cox subpoenaed the tapes. The President refused to produce them and, in a response to a motion filed by the Special Prosecutor, on August 29th, Judge Sirica ordered the tapes to be produced for in camera (the court only) review prior to releasing them to the Special Prosecutor. The President appealed Sirica's order, which was upheld by the U.S. Appeals Court in the District of Columbia on October 17, 1973.[461]

The Saturday Night Massacre .

The President and his legal team still sought to avoid having to pro- duce the actual tapes and had begun negotiations towards a compro- mise with Special Prosecutor Cox before Judge Sirica's order had been affirmed on appeal. The compromise proposal was to have transcripts of the eight tapes prepared, which would be authenticated by Senator John Stennis, who would be allowed to listen to the tapes. However, Nixon was adamant that Cox must also agree not to pursue any further tapes.[462] Cox refused to agree to forgo future efforts to obtain addition- al tapes. The President told his Chief of Staff, General Alexander Haig, to have Cox fired. The order had to come from Richardson. He refused to do it and resigned. Richardson's

459 *Bernstein and Woodward, The Final Days, 57.*

460 *This was the first time that Congress or the Special Prosecutor knew about the White House taping system. Before Butterfield's disclosure, Cox was advised that the President had a tape of an April 15, 1973 meeting with John Dean. When Cox attempted to get a copy of the tape in June 1973, he was told that there was no tape, just a "dictabelt" recording of the President's recollections of the meeting. The White House refused to provide a copy of that recording. See The 1974 House Judiciary Committee Impeachment Report, 123.*

461 *Ibid.*

462 *Bernstein and Woodward, The Final Days; The 1974 House Judiciary Committee Impeachment Report, 123-125.*

Deputy, William D. Ruckelshaus, also refused and resigned. The Solicitor General, Robert H. Bork,was next in line. He issued the order, which not only fired Cox, but also abolished the Office of the Special Prosecutor.[463]

The President over-played his hand. When his press secretary, Ron Zeigler, announced the order on Saturday evening, October 20th, a firestorm of outrage swept the country and Cox's firing went down in history as the "Saturday Night Massacre." The television networks were on the air immediately with hour–long specials; the headline on the front page of the Sunday New York Times screamed in large print "NIXON DISCHARGES COX FOR DEFIANCE; ABOLISHES WA- TERGATE TASK FORCE; RICHARDSON AND RUCKELSHAUS

OUT." Within two days, 50,000 telegrams had arrived in Washington, the largest concentration in Western Union's history. The Deans of the most prestigious law schools demanded that the House begin impeachment proceedings. More ominously for the President, by the following Tuesday, twenty-two bills calling for an impeachment investigation had been introduced in the House.[464]

The Final Battle for the White House Tapes .

In the face of this huge blowback, the President produced some of the tapes on October 23rd and on November 1st he appointed Leon Jawork- si to replace Archibald Cox as Special Prosecutor.[465] Jaworski, a Dem- ocrat, was a lawyer with a formidable track record. He was the son of a Baptist minister, who was on the team that prosecuted German war criminals at Nuremberg. He had served previously as a special prose- cutor in 1962 when he was appointed by then Attorney General Robert

463 The 1974 House Judiciary Committee Impeachment Report, 123-125; Bernstein and Woodward, The Final Days, 70-73.

464 Ibid., 71.

465 By order dated November 14, 1973, after Leon Jaworski had been appointed as special prosecutor by the President, the United States District Court for the District of Columbia ruled in a lawsuit brought by public interest groups that the firing of Archibald Cox was improper. See Nader v. Bork, 366 F. Supp. 104 (D.D.C. 1973).

Kennedy to represent the United States against Mississippi Governor Ross Barnett's attempt to prevent James Meredith's registration as the first black to attend the University of Mississippi. He had a thriving private law practice in Houston and had just completed a one-year term as President of the American Bar Association, a special sign of distinction in the legal profession.[466]

It turned out to be Jaworski's job to take the fight over the White House tapes to its conclusion. On March 1st, seven of the President's former top aides, including Mitchell, Haldeman, and Ehrlichman, were indicted on various federal charges for their role in the Watergate cover-up. In preparation for the trial, Jaworski's team subpoenaed the President to produce additional tapes, which he refused to do, based on a claim of executive privilege. Jaworski promptly moved the court to enforce the subpoena. On May 20th, Judge Sirica who, as Chief Judge, had assigned the case to himself, overruled the President's objection. The President's lawyers promptly appealed. Given the importance of the issue and the need for a quick resolution of the dispute, the Su- preme Court agreed to take the matter before the Court of Appeals had considered the issue. Briefing was conducted on a short schedule and oral argument was held before the Supreme Court on July 8th.

The Supreme Court issued its ruling on July 24th.[467] In a unani- mous decision, including three Nixon appointees, Chief Justice War- ren Burger affirmed Judge Sirica's order, ruling that a general claim of executive privilege like the one made by the President was insufficient to overcome the legitimate need for the documents in a criminal trial.[468] The Supreme Court also ordered Judge Sirica to review the doc- uments before turning them over to the Special Prosecutor. The Court refused to consider the President's cross-appeal of his designation by the grand jury as an "unindicted co-

466 Bernstein and Woodward, The Final Days, 75.

467 United States v. Nixon, 418 U.S. 683 (1974).

468 Justice William Rehnquist did not participate because he had served in the Department of Justice under President Nixon.

conspirator," because that issue was "unnecessary to resolution of the question whether the claim of privilege is to prevail."

The game was up. President Nixon now faced disclosure of tapes of his own voice proving that he had participated in the Watergate cover-up from the very start and lied to the American people about it numerous times.

CHAPTER 17
PRESIDENT NIXON'S "NEAR IMPEACHMENT"

On February 6, 1974, the House of Representatives adopted a resolution, by a vote of 410 to 4, authorizing the House Judiciary Committee to investigate grounds for the impeachment of President Nixon.[469] The Judiciary Committee was given subpoena power. It also had access to the materials gathered by the Senate Watergate Com- mittee and a substantial amount of evidence gathered by the special prosecutor. The Committee conducted public hearings between May 9th and July 17th, in which the President's counsel, James St. Clair, participated.[470] It considered more than 7,200 pages of evidentiary material.[471]

On July 27, 29, and 30, 1974, the House Judiciary Committee voted to approve three articles of impeachment against President Nix- on.[472] This was a week after the Supreme Court had ruled that Nixon had to produce the tapes of his White House conversations, but before the Committee had

469 *The 1974 House Judiciary Committee Impeachment Report, 6.*

470 *Ibid., 8-9.*

471 *Ibid., 9.*

472 *The full text of the articles of impeachment can be found at The 1974 House Judiciary Committee Impeachment Report, 1-4. On July 30th, the Judiciary Committee considered two additional articles of impeachment, both of which were defeated by a vote of 26-12. The first of the rejected articles was based on the President's conduct of a secret bombing campaign in Cambodia, alleging that it was wrongfully concealed from Congress. The second rejected article was based on allegations that the President had wrongfully used public money to improve his properties in Florida and California and that he had under-reported income in his federal tax filings in 1969, 1970, 1971 and 1972. Ibid., 217-223.*

access to them.[473]

Article I.

This Article was passed on July 27th by a vote of 27 to 11, or 71%. All 21 Democrats voted in favor and were joined by six of the 17 Republi- cans on the Committee.[474] This article was aimed at obstruction of jus- tice related to the Watergate break-in. It alleged that the President had:

". . . violat[ed] his constitutional duty to take care that the laws be faithfully executed, has prevented, obstruct- ed, and impeded the administration of justice, in that:

On June 17, 1972, and prior thereto, agents of the Committee for the Re-election of the President committed unlawful entry of the headquarters of the Democratic National Committee in Washington, Dis- trict of Columbia, for the purpose of securing political intelligence. Subsequent thereto, Richard M. Nixon, using the powers of his high office, engaged personally and through his subordinates and agents, in a course of conduct designed to delay, impede and obstruct inves- tigations of such unlawful entry; to cover up, conceal and protect those responsible; and to conceal the ex- istence and scope of other unlawful covert activities."

Then followed a series of nine alleged means that the President had used to implement the impeach- able course of conduct, including: false or misleading statements to investigative officers; withholding rele- vant information from investigators; causing witnesses to give false or misleading information to

473 The Judiciary Committee's Final Report, dated August 1974, included references to the tapes that were available to them after the vote. Although the issue was moot, on August 20, 1974, the House of Representatives adopted H.Res. 1333, by a vote of 412 to 3, which accepted the Judiciary Committee's report and formally recognized the President's resignation.

474 The 1974 House Judiciary Committee Impeachment Report, 335.

investigators; interfering with the conduct of investigations by the Department of Justice, the FBI, the Special Prosecutor and Congressional Committees; bribing witnesses and potential witnesses; endeavoring to misuse the CIA; passing information from the Department of Justice to subjects of investigations; making false andmisleading statements to the American public to deceive theminto believing that a thorough investigation was being conducted; and offering favored treatment to individuals in return for silence or false testimony.

Article II .

This article was passed on July 29th, by a vote of 28 to 10, or 73.6%. All the Democrats and seven Republicans voted in favor.[475] It was broader than Article I, aiming generally at an abuse of power that included the Watergate cover-up, but also went beyond that. It alleged that the President:

". . . in disregard of his constitutional duty to take care that the laws be faithfully executed, has repeatedly en- gaged in conduct violating the constitutional rights of citizens, impairing the due and proper administration of justice and conduct of lawful inquiries, or contravening the laws governing agencies of the executive branch and the purposes of these agencies."

The list of impeachable conduct included: obtaining informa- tion from the IRS for unlawful purposes; misusing the FBI and the Secret Service by authorizing these agencies to conduct electronic surveillance of private citizens; maintaining a secret investigative unit within the office of the President that engaged in unlawful conduct; failing to act when he knew his subordinates were interfering in lawful inquiries and covering up unlawful conduct; and improperly interfer- ing with the FBI, the Special Prosecutor and the CIA.

475 *Ibid., 336.*

Article III .

The final article was passed on July 30th by a vote of 21 to 17, or 55.2%. Unlike the other two articles, this one attracted very little Republican support, with only two voting yes. Two Democrats voted no.[476] This was a narrow article based on the President's alleged wrongful refus- al to produce documents in response to four subpoenas issued by the House as part of its impeachment investigation. The trial on this article would presumably have focused on the President's intent in invoking executive privilege as the grounds for refusing to produce the docu- ments. Had the Judiciary Committee known of the contents of the tape of the June 23, 1972 White House meeting in which the President had directed a cover-up of the Watergate break-in, this article may have drawn greater support.

Were the Articles of Impeachment Based on Impeachable Offenses?

The answer is yes. Articles I and II were based on substantial abuses of presidential power that related directly to Nixon's conduct of the office of the Presidency. Moreover, much of the alleged conduct was criminally indictable. Nixon's actions fell squarely in the category of "abuses of the public trust" that Hamilton wrote about in Federalist 65. Moreover, there was little "taint of partisanship" in the vote on these two articles, each capturing a little more than 70% of the Judiciary Committee.

Article III, which was based on President Nixon's refusal to pro- duce the tapes based on executive privilege, is a closer call. The pa- rameters of the presidential executive privilege were not clear then and remain murky to this day. It would not normally be an impeachable offense for a president to assert executive privilege to protect presi- dential papers and in-house deliberations. However, in Nixon's case, the Supreme Court ruled that executive privilege did not apply to the White House tapes. There is a strong argument that he abused the priv- ilege to keep Congress and the public from knowing that he was direct- ly involved in the Watergate cover-up from the very beginning.

476 *Ibid., 337.*

CHAPTER 18
RICHARD NIXON GIVES IN

"I took kind of a nose count today and I couldn't find more than four very firm votes [for acquittal in the Senate]"[477]

By the beginning of August, it was clear that the President faced two alternatives: a trial in the Senate on the three articles of impeachment that were certainly going to be approved by the full House, or resignation. Nixon had built his career on never giving in, even when the odds were against him. His family was urging him to stay the course and endure a Senate trial in the hope that he might prevail there.

Virtually everybody else disagreed. Once the Supreme Court had ordered Nixon to produce the tapes on July 24th, he had no choice but to confront the fatal blow they would strike against him. The tape of his June 23, 1972, meeting with Haldeman was the "smoking gun" that convinced nearly all of his advisers that resignation was in the best interests of the country and the only realistic alternative. Nixon had staked his future on the lie that he had not known of the Watergate cover-up until March 21, 1973, when he

477 Senator Barry Goldwater's assessment of President Nixon's chances of prevailing in a Senate impeachment trial delivered to Nixon in the aftermath of the House Judiciary Committee's proposal of articles of impeachment to the House, as quoted in Bernstein and Woodward, The Final Days, 415.

had the "cancer on the Pres- idency" meeting with John Dean. Nixon's own voice on the June 23rd tape was devastating.

Even the cold transcript was bad. Haldeman reported that ". . . the FBI is not under control . . .," and ". . . they've been able to trace the money [the $100 bills in the possession of the burglars]." It was clear from the context that this was not the first report Haldeman had given the President on the break-in and efforts to block the FBI inves- tigation. Those efforts were not working. Haldeman suggested that ". .

. the way to handle this now is for us to have Walters [the CIA Deputy Director] call Pat Gray [acting FBI Director] and just say, 'Stay the hell out of this . . .' " The President and Haldeman discussed the best way to use the CIA. This is what the President told Haldeman to do:

> "PRESIDENT: "When you get in these people [the CIA] when you . . . get these people in, say: 'Look, the problem is that this will open up the whole, the whole Bay of Pigs thing, and the President just feels that' ah, without going into details . . . don't, don't lie to them to the extent to say there is no involvement, but just say this is sort of a come- dy of errors, bizarre, without getting into it, 'the President believes that it is going to open the whole Bay of Pigs thing up again, for keeps and that they should call the FBI in and say that we wish for the country, don't go further into this case,'period!
>
> HALDEMAN: OK
>
> PRESIDENT: That's the way to put it, do it straight (Unintelligible)"

Of great significance was the fact that this conversation was unknown to the Judiciary Committee, or any member of the House or the Senate, when the Committee voted on the articles of impeach- ment.[478] On August 5th,

478 *The Judiciary Committee was aware of the 18½ minute gap that existed in a tape recording*

the transcript was delivered by Nixon's lawyer to the Committee's senior staff counsel.[479] It was immediately circulat- ed to the Committee and key members of Congress. This was the final nail in Nixon's presidential coffin. All of the President's supporters on the Judiciary Committee announced that they would vote for im- peachment, as did John Rhodes, the House Minority Leader.[480] It was a foregone conclusion that the President would be impeached. As Barry Goldwater, the old Republican warhorse, who had battled against and alongside Nixon for over two decades, said, "too many lies, too many crimes."[481]

Armed with this startling new information, on August 7th, a three-person Republican Congressional delegation trooped to the White House to share their candid assessment of Nixon's chances of avoiding conviction in the Senate. The group was led by Senator Gold- water. With him were Rhodes and Hugh Scott, the Senate Minority Leader.[482] Goldwater put it bluntly to the President: "I took a kind of a nose count today, and I couldn't find more than four very firm votes [for acquittal], and those would be from older Southerners. Some are very worried about what's been going on, and are undecided, and I'm one of them."[483]

The President went on national television the next day to announce that he would resign. On August 9, 1974, he tendered a one-line letter to Henry Kissinger, the Secretary of State, stating imply that "I hereby resign the Office of President of the United States." The original of the letter contains a hand-written notation by Kissinger indicating that he received it at 11:35

---

of a June 20, 1972 meeting between Halde- man and the President. The President's lawyer had "acknowledged that the only erased portion of the tape was the conversation dealing with Watergate." The Committee's report concluded that "[i]t is a fair inference that the erased conversation . . . con- tained evidence showing what the President knew of the involvement of his closest advisors shortly af- ter the Watergate break-in." See The 1974 House Judiciary Committee Impeachment Report, 126-127.

479 Ibid., f.n., 52.

480 Bernstein and Woodward, The Final Days, 394. After reading the transcript, Rhodes was quoted as saying, "This is it. It's all over. There was the smoking gun. . . . My mind was made up. I would have to vote for impeachment. . . ." Farrell, Nixon, 529.

481 Bernstein and Woodward, All The President's Men, 346.

482 Bernstein and Woodward, The Final Days, 414-415.

483 Ibid., 415. See also Bernstein and Woodward, All the President's Men, 346.

a.m. Nixon and his family then trudged across the White House lawn to board a helicopter that took them away from the seat of presidential power into infamy.

This sad chapter in American history was finally concluded on September 8, 1974, when President Gerald R. Ford issued Presidential Proclamation No. 4311 containing his pardon of the former President: "I . . . have granted and by these presents do hereby grant a full, free and absolute pardon unto Richard Nixon for all his offenses against the United States which he, Richard Nixon, has committed or may have committed or taken part in during the period from January 20, 1969 through August 9, 1974."

PART 4

PRESIDENT WILLIAM JEFFERSON CLINTON

CHAPTER 19
BILL CLINTON – POLITICAL PRODIGY

"I remember meeting Clinton and him telling me within forty-five minutes that he planned to go back to Arkansas to be governor or senator and would like to be a national leader someday."[484]

Boy Wonder Politician .

Those words above from Bill Clinton to one of his fellow Rhodes Scholars in the fall of 1968 when he was 22 years old indicate that, of all our presidents, he was the most intentional about his political life from an early age. His journey to the top began on a hot, humid day at the White House in the summer of 1963, when he was just 16 years old.[485] He was there, along with a large group of other teenage boys for the Boys Nation convocation. These bright and promising adoles- cent boys were delegates selected from the Boys State conventions from all over the country. They were the future leaders of America and were celebrated as such. They

484 *Rick Stearns, one of Bill Clinton's fellow Rhodes Scholars, describing his first conversation with the future President on the S.S. United States as they sailed from New York to England in the fall of 1968 to begin their studies at Oxford University, as quoted in Maraniss, David, First in His Class, The Biography of Bill Clinton (New York, Simon & Schuster, 1996) (hereafter Maraniss, First in His Class),124.*

485 *The story of the handshake with John F. Kennedy is taken from Ibid., 11-20.*

got an up close and personal look at how the national government worked and got to rub shoulders with some movers and shakers. Clinton and his fellow Arkansas delegate,

Larry Taunton, were treated to lunch by their two Arkansas U.S. Senators, John McClellan and J. William Fulbright.

But the highlight was the chance to meet President John F. Kennedy, the young and vibrant proponent of the "New Frontier." The boys were bussed to the White House where they were marshalled into the Rose Garden to hear the President speak. Bill Clinton was instinctively drawn to Kennedy and he wanted to get as close to JFK as he could. Being six foot three and hefty he was able to push his way to the front of the crowd as they waited for the President. After his brief remarks, the President dove into the crowd and the cameras started clicking. Clinton was the first to get his picture taken with the President. As the current and future Presidents shook hands, Kennedy's face can only be seen in profile, but most of Clinton's face was turned toward the camera. What you see is a clean-cut and star-struck teenager setting his jaw and looking the President directly in the eyes, clearlysavoring the auspicious moment. His copy was ready to take home with him to show his Mom the picture that she wanted. And it was a cherished memento that pointed him to a future of public service.

Given his aspirations, it was not surprising that, upon graduation from high school in 1964, Clinton applied for and was accepted to Georgetown University, a well-regarded institution that was the "lo- cal college" of the nation's capital. Capitalizing on his experiences in Boys State and Nation, Clinton immersed himself in campus politics. He ran for and was elected as president of his freshman and sophomore classes.[486] He cut quite the

486 *Ibid., 56, 67.*

figure on campus, with his political ambi- tions out front and his unmatched ability to schmooze both a blessing and a curse. People were never quite sure if he was sincere or manipu- lative, but they enjoyed it enough to back him when he asked for their votes. More than that, his political talents and ambitions were evident to those close to him. His Georgetown girlfriend, Denise Hyland, with whom he was close for several years and knew him well, remarked to a traveling companion in France over the summer between their freshmen and sophomore years, "Remember this name – Bill Clinton– because someday he will be President."[487]

In the summer of 1966, Clinton took his political ambitions back to Arkansas where he worked at the ground level on Democrat Judge Frank Holt's campaign for Governor. This was a grunt-level job that mainly involved the logistics of getting the candidate where and when he needed to be. Thus began a series of campaign assignments that exposed Clinton to the rigors of politics and the organizational tech- niques necessary for a successful election bid. More immediately, it led to a back-office job with Senator Fulbright in D.C., where for a year he saw the inner workings of the office of a major national poli- tician.[488]

Then, during the summer of 1968, he worked on Fulbright's sen- atorial re-election campaign. Once again, the job was not exciting, re- turning cars to dealerships throughout Arkansas that had loaned them to the campaign. But his political aspirations became more directed. He told his traveling companion on one of their long drives around the state that the power job he wanted was Governor of Arkansas and that Attorney General was the best stepping stone to Governor.[489] This aspiration was repeated to his Rhodes classmate that fall and it became his strategy: get a law degree, return to Arkansas and run for Attorney General on the way to becoming Governor.

In the fall of 1968, Clinton took a detour, but an understandable one.

487 Ibid., 68.
488 Ibid., 83-95.
489 Ibid., 113.

In his senior year at Georgetown, Clinton applied for and was awarded a Rhodes Scholarship. Aside from making some useful con- nections for the future (e.g. Robert Reich who became Clinton's Sec- retary of Labor), his time at Oxford really didn't advance his politi- cal football, although it certainly burnished his resume for entry into Yale Law School. Like many of his Rhodes classmates, the Vietnam War and the draft were ever-present worries that intruded on what was supposed to be an idyllic two years in one of the greatest universities of the world, punctuated by extensive travel, mostly on the European continent. Clinton managed to avoid being drafted, but in the process of working the problem, he was back and forth across the Atlantic, never sure if he would be able to devote the time necessary to get an Oxford degree, which he never did.[490]

But, by the fall of 1970, his draft problems behind him, Clinton entered Yale Law School, where he punched his first ticket on the road to Governor and also met the woman who would become his wife. Clinton paid more attention to politics than he did to his law studies. In the summer and fall of 1970, he worked on the Senate campaign of Democrat Joe Duffy, becoming the candidate's favorite organizer.[491] Then, Clinton got a job as one of two coordinators in Texas for George McGovern's 1972 presidential campaign.[492]

So, when Clinton had finished Yale Law School in 1973, he not only had a law degree, he had experienced life in the office of a U.S. Senator and had worked on campaigns for Arkansas Governor, Con- necticut Senator and President of the United States. In the process, he had made contacts in Arkansas and nationally that would serve him well in the years to come. In these pre-laptop days, Clinton had amassed a "contacts file" on index cards that contained names, ad- dresses and phone numbers of a host of people he had encountered in his life as a student and political operative who might

490 *Clinton's Oxford years are recapped in Maraniss, First in His Class, 124-224.*
491 *Ibid., 228.*
492 *Ibid., 263-286.*

help him in his own campaigns.[493] He was ready to hit the ground running in Arkansas.

The future Governor landed a job on the faculty of the University of Arkansas Law School, but it was really just a way station on the highway to politics. In 1974, at the age of 28, he made his first run for political office when he put his hat in the ring to unseat a Republican incumbent who held a seat in the U.S. House of Representatives. No one really expected him to win, but he put in a far better showing than had been predicted and he learned a lot about how to be an effective candidate for elective office.

The next time up for Bill Clinton came in 1976, when he ran for and was elected Attorney General of Arkansas at the age of 30. Two years later, he achieved his goal of becoming the Governor of Arkan- sas at the age of 32, when he was elected for his first of five terms. He got off to a rocky start and was defeated in his first bid for reelection in 1980. The "come-back kid" licked his wounds, absorbed his lessons and returned to the fray in 1982, when he was elected Governor for the second time. He repeated the feat three more times. By 1988, counting primaries, runoffs and general elections, he had been involved in 15 elections in 14 years.[494] By 1990, he had been Governor for ten of the past 12 years.[495]

While Governor, Clinton had begun increasing his national pro- file by being active in the National Conference of Governors, landing speaking assignments at three Democratic National Conventions and promoting himself through his position as chairman of the Democratic Leadership Council, which took moderate positions on issues of inter- est to the white middle class.[496] Over the more than 20 years since his foray into collegiate politics at Georgetown he had amassed a large base of supporters ready to be tapped for a bid on the big enchilada.

---

493 Ibid., 299.

494 Ibid., 448.

495 Ibid., 452.

496 Ibid., 452-453.

He considered, but rejected a run for the presidency in 1988, but made it in 1992, when he unseated incumbent George H.W. Bush, trumping Bush's unquestioned foreign policy credentials by focusing on domestic issues ("it's the economy stupid"). At the age of 46, Bill Clinton shot to the top of America's political mountain. This was a meteoric rise unmatched in the history of the Republic. Then, in 1996, he became the first Democratic president since Franklin Delano Roosevelt to be elected for a second term. No doubt about it -- Bill Clinton was the political genius of his generation. And he had collected a lot of enemies in the process.

The Inveterate Womanizer .

Bill Clinton would hand his enemies the ammunition they needed to take a serious shot at undoing his re-election in 1996, although this did not become evident right away. There is no serious debate about it: Bill Clinton has a long and worrisome track record of womanizing.[497] It's not as if this was a novel thing in American history. Thomas Jefferson, the author of the Declaration of Independence and our third President, fathered children with one of his slaves, Sally Hemmings. Woodrow Wilson and Warren G. Harding both had mistresses. Franklin Roosevelt's mistress, Kate Mercer, visited him on his deathbed. Dwight Eisenhower's driver in London, Kate Summersby, was also his mistress. John F. Kennedy's sexual escapades in the White House are legendary. Donald Trump's presidential campaign was plagued by evidence of his sexual indiscretions but, as with Bill Clinton, it did not keep him from being elected. This is not to excuse Bill Clinton's behavior, but it helps to put the American electorate's reaction to his sexual adventures in context.

By 1988, when Clinton first considered running for president, his sexual track record had been well-established. The summer after his graduation from Georgetown in 1968, when he was back in Arkansas before heading

497 Harris, John F., The Survivor (Random House Trade Paperbacks, New York, 2005) (hereafter Harris, The Survivor), xvii-xviii; Maraniss, First in His Class, 320-321, 439-441, 460-461.

to Oxford, Clinton had four women in play. He was corresponding with two of his Georgetown girlfriends, while spending time with two other women in Arkansas.[498] When Clinton was running for Congress in 1974, and after he and Hillary Rodham had become serious, it was well-known among campaign workers that he had an "intense relationship" with a young woman volunteer, and had other girlfriends in several towns around the district and in Little Rock. Hil- lary reportedly "raised hell about it."[499]

The "infidelity issue" was front and center in Bill and Hillary Clintons' deliberations about his running for president in 1988. Clin- ton consulted with his pollster, Dick Morris about it. Morris advised him that the "sex issue loomed very large" in the public's mind. Others close to Clinton urged him to consider the impact on his eight-year- old daughter of having Clinton's sexual escapades becoming an issue in the campaign, as it almost certainly would. The Clintons were not willing to risk it and he decided not to run.[500]

The same calculus yielded a different result in 1992, when Clinton decided to make the run and take the heat. By the summer of 1991, the Clintons had discussed the issue with people close to them and decided on the strategy for dealing with it. He would say that he and his wife had had some problems, but that they had worked through them and were committed to their marriage.[501] The candidate got the chance to implement the strategy when he faced allegations in early 1992 that he had had a twelve-year affair with Gennifer Flowers, anArkansas state employee and part time cabaret singer. His popularity dropped in the wake of the allegations. On January 26, 1992, the Clintons went before the cameras together on "60 Minutes" to put that issue behind them.[502] With millions of Americans watching them, the Clintons sat close together on a small love seat, occasionally holding hands and Hillary nodding in agreement with her husband's description of their

498 *Ibid., 116.*

499 *Ibid., 320-321.*

500 *Ibid., 439-441.*

501 *Ibid., 460-461.*

502 *See transcript of the interview at http://www.angelfire.com/wa/starreport/60min.html.*

marriage and his behavior that had harmed it. They portrayed themselves as dedicated to their twenty-year marriage and the love they had for each other. Although Hillary claimed that she was not "some little woman standing by my man like Tammy Wynette," that's exactly what she did. They sought to shift the spotlight onto the media, claiming that the American people understood them and their marriage, even if the press did not. While they both denied the Flowers affair, when asked directly by Steve Kroft, "Are you prepared tonight to say that you've never had an extramarital affair," the candidate declined to categorically deny that he had, saying instead ". . . I have acknowledged wrongdoing. I have acknowledged causing pain in my marriage."[503]

It was a bravura performance. Clinton's popularity rebounded. He made a strong second place showing in the New Hampshire primary and then nearly swept the Southern primaries held on Super Tuesday, March 10, 1992. He went on to win the nomination of his party and to win the general election in a three-way race with President Bush and third party candidate Ross Perot.[504] The American electorate had absorbed the news of Clinton's wayward behavior during his marriage and elected him President anyway. It seemed that this problem was now behind him. But, his May 1991 encounter with Paula Jones re- mained to be revealed and his affair with Monica Lewinsky lay in Bill Clinton's future.

The sordid events that led to Bill Clinton's impeachment by the House of Representatives in December 1998 and his acquittal by the Senate less than a month later confer honor on precious few of the par- ticipants in those events. To understand how this happened, we need to look at three strands of seemingly unrelated facts that came together in early 1998: the Paula Jones case against Bill Clinton, his affair with Monica Lewinsky and the independent counsel investigation conduct- ed by Kenneth Starr.

503 *In his deposition in the Paula Jones case, Clinton did admit to having had sexual relations with Gennifer Flowers once in 1977. See transcript at www.washigntonpost.com/wp-srv/politics/special/pjones/docs/clintondep013198.htm , 62-63 of 73.*

504 *https://britannica.com/event/United-States-presidential-election-of-1992.*

CHAPTER 20
PAULA JONES V. WILLIAM JEFFERSON CLINTON

The genesis of President Bill Clinton's impeachment lies not with Monica Lewinsky but in his encounter with another woman, Paula Corbin Jones, in a hotel room in Little Rock, Arkansas in May 1991. That encounter blossomed into a lawsuit brought by Jones against Clinton in Arkansas federal court in May 1994. It is significant to note that whatever happened in that hotel room in 1991 had nothing whatsoever to do with Clinton's conduct as the President of the United States following his inauguration in January 1993.

The road to President Clinton's impeachment began on May 8, 1991, in a private encounter between then Governor Clinton and Paula Corbin, later Paula Corbin Jones, in a room in the Excelsior Hotel in Little Rock, Arkansas.[505] At the time, Paula Jones was a new Arkansas state employee who was working at the registration desk for a confer- ence at the hotel sponsored by the Arkansas Industrial Development Commission at which the Governor was delivering a speech. She and a friend spoke briefly at the registration desk with Danny Ferguson,one of Governor Clinton's state trooper bodyguards.

---

505 The description of this encounter is taken from the Court's ruling on President Clinton's motion for summary judgment found at Jones v. Clinton, 900 F. Supp. 657 (E.D. Ark. 1998), issued on April 1, 1998. As noted in the text, Clinton denies that anything improper occurred.

Ferguson testified in his deposition that he and Clinton had a con- versation about the possibility of meeting with Jones during which the Governor remarked that she had "that come-hither look," i.e., "a sort of [sexually] suggestive appearance from the look of the dress." Some- time later that day the Governor "asked him to get a room because he was expecting a call from the White House and had other calls to make." Ferguson testified that he got the room and the Governor told him that if Jones wanted to meet him, she could "come up."

According to her deposition testimony,[506] Jones was excited about meeting the Governor and went to the hotel room to do so. It is undisputed that Clinton and Jones were alone in the hotel room for some period of time. From here, it becomes a classic "he said/ she said" situation. Under the rules governing the summary judg- ment motion that was before the court, the judge had to assume that Paula Jones's version of what happened was true. According to Jones, during the time that she was alone with Clinton, he un- expectedly reached over, took her hand and pulled her toward him into a close embrace. She then retreated from him, but Clinton ap- proached her again, saying "I love the way your hair flows down your back" and "I love your curves," putting his hand on her leg and started sliding it toward her pelvic area and bent down in an at- tempt to kiss her, all without her consent. She exclaimed "what are you doing?" told the Governor that she was "not that kind of girl" and "escaped" by walking away from him.

She tried to distract Clinton by chatting about his wife and sat down at the end of the sofa nearest the door. Clinton sat down on the sofa next to her "lowered his trousers and underwear, exposed his pe- nis (which was erect)" and told her to "kiss it.'" She was "horrified" by this, "jumped up from the couch," and said she had to go. Clin- ton, while fondling his penis,

506 A deposition is an examination of a witness under oath, just as if the witness were testifying in court. The lawyers for the parties are present, but a judge normally is not. Objections are made, but, unless the question would invade the attorney client privilege, the witness answers, subject to a later ruling by the judge. A court reporter transcribes the questions and answers and then prepares a written version, called a "transcript." Depositions are also frequently videotaped.

said "well, I don't want to make you do something you don't want to do." As she was leaving, Clinton "de- tained" her momentarily, "looked sternly" at her and said, "You are smart. Let's keep this between ourselves."

In his deposition, Clinton denied Jones' version:[507]

> Q: Mr. President, did you ever make any sexual ad- vances towards Paula Jones?
>
> A. I did not.
>
> Q: Did you ever ask Paula Jones to kiss your penis? A: No, I did not.
>
> Q: Now, Mr. President, you've stated earlier in your testimony that you do not recall with any specificity the May 8th 1991 conference at the Excelsior, is that correct?
>
> A: That's correct.
>
> Q: If that is true, sir, how can you be sure that you did not do these things which are alleged in Ms. Jones' complaint?
>
> A: Because, Mr. Bennett, in my lifetime, I've never sexually harassed a woman, and I've never done what she accused me of doing. I didn't do it then, because I never have, and I wouldn't.

All this allegedly occurred in May 1991. Yet, Paula Jones did not file her lawsuit against the President until May 1994, three years later,[508] after she had voluntarily resigned from her job with the State of Arkansas and moved to California with her husband, Steve Jones. Indeed, had it not been

---

507 *Those portions of the deposition transcript that were made public may be found at www.washingtonpost.com/wp-srv/politics/pjones/docs/ clintondep031398.htm.*

508 *The Complaint that initiated the lawsuit can be found at www.washingtonpost.com/wp-srv/politics/pjones/docs/complaint.htm. A detailed account of how this article and the Jones lawsuit were connected is in Jeffrey Toobin's entertaining book, A Vast Conspiracy, The Real Story of t he Sex Scandal that Nearly Brought Down a President, Simon & Schuster (2000) at 3-28.*

for an article entitled "His Cheatin' Heart," which appeared on December 18, 1993 in the little known conserva- tive monthly American Spectator, the lawsuit never would have been filed.[509] The article, written by a hard-hitting conservative journalist named David Brock, was an attack piece that recounted the difficulties Clinton's aides had encountered over the years in keeping his rumored sexual exploits out of the public eye.

Much of the article was based on Brock's interviews with two Ar- kansas state troopers, Larry Patterson and Roger Perry, both of whom had been detailed to Clinton when he was the Governor of Arkansas. Based on those interviews, Brock told a story of an encounter between Clinton and a woman named "Paula" in a room at the Excelsior Hotel in Little Rock. According to the story as told by the trooper to Brock, "Paula" was in the room alone with Clinton for "no more than an hour." When "Paula" left the room, the trooper said "Paula told him she was available to be Clinton's regular girlfriend if he so desired."

The article made a splash in Arkansas. When Paula Jones learned about the article, she knew, of course, that she was the "Paula" who had supposedly been willing to serve as Clinton's "girlfriend." Jones was angry about what she considered to be a false smear on her repu- tation. She complained to a friend, who connected her with a lawyer in Little Rock. After briefly considering and rejecting a defamation suit against the American Spectator, Jones' counsel decided that the better avenue for a quick buck was to go after the President for what the lawyer hoped would be a quick settlement. Also, realizing that he had a potential tiger by the tail and was not up to doing battle in a civil lawsuit against the President of the United States, if it came to that, he brought in reinforcements to draft the complaint and take the lead in representing Paula Jones. What started out as a "shakedown" turned into – well -- a federal case with a life of its own.

---

509 The article can be found at https//spectator.org/49976_his-cheatin-heart/

The complaint alleged a smorgasbord of claims against the Pres- ident, but the golden thread of the case was a civil rights claim that alleged that the Hotel Excelsior encounter amounted to "sexual harass- ment" by then Governor Clinton that deprived Jones of a right to equal treatment in the workplace and caused her damages that were alleged, as allowed by the rules, in vague terms.

The case was assigned to Judge Susan Webber Wright. Born and raised in Arkansas, she graduated from Randolph-Macon Woman's College in 1970 and the University of Arkansas Law School in 1975. While in law school, she took Bill Clinton's admiralty law course, where she had a minor scrape with Clinton over her grade. He had lost all of the final exam papers and offered the entire class a B+ or the op- portunity to retake the test. She elected to retake the test and ended up with an A. Upon graduation, she was law clerk to a judge on the United States Court of Appeals for the Eighth Circuit, a position reserved for the top law school graduates. Law clerks work closely with their judge on researching the law and helping to draft written decision in cases assigned to the judge. After a year as a clerk, she joined the faculty at the University of Arkansas Law School and served there until she was appointed to the Arkansas federal court by President George H.W. Bush in 1989.

In short, Judge Wright was a homegrown elite lawyer and a con- servative Republican who presided with fairness to the parties and re- spect for the Office of the Presidency. Handed an unprecedented and exceptionally difficult case, Judge Wright's rulings demonstrated not only diligence and faithfulness to the law, but also a wisdom that was able to see the line between President Clinton, the Chief Magistrate of the United States, and Bill Clinton, the individual defendant in a private lawsuit.

This was the first time that a sitting president had been sued. Seiz- ing on this, Clinton's legal team asked the court to dismiss the case because, they asserted, the President was immune from being sued until his term had expired. In an order dated December 28, 1994, Judge Wright denied the request. She ruled that discovery could proceed, but concluded that any trial should be stayed until the President was no longer in office.[510] The President appealed to the Eighth Circuit Court of Appeals. The appellate court agreed with Judge Wright that the President was not immune from suit and that discovery was appro- priate, but it reversed the ruling that the trial could not occur whilethe President was in office.[511]

Not surprisingly, the President's team asked the Supreme Court to review the decision and, as expected given the importance of thecase, the Supreme Court agreed to take it.[512] But the wheels of justice grind slowly. It was another two and a half years before the Supreme Court, in a unanimous ruling dated May 27, 1997, affirmed the Eighth Cir- cuit's decision, stating that, "The Federal District Court has jurisdic- tion to decide this case. Like every other citizen who properlyinvokes that jurisdiction, respondent [Paula Jones] has a right to the orderly disposition of her claims."[513] The case was sent back to the trial court, which set a discovery cutoff of January 30, 1998, but did not set a trial date.[514]

At this point, Jones' lawyers took an aggressive position on the scope of what they could ask about Clinton's extra-marital sexual ac- tivity both before and after the May 1991 incident that was the subject of the case.[515]

510 Jones v. Clinton, 869 F. Supp. 690 (1994)

511 Jones v. Clinton, 72 F.3d 1354 (8th Cir. 1996)

512 The appeal from the trial court to the Eighth Circuit is what is called an "appeal as of right," meaning that the Eighth Circuit was required to review the trial court's decision. In contrast, the Supreme Court decides which cases it will take. Given the President's involvement, it was a foregone conclusion that the Supreme Court would agree to take it.

513 Clinton v. Jones, 520 U.S. 681 (1997)

514 "Discovery" is the name given by judges and lawyers to the phase of a civil lawsuit in which the parties are allowed to "discover" the facts of the case from each other and also from people who are not parties to the case. The process typically includes requests for documents, responses under oath to written questions and examinations of witnesses under oath, usually without the presence of the judge, in what are called depositions.

515 Jeffrey Toobin makes a convincing argument that this discovery campaign was driven, not by the needs of the case, but to gather infor- mation on the President's sexual history for use in the public arena to compromise him and his political agenda. See Toobin, Jeffrey, A Vast Conspiracy, the Real Story of the Sex Scandal that Nearly Brought Down a Presidency (Simon & Schuster, New York, 1999) (hereafter Toobin, A Vast Conspiracy).

They sought to gather information that would support an argument at trial that the President had a "pattern" of sexual mis- conduct that would validate Jones' version of what happened behind closed doors at the Excelsior Hotel. In an order dated December 11, 1997, the court ruled that Jones was "entitled to information regard- ing any individuals with whom the President had sexual relations or proposed or sought to have sexual relations and who were during the relevant time frame [of May 8, 1986 up to the present] state or federal employees." This ruling set the stage for the debacle that occurred at the President's videotaped deposition that was taken in his lawyers' downtown Washington, D.C. office on January 17, 1998.

The order was broad enough to include Clinton's White House affair with Monica Lewinsky, because she was a federal employee during 1995 to 1997 when the affair occurred. Her name first popped up in the Jones case on a witness list faxed by her lawyers to the Pres- ident's counsel on December 5, 1997. On that date, Bill Clinton be- lieved that no one other than he and Lewinsky knew about the affair. He was wrong. Linda Tripp, Lewinsky's supposed "friend," had been recording their telephone conversations during which Lewinsky dis- cussed in detail her sexual exploits with the President of the United States. Unbeknownst to Lewinsky, by December 1997, Tripp had been persuaded by the Jones legal team to share her blockbuster information with them.[516]

The President's deposition was looking like a trial lawyer's dream for the Jones lawyers. If they were lucky (and it shouldn't take much luck), they could bait the President into a series of lies about his rela- tionship with Lewinsky that could be used to impeach the President's credibility at trial.

516 *In a roster of unsavory characters, Linda Tripp is near the top. While pretending to be Monica Lewinsky's friend, Tripp was actually promoting her own interests. Her surreptitious re- cordings of the calls with Lewinsky were illegal under Maryland law (where she lived and from where she participated in the calls), a practice that she continued even after her lawyer advised her of its illegality. She did so in the first instance to "protect herself" and to gather information for a book she was hoping to shop. By December 1997, the Jones legal team knew the details of the Clinton/Lewinsky affair, but neither the President nor Lewinsky knew about Tripp's recordings. See Toobin, A Vast Con- spiracy, 177.*

It would also provide juicy material for the leak mill that plagued the case from its inception.

Jones' lawyers could catch Clinton in a lie only if the President didn't come clean with his lawyers. As it turns out, rather than admit- ting to his relationship with Lewinsky, he lied to his lawyers about it. The day after they received the witness list with Lewinsky's name on it, the lawyers met with the President to review it. When his lead law- yer, Bob Bennett, explained that Jones' lawyers were alleging that the President had had an affair with her, according to two people present, Clinton replied, "Bob, do you think I am f------ crazy? Hey, look, let's move on. I know the press is watching me every minute. The right has been dying for this kind of thing from day one. No, it didn't happen. I'm retired."[517]

Bob Bennett and the rest of Clinton's lawyers marched forward believing that there was no affair with Lewinsky. As a result, they walked right into a trap that Bennett himself helped to spring in the deposition on January 17, 1998. In preparation for it, Bennett hadper- suaded the Judge to preside at the deposition to rule on objections. This was highly unusual. Normally, depositions are taken without a judicial officer present. The questions and answers are transcribed by a court reporter. Objections are made, but unless the answer would reveal at- torney-client communications, the answers are still given. Using the transcript of the testimony, the trial judge typically rules on the objec- tions if a party wants to use the deposition testimony at trial. Having Judge Wright present was seen to be an advantage for the President, whose lawyers got the opportunity to limit the examination.

On the appointed day, the President's secret service cavalcade pulled up to his lawyers' office building and he was escorted to a con- ference room where the deposition was held. Around the table were several lawyers as well as Judge Wright and her law clerk. Paula Jones was also present. The lawyer for Jones conducted a generally rambling examination, but did

---

517 Toobin, A Vast Conspiracy , 166-167; Harris, The Survivor, 294 – 295.

manage to elicit a lie from the President about the Lewinsky affair:

> Q: Did you have an extramarital affair with Monica Lewinsky?
>
> A: No.
>
> Q: If she told someone that she had a sexual affair with you beginning in November of 1995, would that be a lie?[518]
>
> A: It's certainly not the truth. It would not be the truth.[519]

That was bad enough, but Bennett, Clinton's own lawyer, acting on the mistaken belief that his client had been honest with him, unwit- tingly compounded the problem by asking the President to comment on the veracity of an affidavit that Monica Lewinsky, who herself had hired a lawyer, had submitted to the court in her attempt to avoid being deposed:[520]

> Q: [By Robert Bennett] In paragraph eight of her [Lew-insky's] affidavit, she says this, "I have never had a sex- ual relationship with the president, he did not propose that we have a sexual relationship, he did not offer me employment or other benefits in exchange for a sexual relationship, he did not deny me employment or other benefits for reflecting [sic] a sexual relationship."
>
> Is that a true and accurate statement as far as you know it?
>
> A: That is absolutely true.[521]

At this point, other than what she learned at the President's depo- sition, and a January 12th hearing that addressed issues related to the President's

518 The "someone" was Linda Tripp, but neither the President nor his lawyers knew that at the time of the deposition.

519 Public partial transcript of the deposition of William Jefferson Clinton, found at www.washingtonpost.com/wp-srv/politics/special/pjones/ docs/clintondep031398.htm, 14 of 73

520 Like Clinton's deposition testimony, Lewinsky's affidavit was perjurious. Ultimately, she was granted immunity by Ken Starr in exchange for cooperating in his OIC investigation against the President.

521 Ibid. at 68 of 73.

deposition, Judge Wright had no idea who Monica Lew- insky was and, like the President's lawyers, she was unaware that the President had lied under oath. In fact, Judge Wright did not learn that the President may have lied under oath until August 17, 1998, when he went on television and acknowledged publicly for the first time that he had had "a relationship with Ms. Lewinsky that was inappropriate and wrong."[522]

A surprise arrived in Judge Wright's courtroom on the afternoon of January 28th, when Kenneth Starr's Office of Independent Coun- sel ("OIC") filed a motion to intervene in the Jones case with an ac- companying motion to stay discovery. Unbeknownst to Judge Wright, on January 16th, the Special Division of the United States Court of Appeals for the District of Columbia Circuit granted a request from Attorney General Janet Reno to expand the jurisdiction of Indepen- dent Counsel Kenneth W. Starr and entered an Order authorizing the Independent Counsel "to investigate . . . whether Monica Lewinskyor others had suborned perjury, obstructed justice, intimidated witnesses, or otherwise violated federal law . . . in dealing with witnesses, poten- tial witnesses, attorneys, or others concerning the civil case Jones v. Clinton."[523]

The OIC asserted that Jones' counsel were deliberately shadow- ing the grand jury's investigation involving Monica Lewinsky and that "the pending criminal investigation is of such gravity and paramount importance that this Court would do a disservice to the Nation if it were to permit unfettered and extraordinarily aggressive efforts cur- rently underway to proceed unabated."[524] It is hard to see how further discovery in the Jones case could have upset the OIC's apple cart, since the cutoff date for discovery was January 30th, only two days after the OIC filed its motion. Nonetheless, Judge Wright took this in stride, responding immediately to this unexpected

522 *Jones v. Clinton, 36 F. Supp. 2d 1118, 1123 (E.D. Ark. 1999)*

523 *Jones v. Clinton, 993 F. Supp. 1217 (E.D. Ark. 1998), is Judge Wright's denial of Jones' motion for reconsideration of the order she issued on January 29th. She took the opportunity to lay out in some detail the grounds for that ruling.*

524 *Ibid., 1219.*

development, which looked like it was going to derail the forward movement of a case that had been on her docket for almost four years.

She convened a telephone hearing with counsel for the parties to the case and the OIC on the morning of the 29th, a day after the OIC's motion was filed. After hearing from all concerned, she solved the problem by taking Monica Lewinsky out of the Jones case, ruling that evidence relating to Lewinsky would not be admissible at trial. In doing so, she noted that, while such evidence "might be relevant to the issues in the case," it is "simply not essential to the core issues in this case of whether plaintiff herself was the victim … of sexual harass- ment, hostile work environment harassment or intentional infliction of emotional distress."[525] In other words, there is an obvious disconnect between an incident of sexual harassment that allegedly occurred in 1991 and a separate episode of sexual impropriety that began in 1995. As additional ground for her ruling, the Judge noted that the substantial interests of the presidency in avoiding delay in the lawsuit and her concern that the "integrity of the criminal investigation" might be "impaired and prejudiced were the Court to permit inquiry into the Lewinsky matter by the parties in this civil case."[526]

This ruling presaged Judge Wright's April 1, 1998 order grant- ing summary judgment to the President and dismissing Jones' claims against him and his co-defendant Trooper Danny Ferguson.[527] Under the federal court rules governing civil cases, a party may ask the court to rule in its favor before trial because, in the words of the rule, "there is no genuine dispute as to any material fact and the movant is entitled to judgment as a matter of law."[528] What this means is that, if all the facts necessary to decide a case under the governing law are undis- puted, there will be no reason to impanel a jury to resolve disputed facts. Since the law is the province of the court and not the jury, if the facts are undisputed, there is nothing for a

525 *Ibid.,1222.*

526 *Ibid., 1219.*

527 *Jones v. Clinton, 990 F. Supp. 657 (E.D. Ark. 1998).*

528 *Rule 56(a) of the Federal Rules of Civil Procedure.*

jury to do. Summary judgment motions are often filed and not very often granted. President Clinton's motion for summary judgment was one of the few.

At the time of Clinton's motion, there were three claims remain- ing in the case: (a) a civil rights claim under the Fourteenth Amend- ment that Governor Clinton had deprived Jones of equal protection by sexually harassing her; (b) a claim that Clinton and Ferguson had conspired to deprive Jones of her right to equal protection; and (c) a claim under Arkansas law that the Governor had inflicted emotional distress or outrage on Jones.

First of all, had the case gone to trial, a jury would have decided the "he said/she said" dispute between Clinton and Jones. However, for purposes of deciding the motion for summary judgment, the court assumed, without deciding, that Jones' version of what happened at the Hotel Excelsior behind closed doors was true. In order to get to a jury on the equal protection claim, there had to be some disputed evidence to show that there was a connection between the assumed harassment by Clinton of Jones at the Excelsior Hotel and a negative impact on Jones in her the work place at the Arkansas Industrial Development Commission (AIDC).

Judge Wright found that the undisputed facts showed that there was no such impact. Jones continued to work in her same job at the AIDC until she [529]voluntarily resigned in February 1993 to move to Cali- fornia with her husband. Jones admitted that no one, including Gov- ernor Clinton, ever told her that if she refused to submit to alleged advances it would have a negative effect on her job, that she had to submit to alleged advances in order to receive job benefits, "or that the Governor would use his relationship with the AIDC Director . . . to penalize her in her job."[530] Judge Wright summed up by saying, "The Court has carefully reviewed the record in this case and finds nothing in plaintiff's employment records, her own testimony, or the testimony of her supervisors showing that plaintiff's reaction to Governor Clin- ton's alleged advances affected tangible aspects

529 *990 F. Supp. at 665 -666.*

530 *Ibid., 670.*

of her compensation, terms, conditions, or privileges of employment."[531] Moreover, it was undisputed that Jones received every merit increase and cost of living allowance for which she was entitled and that she consistently received satisfactory job evaluations.[532] Secondly, with respect to the emotional distress and outrageous conduct claim, the court ruled that, while Clin- ton's alleged conduct was offensive, it was not sufficient under the law to support the claim.

Jones'lawyers appealed the ruling and the parties settled the case on November 13, 1998, while the case was on appeal, with Clinton agreeing to pay Jones $850,000, a large chunk of which went to her lawyers. But Judge Wright's work wasn't done. By this time it had long since become clear that the President had lied in his deposition, while under oath and with Judge Wright sitting at the table. Adiligent federal judge could not let that pass and she didn't.

On April 12, 1999, a month and a half after the Senate acquitted the President of the impeachment charges, and without a request from Jones' lawyers to do so, Judge Wright found President Clinton in civil contempt of court for his "willful failure to obey this Court's discovery

Orders" on her own initiative.[533] In plain language, she found that he had lied in his deposition and needed to be punished for it. In doing so, she drew a clear line between the President's conduct in the lawsuit and his official presidential duties. As she said, "[t]his lawsuit involved private actions allegedly taken by the President before his term of of- fice began, and the contumacious conduct on the part of the President was undertaken in his role as a litigant in a civil case and did not relate to his duties as President."[534]

---

531 Ibid., 671.

532 Ibid., 671-672. Since the conspiracy claim was based on the viability of the sexual harass- ment claim, there was legal basis for an alleged conspiracy between Governor Clinton and Trooper Ferguson and that claim was also dismissed.

533 Jones v Clinton, 36 F. Supp. 2d 1118 (1999).

534 Ibid., 1124.

As a result, Judge Wright punished Clinton in the same fashion as she would any other lawyer who appeared in her courtroom as a liti- gant, with a ringing endorsement for the proposition that we all stand equal before the law: ". . . this Court will not impose greater sanc- tions against the President for his contumacious conduct in this case than would be imposed against any other litigant and member of the bar who engaged in similar misconduct."[535] With that preamble, the court concluded that ". . . the record demonstrates by clear and con- vincing evidence that the President responded to plaintiff's questions [regarding sexual relations with state or federal employees] by giving false, misleading and evasive answers that were designed to obstruct the judicial process."[536] Lest there be any question that this referred to lies about his relationship with Monica Lewinsky, the court quoted at length from Clinton's January 17th deposition and compared it to his August 17, 1998 testimony before a grand jury empaneled by Kenneth Starr, where he had admitted things about that relationship that he de- nied in his deposition.[537]

Finally, the Court noted the importance of making an example of the President to deter others from engaging in similar conduct: "Sanctions must be imposed, not only to redress the misconduct of the President in this case, but to deter others, who, having observed the President's televised address to the Nation in which his defiance of this Court's discovery Orders was revealed, might themselves consid- er emulating the President of the United States by willfully violating discovery orders of this and other courts, thereby engaging in conduct that undermines the integrity of the judicial system."[538]

Taking into consideration Clinton's willful disobedience of her orders, the fact that Clinton had prevailed in the case at the trial court level and that Jones had been made whole in the settlement, the Court ordered Clinton to pay Jones the reasonable expenses, including attor- neys' fees, she incurred

535 *Ibid., 1125.*
536 *Ibid., 1127.*
537 *Ibid., 1127-1131.*
538 *Ibid., 1131.*

as a result of the President's failure to obey the Court's orders. She also ordered Clinton to pay the $1,202 the Court had incurred in attending his deposition in Washington, D.C. Finally, she referred the matter to the Arkansas Supreme Court's Committee on Professional Conduct, which subsequently suspended his license to practice law. These might seem trivial against a person as important as the President of the United States, but for a private litigant before a federal court it was a significant chastisement. The suspension of the President's law license had no impact on his duties as President, but it amounted to a public humiliation of Clinton in the Arkansas legal community.

So, after five years which included a trip to the Supreme Court, the investment of thousands of hours by the respective legal teams, generating what were surely seven figure attorneys' fees bills, as well as the consumption of substantial judicial resources, the presiding judge found in favor of the President and dealt with his misconduct in a civil contempt order that was tailored to fit the magnitude of the wrongdoing and the circumstances of the case.

Sadly, this was not the case with President Clinton's impeach- ment, where those who were out to get him bootstrapped an attempt to hide an affair during discovery in a lawsuit that had nothing to do with his presidential duties into constitutional grounds for undoinghis election as President of the United States. To understand how that hap- pened, we need to dig more deeply into the Monica Lewinsky story and the Ken Starr investigation.

CHAPTER 21
THE MONICA LEWINSKY AFFAIR

Perhaps you have seen the 1998 movie "Sliding Doors." Starring Gwyneth Paltrow, the movie begins in the London underground where Paltrow's character hurries to board a rush hour train that is about to leave the station. The sliding doors open and the mass of people trying to get on jostle with those trying to exit, all rushing to get on or off before the doors slide closed. In one scene, she gets on. In an alternative scene, the doors close before she can get on and the train leaves the station without her. The movie then takes you on two rollicking rides that play out differently.

President Clinton's intimate relationship with Monica Lewinsky began with just such a "sliding door" moment of chance. But for the government shutdown that was forced by Newt Gingrich's petulant behavior in the fall of 1995, Monica Lewinsky would not have been detailed to Chief of Staff Leon Panetta's office in the White House on the night of November 15th. No government shutdown, no rollicking ride toward the Clinton impeachment.[539]

---

539 The description of Monica Lewinsky's affair with President Clinton is taken from the September 9, 1998 Report/"Information" to Con- gress by the Office of Independent Counsel containing what the report refers to as "substantial and credible information that President William Jefferson Clinton committed acts that may constitute grounds for impeachment." References are to the version that is at http://IndexVermont.com. It will be referred to hereafter as "Starr Report." The description of the intimate relationship is based on what Lewinsky told the OIC. See Starr Report, 23-41. Although

On that evening, the second day of the government shut-down, the 21-year-old intern, who was not being paid and therefore could work, was dispatched to the White House to work in Panetta's West Wing

Office. At the same time, the President was in either the Oval Office or Panetta's office. According to Lewinsky, she and the President made eye contact when he came to the West Wing to see Panetta and Deputy Chief of Staff Harold Ickes, then again later that day at an informal birthday event for one of Clinton's staffers. The two had met the pre- vious summer after she had begun working for Panetta. Lewinsky says that, at departure ceremonies and other events, they engaged in what she described as "intense flirting." Lewinsky had told her aunt that the "President seemed attracted to her or interested in her or something." She also told a visiting friend that she was "attracted" to him and had a "big crush on him."

On the evening of November 15th, they talked alone in the Chief of Staff's office. In the course of flirting with him, she raised her jacket in the back and let him see the straps of her thong underwear, which showed above her pants. Later, at about 8 p.m., while she was walking to the restroom, she passed George Stephanopoulos's office, where the President was inside alone. He beckoned her to enter and she toldhim that she had a crush on him. He laughed and then asked if she would like to see his private office. Through a connecting door in Stephano- polous's office they went through the President's private dining room toward the study off the Oval Office. They talked briefly and acknowl- edged that they were both attracted to each other. Then the President asked if he could kiss her and she said yes. Before returning to her desk, Lewinsky wrote down her name and phone number for thePres- ident.

At about 10 pm., Lewinsky was alone in the Chief of Staff's office and the President approached. He invited her to rendezvous again in

acknowledging that he engaged in "inappropriate intimate" acts with Lewinsky, the President has steadfastly refused to say in public or under oath what those acts were.

Stephanopolous's office in a few minutes and she agreed. They met in Stephanopolous's office and went again to the private study. Ac- cording to Lewinsky, they kissed. She unbuttoned her jacket, either she unhooked her bra or he lifted it up and he fondled her breasts. She testified: "I believe he took a phone call . . . [H]e put his hand down my pants and stimulated me manually in the genital area." While the Pres- ident continued talking on the phone, she performed oral sex on him.

Thus began a series of sexual liaisons that occurred sporadically over the period between November 1995 and March 1997. According to Lewinsky, there were a total of ten encounters, only two of which occurred after she took a job in the Pentagon in April 1996, as the Confidential Assistant to the Assistant Secretary of Defense for Public

Affairs.[540] They generally occurred in or near the private study off the Oval Office, most often in the windowless hallway outside the study. They never had intercourse. She performed oral sex on the President, but he never performed oral sex on her, although he did fondle her breasts and genitals. They also engaged in "phone sex," or, in the Pres- ident's articulation, "inappropriate sexual banter," and exchanged gifts on a number of occasions.

Lewinsky never liked her job at the Pentagon. At her request, the President helped her to find employment elsewhere, first through Bill Richardson, who was the United States Ambassador to the United Nations and then through his friend and long-time Democratic oper- ative Vernon Jordan. With Jordan's help, Lewinsky landed a job with Revlon in New York City in January 1998. Whether these efforts were an attempt by the President to assuage Lewinsky's hurt feelings or an attempt to buy her cooperation in the Jones case became an issue in the impeachment imbroglio.

---

540 There is some indication that the transfer was engineered by Deputy Chief of Staff Evelyn Lieberman, who had become concerned about Lewinsky's relationship with the President and the fact that Lewinsky was underperforming on her job. Toobin, A Vast Conspiracy, 108-109.

As the old saying goes, "fact is stranger than fiction." It would be hard to make up a scenario that could inflict greater personal and pro- fessional pain and embarrassment on the Commander-in-Chief than a public airing of the tawdry facts of his sexual relationship in the sanctity of the White House with a young woman who was half his age and not that much older than his own daughter. In an inexplica- ble fit of naïveté, the President apparently thought his secret was safe with Monica Lewinsky. How wrong he was. As it turns out, she told eleven people, including Linda Tripp, about her affair with the Com- mander-in-Chief.[541] And Tripp's tapes of Lewinsky's "kiss and tell" telephone confessions would find their way into the hands of Kenneth Starr and his just-about-out-of-gas team of federal prosecutors.

541 *Starr Report, 21.*

CHAPTER 22
THE STARR INVESTIGATION

On September 9, 1998, Kenneth W. Starr's Office of Independent Counsel ("OIC") submitted its long-awaited report to Congress setting forth what the OIC believed to be "substantial and credible information that President William Jefferson Clinton committed acts that may constitute grounds for an impeachment."[542] Those acts were focused on the President's affair with Monica Lewinsky and his alleged false testimony and other ultimately unsuccessful attempts to cover up that relationship. This was the culmination of yet another string of bizarre and unpredictable events and circumstances. What began in January 1994 as an investigation into the Clintons' and oth- ers' investment in a lakeside property in Arkansas, known as White- water, morphed in January 1998 into a federal investigation into the President's scandalous affair with Monica Lewinsky.

In January 1994, President Clinton's Attorney General, Janet Reno, appointed Robert Fiske, a Republican, as the independent prose- cutor to investigate the Whitewater controversy and the death of White House Counsel, Vincent Foster, who had committed suicide the previ- ous summer. Fiske was a highly respected and experienced trial lawyer who was a partner in a major Wall Street law firm and the former Unit- ed States Attorney for the Southern District of New York. By the end of June, Fiske had released a preliminary report that confirmed Foster's death to have been a suicide and cleared the Clintons of any wrong doing in the Whitewater matter. That

542 *Ibid., 14.*

could very well have closed the books on the Clintons as far as Whitewater was concerned.

But that did not happen. Instead, the same day that the Fiske report was released, President Clinton signed into law the Independent Counsel Reauthorization Act of 1994.[543] That statute abolished the position of special prosecutor and replaced it with the position of independent counsel. In addition, the method for choosing the independent counsel was changed. Instead of the Attorney General, the selection was now to be made by the "Special Division" of the U.S. Court of Appeals for the District of Columbia Circuit.[544] Attorney General Reno requested that Fiske be chosen, but on August 5, 1994, the Special Division chose Kenneth Starr.[545]

Starr, a Republican, was highly credentialed, but his experience was largely in appellate law. He had clerked for Supreme Court Chief Justice Warren Burger. In 1983, he was nominated by President Ronald Reagan, and confirmed by the Senate, as a judge on U.S. Court of Appeals for the District of Columbia. He resigned from that position in 1989, when he was asked to serve as Solicitor General under President George H.W. Bush, a position he occupied until 1993. Significantly, he had no previous experience as a prosecutor. Starr chose to ignore the Fiske conclusions on Whitewater.

Instead, he redoubled efforts to investigate that matter and also sought and received permission to investigate alleged improprieties in the White House travel office, potential abuse of confidential FBI files and the Rose Law Firm where Hillary Clinton had practiced law during the time that her husband was the Governor of Arkansas. By 1998,

Starr's OIC had incurred costs of about $40 million,[546] but had little to

543 *28 U.S.C. §§ 591-599 (1974)*

544 *28 U.S.C. §§ 593.*

545 *Dash, Abraham, "The Office of Independent Counsel and the Fatal Flaw: They Are Left Twisting in the Wind," 60 Md. L. Rev. 26 (2001), 29-30.*

546 *Gordon, Robert W., "Imprudence and Partisanship: Starr's OIC and the Clinton-Lewinsky Affair," Faculty Scholarship Series, Paper 1411 (1999) (hereafter Gordon, "Imprudence and Partisanship"), 641, f.n. 11. GAO accountings show that Starr spent $40 million through September 1998,*

show for it. There were some indictments against former Clinton associates and three convictions for financial crimes in the Whitewater case. However, the OIC had uncovered nothing indictable against the President and his wife and issued no reports to Congress indicating that there was "substantial and credible evidence" that the President had engaged in conduct that might have been impeachable.

It looked as if Starr was about to close up shop when, on Jan- uary 12, 1998, Linda Tripp contacted the OIC and revealed detailed information provided to her by Monica Lewinsky about her relation- ship with the President, including the audio tapes of Tripp's telephone conversations in which Lewinsky described her relationship with the President.[547] Connecting with lawyers for Jones, the OIC quickly es- tablished that Lewinsky had committed perjury in the affidavit she sub- mitted in the Jones case. Starr sought and, on January 16th, was granted permission to expand his investigation to include whether Lewinsky or others had suborned perjury or obstructed justice with respect to discovery in the Jones case. On that same day, Lewinsky was lured by Tripp to a lunch at the Pentagon City Mall, where FBI agents acting for the OIC apprehended Lewinsky and questioned her for eleven hours in the Ritz-Carlton Hotel.[548] The agents made it clear that she was free to leave and she was allowed to contact an attorney during the inter- view. From January through the summer of 1998, the OIC continued to interview Lewinsky, in the presence of her lawyers, while at the same time negotiating the terms of an immunity agreement, which was finally reached on July 28th. Lewinsky testified before the grand jury on August 6th.

---

when he submitted his report to Congress and another $7 million between October 1998 and March 1999.

547 Daniel H. Erskine, "The Trial of Queen Caroline and the Impeachment of President Clinton: Law As a Weapon for Political Reform," 7 Wash. U. Global Stud. L. Rev. 1 (2008), 14, f.n. 98.

548 The Impeachment of President William Clinton: An Account, http://www.famous-trials.com/clinton/884-home at 11-12.

By August, the OIC was ready to press the President to testify before the grand jury. Politically, the President could not avoid doing so without appearing to be hiding something. Moreover, pleading his Fifth Amendment privilege against self-incrimination would be polit- ically unacceptable because it would look like he was trying to hide something. The President was going to have to testify under oath about his relationship with Monica Lewinsky. He was scheduled to appear before the grand jury on August 17th.

Given the precedent-setting nature of his appearance before the grand jury, Clinton's lawyers were able to negotiate a special arrange- ment for the testimony. Rather than having to incur the indignity of the President of the United States walking into a federal courthouse to be questioned by federal prosecutors, the testimony would be taken under oath at the White House, with the grand jurors watching by video from the grand jury room in the courthouse. The testimony, which was also videotaped, was limited to four hours, with his lawyers present. Allowing the lawyers to be there was an almost unheard of concession by the prosecutors, since grand jury witnesses are normally not allowed to have their counsel with them.

Starr's team had done their homework. They had gathered and analyzed thousands of pages of documents. Ultimately, the backup to the report submitted to Congress consisted of over 3,100 pages. They had traveled around the country interviewing scores of witnesses, more than seventy of whom had testified before the grand jury.[549] They focused heavily, of course, on Monica Lewinsky. They had debriefed her in several sessions over the course of seven months. They present- ed her testimony to the grand jury on August 6th. They had also deter- mined, based on a blood sample taken from the President on August 3rd, that it was his semen on a blue dress that Lewinsky had turned over to the prosecutors on the same day she signed the immunity agreement.[550] The OIC's goal was to establish

549 *New York Times, "Lewinsky Said to Detail Clinton Affair," August 7, 1998.*

550 *Lewinsky had been wearing the dress during a tryst with the President on February 28,*

that Clinton had lied in his Jones deposition about the nature of his sexual relationship with Lew- insky and that he had attempted to convince others to lie under oath about the facts of the relationship.

This time, the President's lawyers were no longer in the dark about the President's relationship with Lewinsky. As a result, they had their client well-prepared. Their strategy was three-fold. First, they wanted their client to avoid perjuring himself before the grand jury. Second, they wanted to establish that, while Clinton may have sliced the baloney awfully thin in the Jones deposition, he had not outright lied. Finally, knowing that his testimony would be leaked, the Presi- dent wanted to make his case that he was the subject of unfair attacks by his political enemies who were trying to demean him and his Pres- idency for political advantage.

Although blows were landed by both sides, the President hadthe better day. Early in the deposition, Clinton managed to set the parame- ters to his testimony by delivering a prepared statement, which he read into the record:

> "CLINTON: When I was alone with Ms. Lewinsky on certain occasions in early 1996, and once in early 1997, I engaged in conduct that was wrong. These encounters did not consist of sexual intercourse. They did not constitute sexual relations, as I understood that term to be defined at my January 17th, 1998 deposition.[551]
>
> But they did involve inappropriate, intimate contact. These inappropriate encounters ended at my insistence in early

1997. Starr Report, 39.

551 *The definition was provided by the Jones lawyer who was taking the January 17th deposition and read as follows: "For purposes of this deposition, a person engages in 'sexual relations' when the person knowingly engages in or causes: (1) contact with the genitalia, anus, groin, breast, inner thigh, or buttocks of any person with an intent to arouse or gratify the sexual desire of any person; (2) contact between any part of a person's body or an object and the genitals or anus of another person; or (3) contact between the genitals or anus of the person and any part of another person's body. 'Contact' means intentional touching, either directly or through clothing." This definition is obtuse at best, and indecipherable at worst. One thing is for sure, it leaves a lot of room for different interpreta- tions.*

1997. I also had occasional telephone conver- sations with Ms. Lewinsky that included inappropriate sexual banter.

I regret that what began as a friendship came to include this conduct. And I take full responsibility for my ac- tions. While I will provide the grand jury whatever oth- er information I can, because of privacy considerations affecting my family, myself and others, and in aneffort to preserve the dignity of the office I hold, this is all I will say about the specifics of these particular matters.

I will try to answer to the best of my ability otherques- tions, including questions about my relationship with Ms. Lewinsky, questions about my understanding of the term sexual relations, as I understood it to be de- fined at my January 17th, 1988 deposition, and ques- tions concerning alleged subordination [sic] of perjury, obstruction of justice and intimidation of witnesses."[552]

Clinton's repeated refrain was that he and Lewinsky had not en- gaged in sexual intercourse (which was true according to both Clinton and Lewinsky) and that the undisclosed "inappropriate, intimate con- tact" did not meet the definition of sexual relations used in his deposi- tion, as the President understood it.[553] Not to be deterred, and knowing what Lewinsky had said about the specific acts she and the President had engaged in, the prosecutor turned to some specific questions later in the testimony:

"QUESTION: So touching in your view then [during his deposition] and now – the person being deposed touching

552 *Transcript of the Grand Jury Testimony of William Jefferson Clinton, August 17, 1998 (hereafter Clinton Grand Jury Testimony), 4. The transcript can be found at http://www.enquirer.com/clinton/complete_transcript.html,*

553 *Implicit in Clinton's view of the deposition definition is that he would not be engaging in "sexual relations" if he received but did not give oral sex. As unlikely as that might have seemed to the average person on the street, the obscure nature of the definition made it at least plausible.*

or kissing the breast of another person would fall within the definition?

CLINTON: That's correct, sir.

QUESTION: And you testified that you didn't have sexual relations with Monica Lewinsky in the Jones deposition, under that definition, correct?

CLINTON: That's correct, sir.

QUESTION: If the person being deposed touched the genitalia of another person, would that be in – with the intent to arouse sexual desire, arouse or gratify, as de- fined in definition one, would that be, under your un- derstanding, then and now, sexual relations?

CLINTON: Yes, sir."[554]

Gotcha! Clinton implicitly admitted that he lied in the Jones depo- sition when he said he had not had sexual relations with Monica Lew- insky.[555] This false testimony about the details of what Clinton and Lewinsky had done behind closed doors in the White House became the center-piece of the impeachment charges against the President.

---

554 *Clinton Grand Jury Testimony, 38.*

555 *After seven months of emphatic denials, the President went on national television the evening of his grand jury testimony to admit publicly that he had had an "improper intimate relationship" with Lewinsky. At the same time, he said, "Now, this is a matter between me, the two people I love most – my wife and my daughter – and our God. It's nobody's business but ours. Even Presidents have private lives." New York Times, "Clinton Admits Lewinsky Liaison to Grand Jury; Tells Nation 'It Is Wrong,' but Private," August 18, 1998, hhtps:/partners.nytimes.com/library/ politics/081898clinton-lewinsky.html.*

CHAPTER 23
THE STARRREPORT

On the late afternoon of September 9, 1998, with 15 minutes notice, Kenneth Starr's OIC delivered its report to the House of Representatives, along with two duplicate sets of information filling 36 sealed boxes, which were put under lock and key and guarded by the Capitol Police.[556]

The report was submitted pursuant to a provision in the Independent Counsel Act titled "Information Relating to Impeachment" that stated, "An independent counsel shall advise the House of Representatives of any substantial and credible information which such independent counsel receives, in carrying out the independent counsel's responsibilities under this chapter, that may constitute grounds for impeachment."[557] The report contended that "the information" revealed that President Clinton:

> "-- lied under oath [about his relationship with Monica Lewinsky] at a civil deposition while he was a defen- dant [in the Jones case];
>
> -- lied under oath to the grand jury;
>
> -- attempted to influence the testimony of a potential witness [Monica Lewinsky] who had direct knowledge of facts that

---

556 *http://www.famous-trials.com/clinton/884-home, 15; New York Times, "Congress Is Setting Up Steps for Considering Lewinsky Matter," September 10, 1998.*

557 *28 U.S.C. §§ 595(c).*

would reveal the falsity of his deposition testimony;

-- attempted to obstruct justice by facilitating a wit- ness's [Monica Lewinsky] plan to refuse to comply with a subpoena;

-- attempted to obstruct justice by encouraging a wit- ness [Monica Lewinsky] to file an affidavit the Presi- dent knew would be false, and then by making use of that false affidavit at his own deposition;

-- lied to potential grand jury witnesses, knowing that they would repeat those lies before the grand jury; and

-- engaged in a pattern of conduct inconsistent with his constitutional duty to faithfully execute the laws."[558]

The report claimed that "[i]t is not the role of his Office to de- termine whether the President's actions warrant impeachment by the House and removal by the Senate; those judgements are, of course, constitutionally entrusted to the legislative branch."[559] Thus, Kenneth Starr disavowed the exercise of prosecutorial discretion, purporting to leave it up to the House's discretion to decide whether private sexual indiscretions and attempts to cover up the illicit behavior is a proper subject of impeachment. He did so knowing that the impeachment pro- ceedings in the House and a potential trial in the Senate would neces- sarily entail the public disclosure of the most intimate, practically por- nographic, details of what the report calls "sexual contacts" between the President and Monica Lewinsky:

"It is the view of this Office that the details are crucial to an informed evaluation of the testimony, thecredibility of the witnesses, and the reliability of other evidence. Many of the details reveal highly personal information; many are sexually explicit. This is unfortunate, but it is essential. The

558 *Starr Report, 14..*
559 *Ibid., 16*

> President's defense to many of the al- legations is based on a close parsing of the definitions that were used to describe his conduct. We have, after careful review, identified no manner of providing the information that reveals the falsity of the President's statements other than to describe his conduct with pre- cision."[560]

This admission by the independent counsel underscores the bot- tom line: he was inviting the House to impeach Clinton because the President purportedly lied about the technical details of the sex acts he and Monica Lewinsky performed, even though he had admitted in public and under oath in his grand jury testimony that they had en- gaged in "inappropriate, intimate contact." Most people could fill in the necessary blanks, and besides, what difference did it really make? Did we really need to have the Chief Executive describe in technical detail what he and his lover had done behind closed doors?

Punting to Congress the assessment of President Clinton's con- duct against the constitutional standard for impeachment was a ques- tionable abdication of Starr's duty under the statute. Although unstat- ed, the theory of Starr's "impeachment indictment" of the President was that any lie told under oath is a serious breach of trust that "may" merit removal from office. Quoting Herbert Hoover, the report says: "[t]he Presidency is more than an executive responsibility. It is the inspiring symbol of all that is highest in American purpose and ide- als."[561] There is no doubt that the President of the United States should be a shining example of integrity and prudent behavior. So, the unstat- ed assumption is that any lie under oath by the President is a crime and a loathsome crime at that.

Wait a minute. We all know from our own experience that all lies are not equal and that, under certain circumstances, lies are even al- lowed. As Yale

560 Ibid., 8.
561 Ibid., 16.

Law School Professor Robert Gordon has pointedout, the law recognizes that not all lies are perjury.[562] Yet, the OIC "never stopped to analyze the most important question of all: whether Clin- ton's false statements and Lewinsky's false affidavit denying their af- fair did or could have any serious concrete harm to the interests of justice."[563] That would have entailed consideration of how the Lewinsky affair factored into the issues being litigated in the Jones case. Was the fact that Clinton and Lewinsky engaged in sex beginning four years after the Clinton/Jones encounter "material" to the outcome of that case? The parties to the Jones case never saw it that way. The outcome determinative issues in the case focused on the treatment Paula Jones received in the workplace as a result of her alleged sexual encounter with Clinton, which had nothing to do with the President's relationship with Monica Lewinsky.

Indeed, during the House impeachment hearings, a panel of five Republican and Democratic federal prosecutors concurred that testi- mony concerning the President's relationship with Monica Lewinsky was not material to the Jones lawsuit.[564] They also agreed that criminal law is generally not used to sanction misbehavior that occurs in civil litigation and that the OIC's case against the President would likely not be sustained in court, and, therefore, most prosecutors would not pur- sue it.[565] Judge Richard Posner, a respected jurist and prolific author, disagrees with these conclusions. His view is that the evidence was strong that Clinton obstructed justice by improperly influencing wit- nesses and that he perjured himself in his Jones deposition and in his grand jury testimony. He makes the argument that a prosecutor

562 *Gordon, "Imprudence and Partisanship," 655-656.*

563 *Ibid.*

564 *H. Rept. 105-830, Impeachment of William Jefferson Clinton, President of the United States, https://www.congress.gov/congressional-re- port/105th-congress/house-report/830/1, pp. 233- 236. Similarly, Harvard Law Professor Alan Dershowitz testified before the House Judiciary Committee on December 1, 1998, that, if President Clinton had been a private citizen, he would not have been indict-ed for lying under oath about his affair with Monica Lewinsky. See http://www.constituion.org/lrev/deshowitz_test_981201.htm; see also Pollitt, Donald, "Sex in the Oval Office and Cover-Up under Oath: Impeachable Offense," 77 N.C.L.Rev. 259, 279-280.*

565 *Ibid., 236.*

could legitimately indict a private citizen – and President Clinton – for the conduct described in the OIC report.[566]

The report adduced no exculpatory factors weighing in favor of the President. The Jones case was given short shrift. The report did not mention the fact that the conduct at issue in the Jones case had occurred in May 1991, nearly two years before President Clinton had been inaugurated for his first term. The OIC did not acknowledge that, in January 1998, at the very same time that the OIC had announced its investigation to Judge Wright in the Jones case, the Judge had ruled that evidence relating to Monica Lewinsky was not relevant to the "core issues" in that case, and, therefore, would not be admissible at trial. The report was silent on the Judge's April 1998 summary judg- ment ruling that dismissed Jones' claims against the President.

Finally, the OIC provided no rationale for the implicit conclusion that what the President had been accused of "may" have been impeach-

able, even though there was existing Congressional guidance on that score in the form of a House Judiciary Committee staff report that was prepared in February 1974 at the time of the Watergate Hearings. Nor was there any recognition of the substantial body of scholarly analysis concluding that private conduct that does not involve the exercise of presidential powers is not impeachable.

566 *Posner, Richard A., An Affair of State – The Investigation, Impeachment and Trial of President Clinton (Harvard University Press, 1999), 36 – 56*

CHAPTER 24
IMPEACHMENT OF CLINTON BYTHE HOUSE

President Clinton's impeachment proceedings were launched when the OIC Report was submitted to Congress under seal on Sep- tember 9, 1998. On September 11th, the Report was released to the public and posted on the internet.[567] By this time, the fact of the Lew- insky affair (although not the salacious details) had been public for nine months, and the President had delivered a number of public mea culpas, while continuing to perform his presidential duties. Americans had mostly absorbed the shock of Clinton's outrageous private behav- ior and were ready to move on.[568] The House, under the leadership of the Republicans who held a majority, marched on.

On October 5th, the Judiciary Committee voted along party lines to recommend an impeachment inquiry.[569] Three days later, the full House voted 258 to 176 to conduct an impeachment inquiry.[570] Thir- ty-one Democrats crossed the aisle to join all the Republicans to vote in favor of a resolution that referred the matter back to the Judiciary Committee under

---

567 *http://www.famous-trials.com/clinton/881-chronology.*

568 *New York Times, "House, In Partisan 258-176 Vote, Approves Broad, Open-Ended Impeachment Inquiry," October 9, 1998, https:// partners.nytimes.com/library/politics/100998clinton-impeach.html.*

569 *The Impeachment of President William Clinton: A Chronology, http://www.famous-trials.com/clinton881-chronology.*

570 *Ibid.*

the leadership of Republican Henry Hyde. Chairman Hyde announced that his committee would begin hearings after the mid-term elections that were scheduled for November 3rd.[571] Republicans were hopeful that they could boost their numbers in both the House and the Senate, which would give them renewed public backing for impeachment.[572]

The Republican expectations were dashed on November 3rd. While they retained control of the Senate and House, the Democrats made a strong showing in an off-year election in which the President's party typically loses seats. The partisan break-down in the Senate remained unchanged at 55 Republicans and 45 Democrats. While retaining a majority in the House, the Republicans lost five seats to the Demo- crats, the first time that had happened in a mid-term election in the 20th century. In terms of impeachment arithmetic, this meant that, if the politicians voted along party lines, the President would be impeached by the House, but not convicted in the Senate. Setting arithmetic aside, exit polling showed that the voters were largely approving of the Pres- ident. While the Lewinsky affair cast a shadow over the election, 60% of the voters did not think the President should be impeached.[573]

Despite the strong indications that the electorate was not behind impeachment, House Republicans pushed on. Hearings on impeach- ment were held from November 9th to December 10th. Witnesses were called, including an all-day session on November 9th with nineteen constitutional scholars testifying on the constitutional standard gov- erning impeachment, and another session on December 9th with five former federal prosecutors addressing the standards for perjury and obstruction of justice. However, the committee did not seek testimony from any of the witnesses identified

571 New York Times, "House, In Partisan 258-176 Vote, Approves Broad, Open-Ended Impeachment Inquiry," October 9, 1998, https://part- ners.nytimes.com/library/politics/100998clinton-impeach.html.

572 Ibid.

573 New York Times, "Democrats, Defying Predictions, Bring Home Victories," November 4, 1998, https://partners.nytimes.com/library/ politics/camp/110498eln.html.

in the OIC Report as supporting the allegations of perjury and obstruction of justice against the Presi- dent. The committee was apparently content with relying on theinfor- mation provided by the OIC, implicitly leaving it to the Senate to test the veracity of the OIC information against live testimony from those involved.

On November 5th, the committee also propounded a set of 81 writ- ten questions to the President, to which he responded on November 28th in a document that was undoubtedly written by his lawyers.[574] The questions sought information that largely duplicated what was already in the OIC Report and the President's answers tracked his grand jury testimony. In two introductory paragraphs, the President took the op- portunity to play to the public sentiments that were manifested in the recent elections:

> "I would like to repeat, at the outset, something that I have said before about my approach to these proceed- ings. I have asked my attorneys to participate actively, but the fact that there is a legal defense to various alle- gations cannot obscure the hard truth, as I have said re- peatedly, that my conduct was wrong. I was also wrong to mislead people about what happened and I deeply regret that.
>
> For me, this long ago ceased to be primarily a legal or political issue and became instead a painful personal one, demanding atonement and daily work toward rec- onciliation and restoration of trust with my family, my friends, my Administration and the American people. I hope these answers will contribute to a speedy and fair resolution of this matter."[575]

---

574 *The text of the President's responses can be found at https://partners.nytimes.com/library/politics/112898clinton-text.html.*

575 *Ibid.*

On December 12th, the Judiciary Committee voted along party lines to approve four articles of impeachment for consideration by the full House.[576] The actions taken by the Committee and supporting ar- guments for the majority (Republican) view in favor of the articles and the minority (Democratic) opposition view are contained in a massive committee report.[577] Article I accused the President of perjury in his August 17, 1998 grand jury testimony. Article II was based on alle- gations that he had provided false written discovery responses in the Jones case and that he had lied in his deposition about his relationship with Monica Lewinsky, or, in the words of the article, "a subordinate Government employee." Article III alleged that the President had ob- structed justice by encouraging witnesses in the Jones case and before the grand jury to provide false testimony in support of his efforts to cover up his false testimony about his relationship with Monica Lew-

insky, who remained unnamed in the article. Article IV alleged abuse of power against the President based on allegations that he lied to White House staff and Cabinet members about his affair with Monica Lewinsky, that he "frivolously and corruptly" asserted executive privi- lege, that he "failed and refused to respond" to certain of the Judiciary Committee's 81 questions and that he provided false information in response to others.

On December 19th, the full House approved two articles of im- peachment.[578] Article I alleged that President Clinton lied in his August 17, 1998 grand jury testimony. It was approved by a vote of 228 to 206, with

---

576 *The votes on three of the four articles were 21 to 16, strictly partisan votes. On one of the articles, Republican Congressman Lindsey Graham voted against it, making the vote 20 to 17. https://partners.nytimes.com/library/politics/121298impeach.html.*

577 *H. Rept. 105-830 – Impeachment of William Jefferson Clinton, President of the United States, https://wwww.congress.gov/congressio- nal-report/105th-congress/house-report/830/1. A copy of just the articles of impeachment voted out of the Judiciary Committee can be found at https://part- ners.nytimes.com/library/politics/12098impeach-itext.html.*

578 *Congressional Record, Proceedings and Debates of the 106th Congress in the Senate, First Session, January 7, 1999, records the two articles of impeachment as they were "exhibited" to the Senate by the House managers.*

five Republicans and all Democrats voting against it.[579] Article II alleged obstruction of justice in the Jones case by attempting to suborn perjury by witnesses in that case and the OIC grand jury investigation. It was approved by a vote of 221 to 212, with 12 Republicans voting no and five Democrats voting yes.

The other two articles suggested by the Judiciary Committee were rejected by the full House. Judiciary Committee Article II relating to the President's alleged false testimony in his Jones deposition was de- feated by a vote of 229 to 205, with 28 Republicans joining the Dem- ocrats.[580] Article IV relating to the President's response to the written questions submitted to him by the Judiciary Committee was soundly defeated by a vote of 285 to 148.

Partisanship permeated the impeachment proceedings in the House from start to finish. The Republicans lined up almost four- square to impeach the President while, on the other side, the Demo- crats phalanxed behind the President.

---

579 *New York Times, "President Is Impeached and Faces Senate Trial," December 20, 1998, https//partners.nytimes.com/library/poli- tics/122098impeach.html.*
580 *Ibid.*

CHAPTER 25
THE SENATE TRIAL OF PRESIDENT CLINTON

The political heat was now on the Senate, which was facing only the second impeachment trial of a president in the history of the Republic, and the first-ever trial of an elected President. Having been stung by the bad results of the mid-term elections, the Republican leadership in the Senate was also staring in the face of polls indicat- ing strong support for the President and equally strong opposition to his impeachment and a Senate trial. In a New York Times/CBS News poll that was taken immediately after the House voted in favor of the first article of impeachment, 72% of those polled said they approved of Clinton's job performance.[581] Two-thirds of Americans opposed Clinton's removal from office, while 60% said they thought that the President's impeachment was punishment enough and that there should be no Senate trial.[582] Equally troubling was the strong signal that the impeachment was damaging the Republicans' standing with the electorate. Two-thirds of the people polled said they believed that the Republicans were pursuing impeachment for political gain against Clinton and the Democratic Party.[583] These political realities and the party line-up in the Senate, where the Republicans did not have the two-thirds majority required for conviction, made the President's acquittal likely.

---

581 New York Times, "Public Support for the President and for Closure, Emerges Unshaken," December 21, 1998, https://partners.nytimes. com/library/politics/122198impeach-poll.html.

582 Ibid.

583 Ibid.

The Senate leadership saw no mileage in conducting a "reveal all" trial on the floor of the Senate with live witnesses testifying about inti- mate sexual conduct in a "he said/she said" Congressional extravagan- za. The House Republicans' campaign for political blame by humiliat- ing President Clinton flopped. The Senate had no choice but to play it out with minimal additional damage to the politicians in Washington who had led the charge against the President in a battle most American voters did not want to fight. They would do so by fashioning a "trial" that wasn't. The Senate leadership from both parties cooperated from the outset to keep the trial as short as possible and sanitized, to the extent possible, of the salacious details of the Clinton/Lewinsky affair that were so prominent in the OIC Report.

The proceedings began at 9:45 a.m. on January 7, 1999 when the President, pro tempore, Senator Strom Thurmond, called the Senate to order. Before the Senate got down to business, the Chaplain, Dr. Lloyd John Olgilvie, a Presbyterian minister, offered a prayer, includ- ing these words:

> ". . . Holy God, as this sacred Chamber becomes a court and these Senators become jurors, be omnipresent in the pressures of these impeachment proceedings. Grant the Senators the ability to exercise clear judgment with- out judgmentalism. Today, unite the Senate in nonpar- tisan commitment to the procedures that will most ef- fectively resolve the grave matters before them andour Nation. Bind the Senators together as fellow patriots seeking Your best for our beloved land. . . ."[584]

Having called on the Almighty, at 10:05 a.m., for only the second time in the history of the Republic, a delegation of House managers ap- peared

---

584 Proceedings and Debates of the 106th Congress, First Session, Senate, Thursday, January 7, 1999, Vol. 145, No. 2. The House managers were a delegation of Representatives, all Republicans, who were commissioned by the House to present the case for impeachment in the Senate trial. They were Henry Hyde (Illinois), Chair of the House, Judiciary Committee, James Sensenbrenner (Wiscon- sin), William McCollum (Flor- ida), George Gekas (Pennsylvania), Charles Canady (Florida), Ste- phen Buyer (Indiana), Edward Bryant (Tennessee), Bob Barr (Georgia), Asa Hutchinson (Arkansas), Chris Cannon (Utah), James Rogan (California) and Lindsey Graham (South Carolina).

below the bar of the Senate to deliver articles of impeachment against a President. The newly appointed Senate Sergeant at Arms, James W. Ziglar, announced their presence:

> "Mr. President [pro tempore] and Members of the Sen- ate, I announce the presence of the managers on the part of the House of Representatives to conduct the proceedings on behalf of the House concerning the im- peachment of William Jefferson Clinton, President of the United States."[585]

Senator Thurmond acknowledged their presence and they were escorted to the Senate floor, where the Sergeant-at-Arms intoned:

> "Hear ye! Hear ye! Hear ye! All persons are command- ed to keep silent, on pain of imprisonment, while the House of Representatives is exhibiting to the Senate of the United States articles of impeachment against Wil- liam Jefferson Clinton, President of the UnitedStates."

Henry Hyde, who was leader of the House managers, thereupon read the articles of impeachment. The next order of business was to es- cort the Chief Justice of the United States, William Rehnquist, into the Senate Chamber, where he was first sworn in and then administered the oath called for by the Constitution to the assembled Senators:

> "Do you solemnly swear that in all things appertain- ing to the trial of the impeachment of William Jefferson Clinton, President of the United States, now pending, you will do impartial justice according to the Con- stitution and laws, so help you God?" The Senators answered "I do" and then signed the "Official Oath Book."[586]

---

585 *Ibid.*
586 *Ibid.*

The trial was now officially under way. But this was to be no ordinary trial. Far from it. The next day, Majority Leader Trent Lott, a Republican from Mississippi, and Minority Leader Tom Daschle, a Democrat from South Dakota, jointly submitted Senate Resolution No. 16, which was approved by the Senate.[587] That Resolution estab- lished the procedure that would govern the trial. A subpoena, with the Articles of Impeachment attached, would be issued to the President, who was given until January 11th to file his answer and the House Man- agers were given two days to file their "replication" (response) to that answer. Trial briefs summarizing the parties' cases were allowed and were to be submitted by January 11th by the House and January 13th by the President. The House managers were to make their argument in fa- vor of impeachment beginning January 14th, for a period of time not to exceed 24 hours of the Senate's time.Thereafter, the President's coun- sel[588] would be allowed to make their presentation, also limited to 24 hours. The arguments were to be limited to information in the record, which was voluminous, including all of the materials that supported the OIC Report. Following the presentations by the House managers and the President's counsel, the Senators would be allowed to question the parties' lawyers for a period not to exceed 16 hours.

At this point, before any live witnesses would have been heard, a motion to dismiss the articles of impeachment could be made. This option was designed to delay the issue of live testimony until the Sen- ate had already heard the major arguments based on the written record. Should the motion to dismiss be granted, that would end the trial. If the motion were denied, the Senate would then immediately entertain a motion for live testimony.

---

587 Congressional Bills, 106th Congress, 1st Session, S. RES. 16, https://www.gpo.gov/fdsys/pkg/BILLS-106sres16ats/html.

588 President Clinton's trial team included White House Counsel Charles Ruff, Deputy White House Counsel Cheryl Mills, Deputy White House Counsel Bruce Lindsey, White House Special Coun- sel Larry Breuer and White House Special Counsel Gregory Craig, Williams and Connolly partners David Kendall and Nicole Seligman, and former Arkansas Senator Dale Bumpers.

The process unfolded as planned. The trial briefs submitted by the House managers and President Clinton's counsel summarized the law and facts that they contended supported their positions. The man- agers' trial brief was filed first, on January 11, 1999.[589] The managers contended that conviction was appropriate on both Article I (perjury) and Article II (obstruction of justice.) On the first article, they argued that the facts supported the conclusion that the President had "delib- erately and willfully testified falsely under oath when he appeared be- fore a federal grand jury on August 17, 1998."[590] The brief provided a "non-exhaustive list" of examples of his alleged lies.[591]

On the second article, the managers asserted that "[t]he President engaged in an ongoing scheme to obstruct both the Jones civil case and the grand jury. Further, he undertook a continuing and concerted plan to tamper with witnesses and prospective witnesses for the purpose of causing those witnesses to provide false and misleadingtestimony."[592] As with the perjury allegations, the brief listed a series of examples of the President's obstruction conduct.[593]

The House managers did not contend that the President's conduct had been undertaken in the performance of his duties as the Chief Ex- ecutive, nor did they argue that his conduct adversely impacted the business of the country. Instead, they argued that Clinton engaged in personal criminal conduct that violated his oath to "preserve, protect and defend" the Constitution and ignored his constitutional duty to "take care that the laws are faithfully executed."[594] In effect, they ar- gued that lying under oath

589 *Brief of the House Managers, January 11, 1999, http://www.famous-trials.com/clinton/897-senatebriefs.*

590 *Ibid., 2.*

591 *Ibid., 2-3. The first example was that, at the outset of his testimony, ". . . the President read a prepared statement, which itself contained totally false assertions and other clearly misleading information." This contention is a stretch. Certainly, the statement read by the President was incomplete as to the details, but he admitted the essence of the "charges" of sexual impropriety and the statement itself is not false. See Clinton's statement above at pages 196-197.*

592 *Ibid., 3.*

593 *Ibid., 3-4.*

594 *Ibid., 4-5.*

about a private sexual relationship and oth- erwise attempting to cover up the relationship are serious crimes that justified the President's removal from office. As precedent, they cited the impeachment and conviction of three federal judges based on per- jury,[595] contending that the Constitution makes no distinction between the standard for impeaching judges and other "civil officers," includ- ing the President.[596]

The President's trial brief sought to rebut the House mangers' arguments on a number of levels.[597] First, the President's trial team pointed out that the House was asking the Senate to remove the Pres- ident ". . . because he had a wrongful relationship and sought to keep the existence of that relationship private."[598] They then argued that this private conduct, even though wrongful, was not impeachable. As they put it, "'[H]igh Crimes and Misdemeanors' refers to nothing short of Presidential actions that are 'great and dangerous offenses,' or 'at- tempts to subvert the Constitution.' Impeachment was never intended as a remedy for a private wrong."[599] Therefore, ". . . in all but the most extreme instances, impeachment should be limited to abuse of public office, not private misconduct unrelated to public office."[600] In addition to the statements by the founders at the Constitutional Convention and the ratifying conventions, they relied on the fact that, in 1974, the House Judiciary Committee did not approve an article of impeachment against President Richard Nixon based on the allegation that he had submitted fraudulent tax returns to the Internal Revenue Service.[601]

The President's brief asserted that presidential impeachment is qualitatively different from impeachment of federal judges, who are appointed for life and "during good behavior." Therefore, the only mechanism for removing a

595 *Ibid., 68-74.*
596 *Ibid., 73-75.*
597 *Brief for the President, January 13, 1999, http://www.famous-trials.com/clinton/898-clintonbrief.*
598 *Ibid., 4.*
599 *Ibid., 16.*
600 *Ibid.*
601 *Ibid., 18.*

federal judge is impeachment. In contrast, a President is elected by the nation to a term, limited to a specified num- ber of years, and faces accountability in the form of elections.[602] The brief also distinguished the facts of the three judicial impeachments from the facts before the Senate in the Clinton trial. In the three judi- cial impeachments cited in the House brief, the perjurious statements were immediately and incurably related to the performance of their official duties.[603] That was not the case with the allegations against the President, which admittedly did not directly involve his official conduct.[604] Finally, the President's team set out their version of the facts, arguing that President Clinton had not lied under oath and had not obstructed either the Jones case or the grand jury investigation.[605]

Between January 14th and 25th, the House managers and the President's lawyers made their arguments, followed by a question and an- swer period that also ended on January 25th. The same day, Democratic Senator Robert Byrd of West Virginia submitted a written motion to dismiss the case against the President that was immediately debated by the House managers and the President's counsel.[606] The theory of the motion to dismiss was that, since the President's conduct admittedly did not directly affect his official duties, an acquittal was appropriate without any further fact-finding. This would require two-thirds of the Senators to agree with the President's version of the standard for im- peachment. Given the party makeup of the Senate, that was not going to happen.

Two days later, the roll was called on the motion to dismiss, which was defeated, 56 to 44, with one Democrat (Russ Feingold of Wisconsin) voting with the Republicans.[607] This vote proved what was expect- ed. Although

602 *Ibid., 23.*

603 *Ibid., 24.*

604 *Ibid.*

605 *Ibid., 32 – 94.*

606 *The presentations can be found at Proceedings and Debates of the 106th Congress, First Session, Senate, Monday, January 25, 1999, Vol. 145, No. 13.*

607 *Proceedings and Debates of the 106th Congress, First Session, Senate, Wednesday, January 27, 1999, Vol. 145, No. 15.*

the Republicans had the votes to block a dismissal of the impeachment articles, which would have been an embarrassment to House Republicans, they also did not have the votes for a conviction. It undoubtedly affected what transpired on the witness front. First, the House managers wanted to depose a number of witnesses and the Sen- ate signaled that it would not allow more than three. With that in mind, the managers moved for leave to take the depositions of just three wit- nesses: Monica Lewinsky, Vernon Jordan and Sidney Blumenthal.[608] That request was granted on January 27th by a vote of 56 to 44, essen- tially along party lines.[609] The question of live testimony for the three witnesses to be deposed was left open.

Although not part of the motion, the House managers also pe- titioned the Senate to request the appearance of the President for a deposition and to appear live before the Senate.[610] While the managers contended that it was "exceedingly important" for the President to tes- tify, the Senate disagreed. President Clinton was not deposed, nor was he subpoenaed to testify live.

The videotaped depositions were taken by the House managers on February 1st (Lewinsky) and February 5th (Jordan and Blumenthal).[611] A Senator presided over each deposition and select Senators also at- tended, as did lawyers for the President. All three had testified be- fore the grand jury and those transcripts were already in the record. Not surprisingly, the depositions yielded nothing new and, in the case of the Lewinsky deposition, it actually hurt the House managers' case.[612] Even so, the managers selected

---

608 Proceedings and Debates of the 106th Congress, First Session, Senate, Tuesday, January 26, 1999, Vol. 145, No. 14. Blumenthal was a senior adviser to Clinton, who was called to the grand jury to testify about what the President had told his staff concerning his relationship with Monica Lewinsky.

609 Proceedings and Debates of the 106th Congress, First Session, Senate, Wednesday, January 27, 1999, Vol. 145, No. 15.

610 Proceedings and Debates of the 106th Congress, First Session, Senate, Tuesday, January 26, 1999, Vol. 145, No. 14.

611 The portions of the transcripts that were released to the public can be found at https://australianpolitics.com/1999/02/01/monica-lew- insky-deposition.html; https://australianpolitics.com/1999/02/05/vernon-jordan-deposition.html; https://australianpolitics.com/1999/02/05/ sid-ney-blumenthal-deposition.html.

612 For example, with respect to the false affidavit that Lewinsky had signed in the Jones case, she denied that the President had told her what to say. See Lewinsky deposition, 27, https://austra-

Lewinsky as the only witness they requested to call live. Apparently figuring that calling Lewinsky live would do the Republican Party no good, 25 Republican Senators joined all the Democrats in voting against her live testimony, which was rejected by a 70 to 30 vote. Instead, the Senate decided to play her video deposition to the Senate during floor arguments.[613] The Jordan and Blumenthal depositions would be admitted into evidence, but not played to the Senators on the floor of the Senate.[614]

The limitation on the number of witnesses and the exclusion of any live testimony from the floor of the Senate were fundamentally inconsistent with the fact-finding paradigm of the American trial, the purpose of which is to have the jury decide the facts where they are dis- puted. Under this paradigm, direct live testimony from and cross-ex- amination of witnesses with relevant evidence to offer are essential to the ability of the jury to decide the contested facts. Since, as the pro- ceedings to date had shown, the facts were hotly contested, this was a case that would normally demand live testimony.

However, the vote on the motion to dismiss took the steam out of the House managers' case, to the extent it ever had any. Most of the Senators lost their zeal for continuing the trial, which limped to an an- ticlimactic conclusion on February 12th. Both articles of impeachment failed to get the two-thirds majority necessary for a conviction, with the Senators remaining true to their partisan camps. The vote on Ar- ticle I was 45 guilty and 55 not guilty, including ten Republicans. On Article II, the vote was 50 guilty (all Republicans) and 50 not guilty (including five Republicans).[615] In other words, the "trial" did essen- tially nothing to change the minds of the fact-finding Senators. They had just engaged in a constitutionally mandated process that was noth- ing short of a sham. But at least it was over.

lianpolitics.com/1999/02/01/monica-lewinsky-deposition.html.

613 New York Times, "Senate Votes Not to Call Lewinsky, but Will Show Video Instead," February 5, 1999, https://partners.com/library/ politics/020599impeach-trial.html. See also, Transcript: Senate votes on handling deposition videotapes, February 4, 1999, http://www.cnn.com/ ALLPOLITICS/stories/1999/02/04/transcript/

614 Ibid.

615 Proceedings and Debates of the 106th Congress, First Session, Senate, Friday, February 12, 1999, Vol. 145, No. 26, S-1459.

CHAPTER 26 SHOULDPRESIDENT-CLINTON HAVE BEEN IMPEACHED?

Setting aside the nuances of the criminal law and the dispute over the facts in light of those nuances, President Clinton's behavior was orally repugnant. The essential facts were undisputed and they were not good for the President. He engaged in a sordid affair with a young government employee within the confines of the Oval Office, remembering that the White House was also the home of the President, the First Lady and his family. He demeaned his Presidency right in the very office where the nation's business is conducted and betrayed his family in their home. Then, in a failed attempt to avoid getting caught, he lied under oath and embarked on a campaign to make sure others supported his cover-up. When he got caught, he and his lawyers put together a "defense" that was based on a technicality that allowed him to argue that he had not committed perjury because, under the definition of "sexual relations" used in his deposition, what he and Monica Lewinsky engaged in did not qualify. This was pettifoggery at its worst.

There was also a breathtaking arrogance to what Clinton did. He could have settled the Jones case before he was put under oath, which is exactly what civil litigants do on a regular basis all over America to avoid having to air facts that they would prefer to remain private. Don't Americans have the right to expect better from their President? Didn't his conduct rise to the level of a major breach of trust that justi- fied removing him from office and undoing an election?

This was a question of character. Did Bill Clinton exhibit the character we want in our Chief Executive? Who gets to make that decision: The House of Representatives and the Senate, or the American electorate? By 1992, presidential elections had become ahigh-intensi- ty crucible in which the candidates were subjected to the most search- ing inquiry about every aspect of their lives. Beginning with the 1988 presidential campaign of Senator Gary Hart, the sexual improprieties of the candidates had become fair game. In fact, Bill Clinton's sexual track record was an issue in his 1992 presidential campaign. In early 1992, he confessed on the most watched news show, 60 Minutes, that he had engaged in activity that had brought pain to his family. That's code for "I had affairs." This was known to the electorate and pre- sumably was weighed in the balance when they went to the polls in two separate elections. Both in 1992 and 1996, the judgment by the American electorate was that, viewing all of Clinton's strengths and weaknesses and weighing them against what the other candidates had to offer, he was the preferred choice. They cared more about his public program and capabilities than they did about his private misconduct. That continued to be the case throughout the public airing of his affair with Monica Lewinsky.

Under the Constitution, Congress could reverse Clinton's election only through impeachment for and conviction of "treason, bribery, or other high crimes and misdemeanors."[616] That brings us to this ques- tion: was the conduct alleged in the articles of impeachment passed by the House actually impeachable? To start, don't we have to give great weight to the fact that the House of Representatives voted to impeach the President? After all, the Constitution states that the House ". . . shall have the sole power of

616 *There was never any suggestion that removal under the 25th Amendment was an option.*

impeachment." However, this does not mean that the House's impeachment power is unlimited. That view was soundly rejected by the House Judiciary Committee when it is- sued the articles of impeachment against Nixon in 1974, a rejection that is broadly endorsed by constitutional scholars. Even the most par- tisan Republicans did not make that argument to justify Clinton's im- peachment.

The OIC Report and most Republicans seized on the criminal nature of the President's conduct. The independent counsel could have, but did not, indict the President. There is a constitutional question about the susceptibility of a sitting president to indictment, but Starr could have delayed the indictment until Clinton left office. Had this path been chosen, Clinton would have continued his Presidency with the cloud of the indictment hanging over his head. This could have im- paired his effectiveness, but given the public acceptance of Clinton's behavior, it seems likely that it would not have. Moreover, most pros- ecutors, and certainly those who testified before the House Judiciary Committee, agreed that Clinton's lies about sex, and especially those that were uttered in the Jones case, were typically not prosecuted.

The mere fact that the President's behavior may not have been "criminal" does not end the inquiry. While a crime may be sufficient for impeachment, it is not necessary. Ultimately, the Republican ar- gument was that it was unseemly in the extreme for a President of the United States to have manipulated the judicial system with lies and attempted cover-ups. Testimonial oaths are a sacred and fundamental aspect of our judicial system. For the President to have lied under oath and encouraged others to do likewise were serious violations of the public trust and therefore qualified as "high crimes or misdemeanors." Significantly, this argument assumes that impeachable conduct need not be directly related to the discharge of a president's officialduties.

The overwhelming majority of constitutional scholars believe that President Clinton's impeachment was improper because, although his conduct was morally reprehensible, it did not relate to his presidential duties. This requirement finds its origin in the debates at the Consti- tutional Convention, where George Mason, who sponsored the "other high crimes or misdemeanors" language, included the words "against the State." The Committee on Style's deletion of "against the state" in the final version does not change the result. That Committee, as noted in Chapter 4, had no authority to change the substance of what the Convention as a whole had approved. Moreover, the ratification debates support the Mason language. Writing in Federalist 65, Alex- ander Hamilton noted that impeachable offenses were political in na- ture, relating to "injuries done immediately to society itself." The early commentator, Justice Story, echoed the public service aspect of the definition, noting that impeachable acts would entail conduct under- taken in the "discharge of the duties of political office." The articles of impeachment against Presidents Johnson and Nixon were based on conduct directly related to their constitutional duties.

The Republicans never seriously argued that the President's con- duct (criminal or not) directly affected his official duties. If we take the view – as we must - that impeachment is not for punishment, but rather for removal, it is hard to argue that President Clinton should have been

PART 5

CONCLUSION

CHAPTER 27
WHERE HAVE WE BEEN AND WHERE AREWE GOING?

What does this history tell us about the future? Is it significant that impeachment has been rarely invoked? How did the character of Presidents Johnson, Nixon and Clinton affect what happened? What role has partisan politics played? What is the impeachment stan- dard? How have special prosecutors/independent counsels affected the process? Will President Donald Trump be impeached?

Presidential Impeachment Is Rare .

The first thing the history tells us is that presidential impeachment is rare. In the 229 years since the ratification of the Constitution, only two presidents have been impeached and neither one was convicted. But for Richard Nixon's resignation, he would have been impeached and almost certainly convicted. That makes a total of only three (re- ally two and a half) times in the entire history of the Republic that Congress has thought it necessary to pull the impeachment lanyard. The founders would see this as a good thing. For most of the framers a strong and "energetic" executive was important to the success of the national government. They had lived through the failure of the Articles of Confederation and saw the absence of a well-functioning executive as one of the greatest ingredients in the failure of that scheme of gov- ernment. They wanted an executive that derived its legitimacy from the people, not from Congress. Consequently, they provided for the election of the President separately from Congress.

Under the Constitution, the President and Vice President are the only nationally elected officials. Accordingly, negating the President's election was to be avoided except in the most extreme cases. From the very beginning, presidential elections provided an opportunity to vet the views, virtues and flaws of the candidates. Especially since the advent of television, as well as the increasing role of the media and special interest groups, presidential candidates have been, and will continue to be, zealously scrutinized. For example, during their cam- paigns, both Presidents Clinton and Trump were subjected to "no holds barred" examinations of every facet of their professional and personal lives. By the time Richard Nixon won the presidency in 1968, he had been in politics for 22 years and his strengths and weaknesses were well-known. No one could seriously argue that the character flaws of these three men were not known to voters when they entered the poll- ing booths. Whatever those flaws may have been, they were voted into office in accordance with the constitutionally mandated process. For the framers, the people's decision should not be lightly disturbed.

The founders were also concerned about the President's ability to hold his own against Congress. As James Madison pointed out in Federalist 51, in a republican form of government, ". . . the legislative authority necessarily predominates." Recognizing Madison's point, in including impeachment in the Constitution, the founders were keen to ensure that it did not become an instrument of congressional domi- nance over the executive. They decided against a parliamentary form of government like Great Britain's, in which the executive was a crea- ture of and beholden to the legislature. Instead, they saw impeachment as a check and balance of last resort, to be invoked only in cases of the most egregious breaches of the public trust. Thus, it is appropriate that, for 42 of our 45 presidents, the day-to-day checks and balances avail- able to Congress and the Judiciary have operated to keep the President reasonably within the boundaries of the governmental playing field.

The Presidents' Personal Flaws Contributed to Their Impeachments.

What unifies the three presidential impeachment episodes that are the subject of this book is that each of the presidents had fundamental character flaws that became the precipitating ingredient in the consti tutional confrontations they faced. Accordingly, the presidents them- selves must bear a significant share of the blame for what they endured. For President Johnson, it was his unbending refusal to compro-

mise with the Congressional Republicans and to accept the fact that the Civil War had eliminated the extreme states' rights view of the Constitution on which his Reconstruction policy was based. His op- ponents were rightly outraged that he was determined to return the South to the very people against whom the war had been fought and won. His conduct was especially lamentable given the fact that he was an "accidental" President. It is true that Abraham Lincoln and Johnson ran on the same ticket and that Johnson was elected in his own right as Vice President. However, it was Lincoln and his policies that were at stake in the presidential election of 1864. Lincoln's victory gave him, not Johnson, the imprimatur of election by the people. Therefore, Johnson did not enjoy the full deference of election by the people that the founders saw as the source of independent presidential legitimacy.

A more thoughtful, less stubborn person would have appreciated the need for compromise with Congress called for by the circumstanc- es, rather than waging an outright battle against the legislative branch. Johnson sealed his own fate when he chose to fire Secretary of War Edwin Stanton, even if subsequent history proved him right about his power to do so. He had managed to avoid impeachment for nearly two years. He could have avoided it altogether had he been willing to com- promise with Congress to pick a Stanton successor agreeable to both. To put it another way, Johnson may have had the constitutional right to do what he did, but a more discerning President would have seen that forgoing the exercise of that right was the wise thing to do.

President Nixon's personal flaws were every bit as central to the process that led to his resignation. Nixon brought a deep-seated inse- curity to his political career. From his very first campaign in 1946, he fought to win, no matter what lies might have to be told to achieve it. He viewed politics as a kind of war without a Geneva Convention to protect the combatants. By his second term as President, he trusted no one and saw no limits on the skullduggery employed by his minions to ensure political victory. He had presided over an elaborate, if ultimate- ly inept, clandestine team authorized to commit crimes to ensure his political success. In short, despite his public denials, he was a crook. When it looked like he was about to be discovered, Nixon employed the powers of the Presidency to cover it all up. A substantial majority of Americans agreed that he got what he deserved.

While Johnson's and Nixon's personal flaws directly impacted the conduct of their office, President Bill Clinton's did not. Clinton's was a very intimate flaw. He was a womanizer, a sexual cheat. The people most profoundly wounded by his personal conduct were his wife, his family and Monica Lewinsky. The American people had been warned of his womanizing during his first presidential campaign in 1992. They still voted him into office, twice. They were apparently willing to ac- cept that flaw so long as he governed effectively, which by and large, he did. Reprehensible as his conduct was, his removal from office was never a real threat. Nonetheless, he handed his political enemies the only ammunition they had to remove him from office. If he had only controlled his libido, he would not have been put to the shame of the lengthy public spectacle his impeachment and trial became.

Politics Has Played an Out-Sized Role in Impeachment .

Contrary to the founders' intent, the impeachments and trials of Presidents Johnson and Clinton were highly partisan enterprises. That's not to say that the founders were not aware of the risk that political passion would pose for the integrity of the process. In the words of Hamilton's Federalist 65, they knew that impeachment would present ". . . the greatest danger, that the decision will be regulated more by comparative strength of the parties than by the real demonstrations of innocence or guilt." But it was their hope that this check and balance of last resort would not be wielded by Congress as a mechanism for bending the President to the will of Congress.

Johnson's impeachment was the result of an epic struggle be- tween the President and the Republican-dominated Congress over the Reconstruction of the South. Big policy issues were at stake. The Radical Republicans wanted him out of the way and saw im- peachment as a means of accomplishing that goal. Indeed, Radicals Thaddeus Stevens in the House and Charles Sumner in the Senate believed that there were no limits on Congress's ability to impeach and convict a President. As Sumner put it, when it came to impeachment, Congress was ". . . a law unto itself." All Senators who voted to convict Johnson were Republicans. All Democrats voted to acquit. Johnson was spared from removal by a single vote. What saved him was the political courage of the seven Republican "recusants" who were willing to forsake their political party in favor of fidelity to the Constitution.

Clinton's impeachment was mundane compared to Johnson's. It did not occur amidst a national crisis like the one that faced the country after the Civil War. There were no great policy issues hanging in the balance. His impeachment was a roundhouse punch thrown by an opposing party that wanted to get rid of "Slick Willy" Clinton. The House impeached the President on a strict party line vote. By the time the House managers arrived at the Senate for Clinton's impeachment trial, the American people were fed up with the process and generally happy with the job Clinton was doing as President. There was no pressing need to reverse his election and no major breach of public trust that adversely affected the United States government. The Senate leadership pared back the "trial" to the point that it became a sham. Everyone knew the outcome when the trial started. It apparently had little, if any, impact on the minds of the impeachment court. The final Senate vote was also partisan.

The Nixon "near impeachment" was the exception that proved the rule. By July 1974, after nearly two years of intense investigation by both Houses of Congress, as well as two special prosecutors, it was clear that the President had seriously abused the powers of the pres- idency to cover up the Watergate break-in. The impeachment vote in the House Judiciary Committee was bipartisan.

It is hard to draw hard and fast conclusions from a universe of three impeachments. However, it can be said with confidence that politics can never be eliminated from the process. By committing the impeachment power to the political branch, rather than the Judiciary, the foundersknew that, at some basic level, it would be a political process. So, it is not a question of whether politics should be involved, it is a question of how much politics there should be and how best to prevent unbridled politics from taking over, as it almost did in the Johnson impeachment. In the divided world we live in today, "tribal politics" makes one skeptical about the ability of members of Congress to set aside their deeply entrenched partisan loyalties to make a non-partisan impeachment decision and for the Senate to sit as an impartial impeachmentcourt.[617]

What Does " Other High Crimes and Misdemeanors" Mean?

What does history teach us about the meaning of the term ". . . other high crimes and misdemeanors." Ultimately, the application of that term is

617 *For a cogent discussion of the impact of "tribal politics" on our current political system see Tribe, Laurence and Matz, Joshua, To End A Presidency, the Power of Impeachment, Basic Books (2018), Chapter 6, pp. 197-241.*

left by the Constitution to be worked out by the House of Rep- resentatives in the first instance, and ultimately by the Senate. It is simply impossible to define impeachment with any precision. Howev- er, we do have a substantial contemporaneous historical record from the Constitutional Convention and the ratification debates with which to work. Congress has also left extensive records from the Johnson, Nixon and Clinton cases that give some helpful guidance.

In President Johnson's impeachment and trial in 1868, there were two polar opposite impeachable offense definitions that had signifi- cant support. At one pole was the Stevens/Sumner view that there are no limits. Congress alone decides what is impeachable and whatever conduct captures the requisite constitutional votes is "impeachable." This view was last espoused by then-Congressman Gerald Ford in a judicial impeachment in 1970. It was rejected by the House Judiciary Committee in its impeachment investigations of Presidents Nixon and Clinton. The rejection is documented in Judiciary Committee reports and hearing transcripts. While Congress is not obligated to do so, it is likely to draw upon this precedent in any future impeachment pro- ceedings. This conclusion is also overwhelmingly supported by the academic community.

At the other extreme is the view that impeachable offenses are limited to indictable crimes. This view, which is not supported by the record of the Constitutional Convention and the ratification debates, drew substantial support from the Democrats during the Johnson im- peachment. James St. Clair, President Nixon's impeachment defense counsel, attempted to resurrect it in Nixon's impeachment investiga- tion. It too was rejected by the Judiciary Committee. In the Clinton impeachment the argument was not even advanced by the President's defense team. This view is also rejected by virtually all scholars.

There is a third definitional question: can personal conduct that does not impact the government or the political system be the basis for impeachment?

For those who answer that question yes, this might be termed the "chief magistrate as exemplar" view of an impeachable of- fense. The argument in favor of making personal crimes impeachable is that, since the President is charged with the "faithful execution of the laws," any significant personal crime committed by him is a ma- jor abuse of trust that detracts from the integrity of government. This question was addressed to some extent in the Nixon case and to a large extent in the Clinton impeachment.

In the Nixon case, one of the articles of impeachment rejected by the Judiciary Committee related to alleged income tax evasion by the President. While tax evasion is certainly a crime, the fact that the President may have committed tax fraud has no impact on the Presi- dent's discharge of his duties. The fact that the Judiciary Committee voted against including this article is some indication that this "private crime" was not impeachable.

The issue of public versus private criminal conduct was at the very core of the Clinton impeachment case. The independent coun- sel, Kenneth Starr, explicitly argued that the President's perjury, even though it related to his personal conduct before he was elected to the Presidency, was a serious breach of public trust that could merit re- moval from office. The weight of academic authority was against this view for one of two reasons and perhaps both. First, the majority of prosecutors who expressed their views on the public record asserted that the perjury that the President was accused of would not have been prosecuted had he been a private citizen, and, therefore, should not be impeachable.

Second, even if it were a crime, most academics agreed that, since the perjury involved a private sexual transgression, it was not the type of significant breach of public trust the Framers had in mind for im- peachment. Given the highly partisan vote in both the House and the Senate, it is difficult to draw any solid conclusions on what impeach- ment definition the individual Representatives and Senators used in reaching their decisions. What we do know is that, in both the Nixon and Clinton cases, the private crimes they were accused of did not suf- fice as grounds for impeachment.

In conclusion, the following can be said about "other high crimes and misdemeanors" in light of the Johnson, Nixon and Clinton expe- riences:

-- While an indictable crime could support im- peachment, Congress is not limited to such a crime in exercising the impeachment power. The touchstone isa significant breach of the public trust widelyrecognized as egregious, or, as Senator William Fessenden said it in 1868, the conduct on which impeachment is based ".

. . should be of such a character as to commend itself at once to the minds of all right thinking men as, beyond all question, an adequate cause, . . . free from the taint of party." (emphasis added)

-- There should be a nexus between the conduct on which impeachment is based and the discharge of the President's duties.

-- Purely private conduct bearing on the character of the President, especially if it has been vetted in the election process, should not support impeachment, ex- cept in the most extreme circumstances.[618]

Independent Federal Prosecutors Have Impacted the Impeachment Process .

When Andrew Johnson was impeached, the investigation was handled in its entirety by the House Judiciary Committee. The deputizing of federal prosecutors[619] to investigate presidential conduct has changed the process,

618 *For example, it would be repugnant to allow a president who had murdered someone to remain in office.*

619 *Before 1983, these independent prosecutors were known as "special prosecutors." Since then, they have been called independent counsel. The text uses the title in effect at the time the investigation was conducted.*

without taking the ultimate decision on impeachment away from the House of Representatives. This happened to Presidents Nixon and Clinton. It is now happening, as of this writing, to President Trump.

In Nixon's case, the special prosecutor's investigation unfolded relatively quickly. Archibald Cox was appointed special prosecutor by Attorney General Elliott Richardson in May 1973. Nine months later, in February 1974, the House Judiciary Committee began its impeach- ment investigation. Although there was cooperation between Congress and the special prosecutor, the House did not request an "impeachment report" from the special prosecutor. The Judiciary Committee's inves- tigation was completed in late July 1974, when it issued its proposed articles of impeachment. The special prosecutor investigation was also effectively concluded as to the President at that time, except for the battle over production of the secret White House tapes.

In Clinton's case, an independent counsel was appointed to investigate the Whitewater real estate investment scandal in January 1994. The investigation lasted more than four years, during which time the subject changed from Whitewater to the Monica Lewinsky affair. The independent counsel's report, which became the basis for Clinton's impeachment, was submitted to the House on September 9, 1998.

On May 17, 2017, Former FBI Director, Robert Mueller, was appointed independent counsel to investigate allegations of Russian meddling in the 2016 presidential election. The investigation is on- going as of this writing in the summer of 2018. It seems likely that it will not be concluded before the mid-term elections in November. It is widely believed that Mr. Mueller's investigation will have a significant impact on any impeachment deliberations in the House.

These prosecutorial investigations have significantly affected the impeachment process. Since the independent counsel's work is sup- posed to be clothed in secrecy, the very existence of the investigations has become the subject of virtually continuous speculation about what the inquiry may or may not be doing to the President's impeachment status on any given day. This has been especially true of the Mueller investigation, which is a tight ship as compared to the constant leaks that came from the Starr team. There seems to be no limit on the imag- ination of the media and the White House in spinning the scraps of supposed facts that find their way into the public arena.

This has generated at least four unintended consequences with re- spect to the impeachment process as it relates to Donald Trump. First, it has lengthened the "debate" over impeachment to coincide with the time it is taking for the independent counsel to conduct his investiga- tion. Second, it has cheapened the debate because it is not tethered to substantial facts. Third, it is providing a vehicle for ongoing conflict between the President and the federal prosecutors. Fourth, and related to the third, the constant attacks by President Trump on the integrity of the Mueller investigation are eroding public confidence in our criminal justice system.

These factors taken together create the impression, if not the fact, of a Presidential Administration under siege. They promote counter- productive speculation and excite the media, which is prone to hype a "constitutional crisis" whenever to do so will sell newspapers or tele- vision/cable advertising. In the process, impeachment is trivialized. The remedy is for our political leaders, beginning with the President, and the media to exercise the discipline to let the independent counsel do his work without constant kibitzing. That is a remedy that appears beyond reach. It will not happen unless Americans deliver a clear and strong message that they expect such discipline to be exercised.

Will President Donald J . Trump Be Impeached?

Many Americans, including most Democrats, are appalled by the depth and degree of President Trump's character flaws and his conduct that debases the dignity of the Presidency. Millions of people believe he is unfit to be President. At the same time, most Republicans, also mil- lions of people, believe that the President is doing a good job, even if many of them cringe at his boorish behavior. It is too early to makean informed assessment of the strength of an impeachment case against the President. We just don't have the facts yet.

> While we don't yet have the answers, we do know what questions we should be asking:
>
> -- Has the President committed an indictable crime and/or engaged in conduct that amounts to a sig- nificant breach of the public trust?
>
> -- Was that crime and/or abuse of trust committed in discharge of his official duties as President and/oras part of his efforts to obtain the Presidency?
>
> -- Is the conduct sufficiently egregious to attract the support of a large bipartisan majority of Americans for his removal from office?

This is a high bar, but it's the bar the founders included in the Constitution. This was the bar against which Richard Nixon's conduct was measured. When all the facts were known, it became clear that there was significant non-partisan support for his removal from office and that his removal was appropriate under the Constitution. President Nixon's resignation was his unspoken admission of that fact.

It may be that we are so "tribalized" that our politicians are in- capable of making the non-partisan decision called for by the Con- stitution to remove a president. If our leaders vote as tribes, as they did in the Clinton impeachment and trial, and to a large extent in the Johnson case, the impeachment of President Trump would be ill-ad- vised, because it would be doomed to failure. The party line-up in the House as of April 2018 was 236 Republicans and 193 Democrats. In order to achieve a majority in the House, the Democrats need to net plus-22 seats in the mid-term elections. That seems achievable. For our purposes, let's assume that happens. That would get the President impeached. The prospects for getting a two-thirds vote for conviction in the Senate on a "tribal" vote are dim. In order to do that, the Demo- crats need to net a plus-17 seats in the Senate in the mid-term elections. That seems unlikely.

This suggests that Americans should wait and watch carefully to see if there will be substantial evidence of an impeachable offense and a growing sentiment amongst the American electorate and its leaders to support Trump's removal from office.[620] Once again, Nixon's case is instructive. The country was also divided in the 1970's. It took two years and the production of overwhelming evidence demonstrating his abuse of power before the requisite votes for removal appeared in Con- gress. What this shows is perhaps the obvious: impeachment is amea- sure of last resort. It can only be properly wielded when the grounds for removal are well-established and widely recognized as supporting the extreme measure of undoing the election of a President of the Unit- ed States.

620 *Professor Dershowitz argues that collusion by President Trump with the Russians to achieve electoral victory in 2016, if proved, would not be impeachable because to do so would not be a crime, even though he also acknowledges that ". . . plainly, collusion with Russia would be a breach of the public trust and fulfill Hamilton's criteria for impeachment (if Hamilton intended those criteria to be a substitute for, rather than an addition to, the enumerated criteria)." (emphasis in the original) See Dershowitz, The Case Against Impeaching Trump," 24-25. To the contrary, this book has shown that Hamilton, who participated in the Constitutional Convention and wrote Federalist 65, as well as most of his founding contemporaries, would find collusion by a presidential candidate with a foreign power to effect his election to be an egregious breach of the public trust and, therefore, an impeachable offense under the Constitution. As such, it would be grounds for removal upon conviction by a two-thirds vote in the Senate.*

Bibliography

History of Impeachment in the Constitution

Constitution, Statutes and Other Legal Authority

Declaration of Independence.

Articles of Confederation of the United States of America.
Constitution of the United States of America

General Government Sources

Constitutional Grounds for Impeachment, Report by the Staff of the Impeachment Inquiry, Committee on the Judiciary, House of Representatives, Ninety-Third Congress, Second Session, February 1974. Congressional Resolutions on Presidential Impeachment: A His- toric Overview, Updated September 16, 1998, Congressional Research

Service, The Library of Congress.

Department of Justice Office of Legal Counsel Memorandum to Attorney General, Regarding a Sitting President's Amenability to In- dictment and Criminal Prosecution, October 16, 2000.

Books

Berger, Raoul, Impeachment, the Constitutional Problems, En- larged Edition (Cambridge, Harvard University Press, 1974).

Dershowitz, Alan, The Case Against Impeaching Trump (New York, Hot Books, 2018)

Ellis, Joseph J., The Quartet (New York: Vintage Books, 2015). Farrand, Max (ed.), The Records of the Federal Convention of

1787, Volumes I – III (New Haven, Yale University Press, 1911).

The Federalist Papers (Odins Library Classics, 2018).

Gerhardt, Michael J., The Federal Impeachment Process, A Constitutional and Historical Analysis (Princeton University Press, 1996). Ketcham, Ralph (ed.), The Anti-Federalist Papers and the Consti-

tutional Convention Debates (New York, Signet Classics, 2003).

Posner, Richard A., An Affair of State – The Investigation, Impeachment and Trial of President Clinton (Cambridge, Harvard Uni- versity Press, 1999).

Rakove, Jack N., Original Meanings: Politics and Ideas in the Making of the Constitution (New York, Alfred A. Knopf, 1996).

Rakove, Jack N. (ed.), Annotated U.S. Constitution and Declara- tion of Independence (Cambridge, The Belnap Press of Harvard Uni- versity Press, 2009).

Sunstein, Cass R., mpeachment, A Citizen's Guide (Cambridge, Harvard University Press, 2017).

Tribe, Laurence and Matz, Joshua, To End a Presidency, the Pow- er of Impeachment (Basic Books, New York, 2018).

Articles

Dash, Abraham, "The Office of Independent Counsel and the Fatal Flaw: They Are Left to Twist in the Wind," 60 Md. L.Rev. 26 (2001). Erskine, "The Trial of Queen and the Impeachment of President Clinton: Law As a Weapon for Political Reform," Wash. U. Global

Stud. L. Rev. 1 (2008).

Pollitt, Daniel H., "Sex in the Oval Office and Cover-Up Under Oath: Impeachable Offense?", 77 N. C. L. Rev. 259 (1998); available at http://scholarship.law.unc.edu/nclr/vol77/iss1/7.

Sunstein, Cass R., "Impeaching the President – An Essay," 147 Univ. Penn. L. Rev. 279 (December 1998).

Turley, Johnathan, "Senate Trials and Factional Disputes: Im- peachment as a Madisonian Device," 49 Duke L. J. 1 (Oct. 1999).

Weeden, L. Darnell, "The Clinton Impeachment Indicates a Presidential Impeachable Offense is Only Limited by Constitutional Pro- cess and Congress' Political Compass Directive," William Mitchell Law Review, Vol. 27: Iss. 4, Article 7 (2001), available at: http://open. mitchellhamline.edu/wmlr/vol27/iss4/7.

President Andrew Johnson Impeachment and Trial Legal Authority

Myers v. United States, 272 U.S. 52 (1926).

Government Sources

The Civil Rights Act of 1866, http://teachingamericanhistory.org/library/document/the-civil-rights-act-of-1866/

Emancipation Proclamation, January 1, 1863, https://www.loc. gov/rr/program/ourdocs/EmanProc.html.

The Proclamation of Amnesty and Reconstruction by the Presi- dent of the United States of America, December 8, 1863, http://www. freedmen.umd.edu/procamn.htm.

Proclamation of Amnesty and Reconstruction, May 29, 1865, https://cwnc.omeka.chass.ncsu.edu/items/show/13.

Proclamation 135 – Reorganizing a Constitutional Government in North Carolina by the President of the United States ofAmerica, May 29, 1865, http:www.presidency.ucsb.edu/ws/index.php?pid=72403.

President Andrew Johnson's Veto of the Freedmen's Bureau Bill, http://teachingamericanhistory.org/library/document/veto-of-the- freedmens-bureau.bill/

President Andrew Johnson's Veto of the Civil Rights Act, 1866, Richardson, ed., Messages and Papers, Vol. VI, p. 405ff.

Reconstruction Acts of 1867, https://www.tsl.texas.gov/ref/about- tx/secession/reconstruction.html.

Tenure of Office Act, March 2, 1867, http://teachingamericanhis- tory.org/library/document/tenure-of-office-act/.

President Andrew Johnson's Third Annual Message to Congress, December 3, 1867, https://millercenter.org/the-presidency/preseiden- tial-speeches/decemebr-3-1867.

Speech of Honorable George S. Boutwell of Massachusetts, in the House of Representatives, December 5 and 6, 1867.

December 12, 1867: Message Regarding the Suspension of Secretary Stanton, https://millercenter.org/the-presidency/presiden- tial-speeches/december-12-1867-message

Articles of Impeachment against President Andrew Johnson, March 4, 1868, https://www.nps.gov/anjo/learn/historyculture/the-ar- ticles-of-im-impeachment.htm.

Trial of Andrew Johnson, President of the United States, before the Senate of the United States, Impeachment by the House of Repre- sentatives for High Crimes and Misdemeanors, Vols. I – III, published by Order of the Senate, Government Printing Office, 1868.

Books

Benedict, Michael Les, The Impeachment and Trial of Andrew Johnson (New York, W.W. Norton and Company Ltd., 1999).

Foner, Eric, Reconstruction, America's Unfinished Revolution, 1863 – 1877 (New York, Harper Perennial Modern Classics, 2002).

Gordon-Reed, Annette, Andrew Johnson (New York, Times Books, Henry Holt and Company, 2011).

Hearn, Chester G., The Impeachment of Andrew Johnson (New York, McFarland & Company, 1993).

Kennedy, John F., Profiles in Courage, (New York, Harper Peren- nial Modern Classics, 2000).

Rehnquist, William H., Grand Inquests – The Historic Impeach- ments of Samuel Chase and President Andrew Johnson (New York, William Morrow and Company, Inc., 1992).

Stahr, Walter, Stanton, Lincoln's Secretary of War, (New York, Simon & Schuster, 2017).

Stewart, David O., Impeached – The Trial of Andrew Johnson and the Fight for Lincoln's Legacy (New York, Simon & Schuster Paperbacks, 2009).

Trefousse, Hans L., Andrew Johnson – A Biography (New York, W.W. Norton & Company, 1989).

Trefousse, Hans L., Impeachment of a President – Andrew Johnson, the Blacks and Reconstruction (New York, Fordham University Press, 1999).

Articles

Lawrence, William, "The Law of Impeachment," The American Register (1852-1891), Vol. 15, No. 11, New Series Volume 6 (Sep. 1867), 641 -680.

Dwight, Theodore W., "Trial by Impeachment," The American Register (1852-1891), Vol. 15, No. 5, New Series Volume 6 (Mar. 1867), 257-283.

Newspaper Articles

Harper's Weekly, "Editorial: Impeachment and General Butler,"December 15, 1866, http://www.andrewjohnson.com/06FirstImpeachmentDiscussions/iiib-16.htm.

Harper's Weekly, "Editorial, Impeachment," October 5, 1867, http://www.andrewjohnson.com/08OvertObstruction OfCongress/v-23.htm.

Harper's Weekly, "Editorial: The President and the Law," March 7, 1868, http://www.andrewjohnson.com/09ImpeachmentAndAcquittal/vi-2.htm.

Harper's Weekly, "The Impeachment Trial" April 18, 1868, http://www.andrewjohnson.com/09ImpeachmentAnd Acquittal/vi-46.htm.

Website Materials

Speech to the Citizens of Washington, Andrew Johnson, February 22, 1866, http://teachingamericanhistory.org/library/document/speech-to-the-citizens -of-washington/.

Cleveland Speech, Andrew Johnson, September 3, 1866, http://www.let.rug.nl/usa/presidents/andrew-johnson-september-3-1866.

Freedmen's Bureau Acts of 1865 and 1866, https://www.cop. senate.gov/artandhistroy/history/common/generic/FreedmensBureau. htm.

President Richard Nixon

Legal Authority

United States v. Nixon, 418 U.S. 683 (1974).

Nader v. Bork, 366 F. Supp. 104 (D.D.C. 1973).

Government Sources

Articles of Impeachment against President Richard M. Nixon as Voted by House Judiciary Committee, July 27, 1974, http://watergate. info/impeachment/articles-of-impeachment.

Impeachment of Richard M. Nixon, President of the United States, Report of the Committee on the Judiciary, House of Representatives, August 20, 1974, U.S. Government Printing Office, 1974.

Books

Bernstein, Carl and Woodward, Bob, All the President's Men (New York, Simon & Schuster Paperbacks , 2014).

Bernstein, Carl and Woodward, Bob, The Final Days (New York, Simon & Schuster (1976).

Farrell, John F., Nixon, The Life (New York, Doubleday, 2017). Mazo, Earl and Hess, Stephen, Nixon, a Political Portrait (New York, Harper & Row, 1968).

Nixon, Richard M., Six Crises (New York, Doubleday & Compa- ny, Inc., 1962).

The Senate Watergate Report (Abridged) (New York, Carroll & Graf, 2005).

The Whitehouse Transcripts, (New York, The Viking Press, 1974).

Wills, Garry, Nixon Agonistes , the Crisis of a Self-Made Man (Boston and New York, Houghton Mifflin Company, 2002).

Newspaper Articles

Washington Post, “5 Held in Plot to Bug Democrats’ Office Here,” June 18, 1972, http://www.washingtonpost.com/wp-dyn/content/arti cle.

Washington Post, “GOP Security Aide Among Five Arrested in BuggingAffair,” June 19, 1972, http://www.washingtonpost.com/pol- itics/gop-security-aide-among-five-arrested-in-bugging-affair.

Washington Post, “Bug Suspect Got Campaign Funds,” August 1, 1972, http://www.washingtonpost.com/politics/bug-suspect-got-cam- paign-funds.

Washington Post, “Mitchell Controlled Secret GOP Fund,” Sep- tember 29, 1972, http://www.washingtonpost.com/politics/mitchell- controlled-secret-gop-fund.

Washington Post , “FBI Finds Nixon Aides Sabotaged Demo- crats.” October 10, 1972, http://www.washingtonpost.com/politics/ fbi-finds-nixoon-aides-sabotaged-democrats.

Washington Post, “Nixon Wins Landslide Victory; Democrats Hold Senate, House,” November 8, 1972, http://www.washington- post.com/politics/nixon-wins-landslide-victory-democrats-hold-sen- ate-house.

The Guardian, “Nixon Wrecked Early Peace in Vietnam,” Mar- tin Kettle, August 8, 2000, https://www.theguardian.com/world/2000/ aug/09/martinkettle.

The New York Times, John A. Farrell, “Nixon’s Vietnam Treach- ery.” December 31, 2016, https://www.nytimes/2016/12/31/opinion/ sunday/nixons-vietnam-treachery.html.

The New York Times, Peter Baker, "Nixon Tried to Spoil Johnson's Vietnam Peace Talks in '68, Notes Show," https://www.nytimes.com/2017/01/02/politics/nixon-tried-to-spoli-johnsons-vietname- peace-talks.

Website Materials

Richard Nixon's Checkers Speech, http://watergate. info/1952/09/23/nixon-checkers-speech.html.

James McCord's March 19, 1973 Letter to Judge John Siri- ca, March 19, 1973, http://watergate.info/1973/03/19/mccord-let- ter- to-judge-sirica.html.

President Bill Clinton Impeachment and Trial Legal Authority

The Independent Counsel Reauthorization Act of 1994, 28 U.S.C.

§§ 591 – 599 (1994).

Clinton v. Jones, 520 U.S. 681 (1997).

Jones v.Clinton, 869 F. Supp. 690 (E.D. Ark. 1994).

Jones v. Clinton, 990 F. Supp. 657 (E.D. Ark. 1998)

Jones v. Clinton, 993 F. Supp. 1217 (E.D. Ark. 1998)

Jones v. Clinton, 36 F. Supp. 2d 1118 (E.D. Ark. 1999)

Nixon v. United States, 506 U.S. 224 (1993).

Government Sources

Report of the Office of Independent Counsel Regarding President William Jefferson Clinton, September 1998.

Congressional Bills, 106th Congress, 1st Session, S. RES. 16 (to provide for issuance of a summons and related procedures concerning the articles of impeachment against William Jefferson Clinton, Presi- dent of the United States), January 8, 1999, http://www.gpo.gov/fdsys/ pkg/BILLS-106sres16ats/html.

H. Rept. 105-830 – Impeachment of William Jefferson Clinton, President of the United States, Committee on the Judiciary, House of Representatives, December 16, 1998, https://www.congress.gov/congressional-report/105th-congress/house-report/830/1.

Impeachment of President William Jefferson Clinton, The Evi- dentiary Record Pursuant to S. Res. 16, Volume XX, Hearing of the Subcommittee on the Constitution –Background and History of Im- peachment, November 9, 1998, Ser. No. 63, U.S. Government Printing Office (1999).

Congressional Record of the Senate's Proceedings for Monday, January 7, 1999, Proceedings and Debates of the 106th Congress, First Session, Vol. 145, No. 2 (containing the Clinton Articles of Impeach- ment as exhibited to the Senate by the House managers).

Congressional Record of the Senate's Proceedings for Monday, January 25, 1999, Proceedings and Debates of the 106th Congress, First Session, Vol. 145, No. 13 (containing debate on motion to dismiss articles of impeachment against President William Jefferson Clinton) . Congressional Record of the Senate's Proceedings for Tuesday, January 26, 1999, Proceedings and Debates of the 106th Congress,

First Session, Vol. 145, No. 14.

Congressional Record of the Senate's Proceedings for Wednes- day, January 27, 1999, Proceedings and Debates of the 106th Con- gress, First Session, Vol. 145, No. 13 (containing the vote on motion to dismiss articles of impeachment against President William Jefferson Clinton)

Congressional Record of the Senate's Proceedings for Friday, February 12, 1999, Proceedings and Debates of the 106th Congress, First Session, Vol. 145, No. 26.

Brief of House Managers in the Senate, Impeachment of Pres- ident William Jefferson Clinton, http://www.famous-trials.com/clin- ton/897-senatebriefs.

Brief for the President in Senate, Impeachment of President William Jefferson Clinton, http://www.famous-trials.com/clin- ton/898-clintonbrief.

Books

Harris, John F., The Survivor (New York, Random House, 2006) Maraniss, David, First in His Class (New York, Simon & Schuster, 1996).

Toobin, Jeffrey, A Vast Conspiracy (New York, Simon & Schus- ter, 1999).

Articles

Dash, Abraham, "The Office of Independent Counsel and the Fatal Flaw: They Are Left Twisting in the Wind," 60 Md.L.Rev. 26 (2001).

Gordon, Robert W., "Imprudence and Partisanship: Starr's OIC and the Clinton-Lewinsky Affair," Faculty Scholarship Series, Paper 1411 (1999).

Newspaper Articles

New York Times, "Lewinsky Said to Detail Clinton Affair," Au- gust 7, 1998, https://partners.nytimes.com/library/politics/080798clin- ton-starr. html

New York Times, "Clinton Admits Lewinsky Liaison to Grand Jury; Tells Nation 'It Was Wrong,' but Private," August 18, 1998. https://partners. nytimes.com/library/politics/081898clinton-lewinsky. html.

New York Times, "Congress Is Setting Up Steps for Considering Lewinsky Matter," September 10, 1998, https://partners.nytimes.com/ library/politics/091098clinton-starr.html

New York Times, "House In a Partisan 258-176 Vote, Approves Broad, Open-Ended Impeachment Inquiry," October 9, 1998, https:// partners. nytimes.com/library/politics/100988clinton-impeach.html.

New York Times, "Democrats, Defying Predictions, Bring Home Victories, "November 4, 1998, https://partners.nytimes.com/library/ politics/camp/110498eln.html.

New York Times, "Text of President's Responses to House Ju- diciary Panel's Questions," November 28, 1998, https://partners.ny- times.com/ library/politics/112898clinton-impeach-text.html.

New York Times, "A Draft of the Four Articles of Impeachment and a Censure Alternative," December 10, 1998, https://partners.ny- times.com/ library/politics/121098impeach.html

New York Times," Panel, on Party Lines, Votes Impeachment; Clinton Voices Remorse, Invites Censure," December 12, 1998, https:// partners. nytimes.com/library/politics/121298impeach.html.

New York Times, "President Is Impeached and Faces Senate Tri- al," December 20, 1998, https://partners.nytimes.com/library/poli- tics/122098impeach.html.

New York Times, "Public Support for the President, and for Clo- sure, Emerges Unshaken," December 21, 1998, https://partners.ny- times.com/ library/politics/122198impeach-poll.html.

New York Times, "Senate Votes to Call Lewinsky, but Will Show Videotape Instead, New York Times," February 5, 1999, https://part- ners. nytimes.com/library/politics/020599impeach-trial.html.

New York Times, "From the Defense: Preserve That Which the Founders Gave Us," February 9, 1999, https://partners.nytimes.com/ library/politics/020999impeach-ctext.html.

New York Times, "Clinton Acquitted Decisively: No Majority for Either Charge," February 13, 1999, https://partners.nytimes.com/li- brary/ politics/021399impeach-rdp.html.

Website Materials

Famous Trials: The Impeachment Trial of President William Clin- ton: An Account, http://www.famous-trils.com/clinton/884-home.

Famous Trials: The Impeachment Trial of President Wil- liam Clinton: A Chronology, http://www.famous-trials.com/clin- ton/881-chronology.

Impeachment Law, https://www.britannica.com/topic/impeach mentTestimony of Alan Dershowitz before House of Representatives Judiciary Committee, December 1, 1998, http://www.constituion.org/ lrev/ dershowitz_test_981201.htm.

Transcript of Interview of Bill and Hillary Clinton, 60 Minutes, January 26, 1992, www.angelfire.com/wa/starreport/60min.html.

Transcript of January 17, 1998 Deposition of William Jefferson Clinton in Jones v. Clinton at http://www.washigntonpost.com/wp-srv/ politics/ special/pjones/docs/clintondep01398.htm.

United States Presidential Election of 1992, https://www.britanni-ca.com/event/United-States-presidential-election-of-1992.

February, 8, 1999: House Managers' Closing Argument, http:// washingtonpost.com/wp-srv/politics/special/clinton/stories/manager-stext020899.

Transcript: Senate votes on handling deposition videotapes, http:// www. cnn.com/ALLPOLITICS /stories/1999/02/04/transcript.

Clinton Impeachment Trial: Monica Lewinsky's Deposition, Feb- ruary 1, 1999, https://australianpolitics.com/1999/02/01/monica-lew-insky-deposition.html.

Clinton Impeachment Trial: Vernon Jordan's Deposition, Feb- ruary 5, 1999, https://australianpolitics.com/1999/02/05/vernon-jor- dan-deposition.html

Clinton Impeachment Trial: Sidney Blumenthal's Deposition, February 5, 1999, https://australianpolitics.com/1999/02/05/sid- ney- blumenthal-deposition.html

CPSIA information can be obtained
at www.ICGtesting.com
Printed in the USA
FSHW020947260419
57612FS